T0299090

THE ECONOMIC DYNAMICS OF LAW

This book offers a dynamic theory of law and economics focused on change over time, aimed at avoiding significant systemic risks (like financial crises and climate disruption), and implemented through a systematic analysis of law's economic incentives and how people actually respond to them. This theory offers a new vision of law as fundamentally a macro-level enterprise establishing normative commitments and a framework for numerous private transactions, rather than as an analogue to a market transaction. It explains how neoclassical law and economics sparked decades of deregulation culminating in the 2008 financial collapse. It then shows how economic dynamic theory helps scholars and policymakers make wise choices about how to avoid future catastrophes while keeping open a robust set of economic opportunities, with individual chapters addressing the law and economics of financial regulation, contract, property, intellectual property, antitrust, national security, and climate disruption.

David M. Driesen is University Professor at Syracuse University, the thirteenth person in the university's history to hold this campus-wide position. He is the author of *The Economic Dynamics of Environmental Law*, winner of the Lynton Keith Caldwell award, and *Environmental Law: A Conceptual and Pragmatic Approach, 2nd edition* (with Robert Adler and Kirsten Engel), and is the editor of *Economic Thought and U.S. Climate Change Policy* and *Beyond Environmental Law* (with Alyson Flournoy). His articles have appeared in *Cornell Law Review, Ecology Law Quarterly, Harvard Environmental Law Review, Virginia Journal of International Law*, and other leading journals. He was an attorney with the Natural Resources Defense Council before entering academe.

The Economic Dynamics of Law

DAVID M. DRIESEN

Syracuse University College of Law

CAMBRIDGE
UNIVERSITY PRESS

CAMBRIDGE
UNIVERSITY PRESS

32 Avenue of the Americas, New York NY 10013-2473, USA

Cambridge University Press is part of the University of Cambridge.

It furthers the University's mission by disseminating knowledge in the pursuit of
education, learning and research at the highest international levels of excellence.

www.cambridge.org
Information on this title: www.cambridge.org/9781107699465

© David M. Driesen 2012

First published 2012
First paperback edition 2013

A catalogue record for this publication is available from the British Library

Library of Congress Cataloguing in Publication data
Driesen, David M.
The economic dynamics of law / David M. Driesen.
p. cm.
Includes bibliographical references (p.) and index.
ISBN 978-1-107-00485-6 (hardback)
1. Law and economics. I. Title.
K487.E3D75 2012
340.1–dc23   2011050683

ISBN 978-1-107-00485-6 Hardback
ISBN 978-1-107-69946-5 Paperback

To my parents, George and Sue Driesen, who have always worked hard to make the world a better place, for me, my siblings, and everybody else.

Contents

Preface

Many scholars have criticized neoclassical law and economics. But very few have proposed viable alternatives. This book presents an alternative economic approach to law, the economic dynamic approach.

My work on economic dynamic theory began with a previous book, *The Economic Dynamics of Environmental Law* (MIT Press, 2003). Although that book developed the theory in the context of environmental law, it also claimed that the theory applied to law more generally and used it to analyze the law of regulated industries, an area different from environmental law, to demonstrate the theory's generality.

That book won the Lynton Keith Caldwell Award in 2004, but that award goes to the best book on environmental policy and politics. The book's claim that the theory applied more generally did not matter in that context and the book's readers came from the world of environmental policy.

I realized that the theory required explicit application to a variety of subject matter areas before readers would appreciate its generality. But I found the task of applying it to a large number of areas, many of which I am not an expert in, rather daunting.

After the 2008 economic crisis, a number of prominent economists began to sound a lot like proponents of economic dynamic theory. Paul Krugman, Joseph Stiglitz, and many others took neoclassical economics to task for creating the intellectual climate that led to disastrous deregulation. This linking of neoclassical law and economics to unwise deregulation echoed a theme of *The Economic Dynamics of Environmental Law* and my edited volume, *Economic Thought and U.S. Climate Change Policy* (MIT Press, 2010). Also, policymakers had spared the world's economy a much more prolonged and deeper debacle, at least temporarily, only because they responded to the crisis in an economic dynamic way. The time had come to make the economic dynamic theory's generality and value apparent to a wider audience. Thus, the current volume aims to establish the generality of the theory more firmly by demonstrating how it has implicitly influenced the law and legal scholarship in a number of fields and how recognizing the theory explicitly might help us advance law and scholarship further.

As I thought about the theory anew, I also perceived the need to develop it further. A major change involves identifying the avoidance of systemic risk (while keeping open a robust set of economic opportunities) as a normative goal for economic dynamic theory. The presentation in *The Economic Dynamics of Environmental Law* had argued for a focus on change over time and for the use of economic dynamic analysis as an analytical technique, but the embrace of an explicit normative goal is new to this book. I have further developed the method of economic dynamic analysis that I argued for in the earlier book, principally by embracing scenario analysis as a way of understanding and preparing for the future without creating the illusion that we know its precise contours. So the theory has evolved.

The world currently copes with a number of problems, such as climate disruption, terrorism, and a fragile economy, that require the long-term focus at the heart of the economic dynamic theory. Yet the United States in particular has often employed a myopic approach to the problems confronting us, often ignoring or clumsily responding to potential long-term threats in a way that reflects an excessive preoccupation with short-term costs and benefits and a failure to think about long-term economic dynamics. In the absence of any theory or method for thinking about change over time, the polity too often divides into warring factions based on people's faith (or lack thereof) in markets and governments, respectively. The economic dynamic theory calls for a serious focus on the shape of change over time and provides tools to make efficacious policy choices in addressing long-term problems. We do not want society to efficiently drive itself off a cliff. Instead, we need it to look ahead, see where it is going, and steer in an appropriate direction to avoid disasters and get to a reasonably pleasant place. Hence, this book embraces a macroeconomic approach to law that sees law as a force shaping society's overall direction, rather than as a mere set of resource-allocating transactions.

As I wrote the book, though, I found that economic dynamic theory already plays a surprisingly robust role in the law and legal scholarship. Furthermore, it plays this role not only in the public law, but also in common law areas such as property and contract. Yet, in recent years, a narrow short-term view of the law as a set of either efficient or inefficient transactions has tended to dominate legal scholarship and guide policy change, with some disastrous results. This book provides a systematic way of using neoclassical law and economics' key insight about economic incentives' importance in order to achieve important and appropriate societal goals, such as preventing catastrophes. I hope readers will make use of the book's insights to help guide society to a better and less contentious future.

As I wrote this book I benefited greatly from informal peer reviews, including several from experts in the fields that I was learning about for the first time or at least revisiting for the first time since law school. I thank the following readers of the book proposal, the book itself, articles destined to become book chapters, or individual chapters: Aviva Abromovsky, Rakesh Anand, William C. Banks, Keith Bybee, Peter Carstensen, Shubha Ghosh, James Hackney, Douglas Kysar, Andrew Long, Robin Malloy, David Popp, Eric Posner, Lynn Stout, Spencer Waller, and participants in a Syracuse University College of Law Workshop. I take responsibility for any errors.

I would also like to thank Myriah Jaworski, Meredith Lee-Clark, and Maria Scandia for research assistance; Christy Ramsdell for administrative support; and John Berger for his support and encouragement. Syracuse University made such an ambitious book possible by offering me a University Professor position, which provides enormous support for research, so I thank Vice-Chancellor Eric Spina and Law School Dean Hannah Arterian for that. I also benefited from a research leave offered specifically to support this project. Finally, I am grateful to the staff of the H. Douglas Barclay Law Library at Syracuse University College of Law for their prompt responses to my never-ending stream of requests.

An Introduction to the Economic Dynamics of Law

Law influences the future, not the past.[1] Legislative bodies may write laws in response to a past event, such as the recent financial crisis. But legislative bodies around the world can no longer prevent the crisis of 2008; they can only seek to prevent a different financial crisis from occurring in the future. A vigorous and appropriate response to the 9/11 attacks might conceivably prevent future terrorist attacks, which might or might not use airplanes, but by 9/12, keeping the World Trade Center from collapsing lay beyond human power. Attempts to address climate disruption[2] cannot lower last year's temperature; they can only ameliorate future flooding, drought, disease, and ecosystem destruction.

Even common law (judge-made law), which scholars think of as retrospective, does not alter the past. A court may order damages to compensate a spouse for the death of his or her partner. But the most powerful judge in the world cannot bring the spouse back to life. The judge can only order compensation in hopes that this solicitude will somehow comfort the bereaved (beginning

---

[1] Cf. Jed Rubenfeld, *Freedom and Time: A Theory of Constitutional Self-Government* 85 (2001) (pointing out that law exists *"over time,"* because law implies that after a rule is established it is followed) (emphasis in original).

[2] I use the term "climate disruption" because scientists expect warmer average surface temperatures to disrupt global ecosystems. See Perry Wallace, "An Overview of This Issue: Climate Change in 2009," 9 *Sust. Development L. & Pol'y* 2 (2009) (listing threats to food production, contamination of fresh water, catastrophic flooding, and pests in new terrain as potential consequences of climate change). The literature more often refers to climate disruption as either "climate change" or "global warming." See, e.g., *Climate Change 2007: Impacts, Adaptation, and Vulnerability*, vii (Michael Parry, et al., eds. 2007) (hereinafter *Impacts*). The "global warming" term describes a central scientific finding that human emission of greenhouse gases has warmed the earth's average surface temperature, but says nothing about why this warming presents a problem and suggests, wrongly, that no local cooling is possible. The term "climate change" is accurate, but conveys nothing substantive about the change's nature. Cf. *Impacts*, supra (assessing the nature of anticipated changes in detail). Hence, "climate disruption" more cogently describes the heart of the phenomenon.

on the day he or she renders judgment) and provide an incentive for the
defendant and other potential wrongdoers to act more carefully in the future.
Even the judicial practice of adhering to precedent influences the future, by
helping establish the legitimacy of judicial decisions in order to allow the
custom of accepting judicial interpretation of law to continue into the future.
That custom of accepting judicial rulings, in turn, becomes a force that allows
legislative actions, even legislative actions radically changing course, to gain
influence over the future through judicial enforcement of the legislation.

Because law aims to influence the future, rather than the past, its architects
must often address surprise, change, and uncertainty. In other words, we must
deal with the dynamics of an unknowable future.

These dynamics often prove nonlinear and make at least the magnitude
and timing of consequences unpredictable. For example, when we started
launching rockets, satellites, and other objects into space, we began to create
space debris, cast-off rocket shells, abandoned satellites, and so on.[3] A little
debris in space does not matter a lot; collisions appear unlikely in the vastness
of space. But those studying space debris' dynamics pointed out that at some
point collisions could increase rapidly and cause serious problems. For once
two pieces of space debris collided, they could break into many pieces, thereby
multiplying the probabilities of another collision. The many pieces created
by a couple of collisions might create several more hits, each multiplying the
dangers of yet more collisions, and so on. Hence, scientists, while unable to
correctly quantify the number of collisions, could predict from their dynamics
that space debris eventually would create a lot of risk for satellites and other
objects in space, unless addressed properly.[4] While a major collision occurred
in 2009, measures to reduce space debris and the fortuitous demise of the
Soviet space program have at least delayed the onset of the type of cascade
of collisions predicted in the 1970s, but scientists still consider space debris as
subject to a dangerous nonlinear dynamic.[5]

These same sorts of dynamics influence the future events law often addresses
here on earth. For example, bank failures occur every year without having broad serious consequences, thanks to deposit insurance. But during the
recent financial crisis, policymakers realized that if large financial institutions
involved in a vast web of transactions went bankrupt, their failure could set off
a chain reaction not unlike one that space debris might cause. While nobody

[3] See generally Donald Kessler, *The Kessler Syndrome*, webpagescharter.net (2009). I thank
Douglas Kysar for suggesting this example.
[4] See id.
[5] Id.

could quantify the costs such a disaster would impose or reliably predict what threshold event might push the economy over the edge, policymakers recognized that failing to take these dynamics seriously could lead to a long-term global economic collapse. Arguably, their actions in response to these economic dynamics converted a catastrophic long-term economic collapse into a serious, but not immediately fatal, setback.

Indeed, many of our most important challenges stem from the possibility – even the likelihood – of serious problems developing in the future. Global climate disruption and terrorism provide prominent examples.

NEOCLASSICAL LAW AND ECONOMICS

Unfortunately, the dominant policy approach of the past thirty years – the approach emanating from neoclassical law and economics – is ill equipped to deal with dynamic and potentially catastrophic phenomena. This approach treats government decisions that should decisively shape our future direction as mere resource allocation decisions. Furthermore, this approach tends to focus policymakers on the static normative criterion of allocative efficiency: the goal of choosing actions that balance costs and benefits at the margin for a fixed technological state (in spite of the existence of dynamic economic models not defined in terms of a fixed technological state). This goal leads to an attempt to quantify, and then convert to dollar values, all of an action's consequences, in order to formulate "optimal" policies. Unfortunately, cost-benefit analysis (CBA) in a strict quantitative sense becomes impossible or incomplete and unreliable when we face important future consequences. Subsequent chapters will defend the proposition that too much reliance upon CBA can prove quite destructive when serious systemic risks loom and when our primary concern is with the future, because CBA tends to focus policymakers on the most easily quantifiable aspects of a problem, rather than its most important dimensions. It helps us mask, rather than seriously confront, the dangerous, uncertain world we live in. Since CBA defines costs in terms of the difficulty of departing from the status quo, this methodology reinforces conservatism even when looming systemic risks suggest a strong justification for departures from the status quo.

While economists formulated neoclassical theory to describe markets, rather than dictate policy, the U.S. law and economics movement used this theory as an underpinning for advocating massive deregulation. This movement's work extolling the virtues of spontaneous private ordering and expressing skepticism about government "intervention" in the marketplace helped support rising faith in free markets which dominated U.S. – and, to some extent, British – policy throughout the late twentieth century and beyond. This enthusiasm for free markets led to a disdain for regulation, a disdain that has played a key role in increasing systemic risks. For example, the U.S. Congress repealed the Glass-Steagall Act – a Depression-era law designed to limit systemic risks by separating retail banking from the sale of securities. This repeal set the stage for the sales of securities backed by subprime mortgages at the heart of the financial meltdown. The United States also deliberately left unregulated derivatives (securities that derive their value from other securities' performance) that investors can use to try to reduce risks, but that can increase systemic risk.

Many of the corporations involved in pushing this deregulation either directly or through the funding of conservative think tanks, such as the Heritage Foundation, relied heavily on the teachings of neoclassical law and economics to support their agenda. These advocates pushed a worldview in which markets basically regulate themselves, often a logical corollary of assuming that market actors are rational and systematically consider all available information to arrive at good decisions. That view enjoyed sufficient support in government to lead policymakers to assume quite often that the costs of regulation must be high and its benefits low. Economists and other economically sophisticated academics understood that the rational market actor and the perfect information assumptions in neoclassical economics function as simplifications to facilitate economic modeling, but do not accurately describe the world. Yet law and economics – and to some extent, economics itself – tended to minimize the significance of the variances between neoclassical economics' assumptions and the real world, treating these assumptions as "good enough" for their purposes. And these apologists for artificiality may have been right that for purposes of facilitating economic modeling exercises, simplifying assumptions can sometimes prove "good enough" and even illuminating. But influential conservative think tanks, corporations, and some adherents of the law and economics school sought to apply the teachings of neoclassical economics to contexts, such as contexts implicating systemic risk, where these assumptions are not good enough, indeed where these assumptions undermine sound policy.

More fundamentally, the whole emphasis of modern law and economics on microeconomics – the study of individual actors' economic behavior – as a guide to government decision making equips policymakers poorly when they seek to address the most central questions they must confront. Policy is often about macro-level change, not about the fine-grained decisions that economists designed microeconomics to model. And macroeconomics, not microeconomics, studies the economy as a whole and therefore focuses on the systemic risks and economic development opportunities that should constitute a major focus for policymakers.

Fortunately, the policymakers who confronted the risk of an economic collapse in 2008 did not rely on a quantitative analysis of costs and benefits aimed at identifying an economically efficient course of action for a fixed state of technology; instead, they employed an economic dynamic analysis of the crisis to envision the future direction of change over time. They then chose among a limited set of alternative policies to countervail a destructive dynamic. I will argue that leaders in Europe did much the same thing to address risks of catastrophic climate disruption and that thoughtful analysts of counterterrorism policy likewise evaluate the economic dynamics of terrorism in order to take effective action against it, with quantification of costs and benefits of their actions playing little or no role. Furthermore, many thoughtful scholars in intellectual property, financial regulation, property, and other fields implicitly analyze law's economic dynamics, rather than its efficiency.

ECONOMIC DYNAMIC THEORY

This book develops an account of law's economic dynamics to help us understand what thoughtful policymakers and scholars have been doing and to help us craft future policy in the world we live in, a world where the future's uncertainty makes it impossible to accurately calculate law's costs and benefits, but where careful thought and analysis might allow us to discern the future's general shape and dynamics. Chapter 4 elaborates and defends this account in greater detail, but setting out its basic contours here will orient the reader.

The economic dynamic theory focuses on the shape of change over time. It adopts avoidance of systemic risk while keeping open a reasonably robust set of economic opportunities as a minimum governmental goal. And it employs economic dynamic analysis to guide decisions minimizing systemic risks, while providing basic institutional support for economic development. Just as neoclassical law and economics changed law's goals, focus, and methods, so too does the economic dynamic approach.

The Focus on Change Over Time

Economic dynamic theory demands a change in focus that flows directly from the economic dynamic perception of the world articulated above. Law should focus on change over time. Its architects should concern themselves with the direction in which we are headed and with the future. The known costs and benefits of the past should concern policymakers less than they do. As such, the economic dynamic approach makes change, not the tendency toward equilibrium, the primary object of study.

The Goal of Avoiding Significant Systemic Risk

An economic dynamic approach makes avoidance of serious systemic risk a major goal for policymakers. We do not and cannot expect policymakers to ensure our future happiness or make perfectly efficient decisions, but we do expect them to take reasonably effective actions to avoid catastrophes, such as ecological collapse, financial meltdowns, and horribly destructive terrorist attacks. Economic dynamic analysis builds on Douglas North's idea of adaptive efficiency, the idea that when we cannot quantify costs and benefits, we should aim to preserve future options.[6] That is, we should take actions to avoid incurring irreversible consequences that limit future possibilities. This approach fits actions addressing the future, especially when we tread down a self-destructive path requiring alteration.

At the same time, an economic dynamic approach recognizes that not all areas of law have avoidance of systemic risk as a primary concern. This theory views areas of law traditionally thought of as providing stable and basic infrastructure for markets, such as contracts and property, in more dynamic terms as well. It sees these foundational areas as providing a framework establishing the requisites of economic development, rather than as ensuring economic efficiency. Indeed, Chapter 4 argues that economic development frequently requires economically inefficient actions and that a tension exists between enhancing desirable and sustainable economic development and maximizing static allocative efficiency.

The goal of avoiding serious systemic risks while leaving open substantial opportunities for economic development provides a much more important, modest, and realistic role for government than the goal of achieving static allocative efficiency. With respect to importance, this book argues that economic equilibria are temporary and not terribly important phenomena. They come and go as technology changes and the economy grows or shrinks. While nobody should desire massive inefficiency, the most important attributes of economies involve progress toward sustainable development tied more to technological innovation and change than to achievement of equilibria.

I focus here on static efficiency because the Chicago School of Law and Economics has focused on static efficiency even in areas like antitrust law, where most economists find dynamic efficiency – efficiency over long time periods[7] – much more important. Of course, if neoclassical law and economics' static nature constituted its sole problem, then an update to focus more on

---

[6] See Douglas C. North, *Institutions, Institutional Change, and Economic Performance* 81 (1990).
[7] See David M. Driesen, *The Economic Dynamics of Environmental Law* 71 (2003).

dynamic efficiency would provide a sufficient cure. But the problem goes much deeper.

The neoclassical vision of government as an optimal resource allocator offers an unrealistically ambitious role for government, and a move toward focusing on dynamic efficiency would only exacerbate that problem. One of the major justifications for capitalism involves the inability of governments to process the information needed to make efficient resource allocation decisions. We need capitalism, precisely because it gets around this informational problem by allowing individuals to make fine-grained resource allocation decisions through the market. Yet, the neoclassical model of government decisions posits that government should view every policy decision it makes not as a decision about the type of society we want to live in or about how to prevent the most serious dangers from destabilizing society, but as a resource allocation decision made through comprehensive analysis of costs and benefits. The economic dynamic goals of providing a framework for economic development while heading off serious systemic risks offer government a distinctive and appropriate role that does not require unachievable fine-grained accuracy implicit in the vision of government as optimal resource allocator.

The economic dynamic model is also more realistic in the sense that it tracks what government actually does. While government surely allocates resources when it acts as a market participant, many government regulatory decisions do not allocate resources directly. Instead, they provide a framework for private resource allocation decisions. This means that private companies often have room to adjust for nominally inefficient government decisions. For example, if government establishes a requirement to reduce pollution, companies may have flexibility in choosing the precise means of compliance and will generally choose the least costly compliance method available. The dynamism inherent in government providing a framework influencing allocation, rather than directly determining what gets produced and by whom, means that prediction of regulation's costs and benefits often proves wrong and, anyway, less important than it might otherwise be. The economic dynamic theory's modest and realistic view of government's appropriate role takes into account both the limits of government information generation and processing ability and the capacity of market actors to adjust to inefficient decisions with decisions of their own to reduce or eliminate inefficiencies.

Economic Dynamic Analysis

To achieve these goals of minimizing systemic risks while preserving basic economic opportunities, policymakers need to employ economic dynamic analysis. Economic dynamic analysis employs systematic analysis of economic incentives to choose courses of actions that effectively avoid serious systemic risks and keep open basic economic opportunities under conditions of uncertainty. Economic dynamic analysis constitutes a form of institutional economic analysis. Perceptive legal analysts frequently employ components of economic dynamic analysis, but have not hitherto explicitly recognized it as an analytical method.

Economic dynamic analysis begins by clarifying possible future consequences of current courses of development. Even when we cannot quantify the magnitude and dollar value of our actions' future consequences, we often can know something about their dynamics, shape, and nature. Even though the federal government had no way of calculating a bank bailout's costs and benefits, it could understand that absent a bailout or some other vigorous intervention, the economic dynamics of the situation could lead to a depression. This book offers many other examples of this sort of situation, where we understand a problem well enough to identify a solution or a limited set of reasonable solutions, but for which CBA would provide limited aid in grappling with a serious problem.

Economic dynamic analysis embraces neoclassical law and economics' emphasis on economic incentives' importance, but aims to make analysis of economic incentives broader and more systematic than the analysis legal scholars typically employ. Almost all legal scholars now consider the law's creation of economic incentives, but most "analysis" consists of a few observations about the incentives law creates, with no serious consideration of whether these incentives actually change conduct. This failing arises even more frequently in policymakers' analysis and observations. A good example of this primitivism comes from the debate about the "tax on marriage," the U.S. law's creation of tax rates for married taxpayers that frequently exceed the tax rates two single people with identical incomes would pay if they lived together and filed separate tax returns. Many policymakers and some academics note that this "tax on marriage" creates a disincentive to marry. But they usually fail to consider whether the tax differential actually influences decisions about whether to marry or not.

Evaluating Incentives' Influence Through Bounded Rationality
Economic dynamic analysis requires consideration of the question of whether an incentive nominally present in the law actually influences behavior. In analyzing this question, economic dynamic analysis assumes that individuals and institutions ignore some incentives and pay attention to others. Institutional economics provides key insights that shape economic dynamic inquiry

into how incentives actually influence behavior. Actors do not have perfect information about everything objectively relevant to their behavior, because nobody has enough time to pay attention to all relevant incentives. People and institutions exhibit "bounded rationality," paying attention to information that their habits, routines, and identity make them pay attention to, while ignoring everything else.[8] Thus, a policymaker trying to analyze the question of whether a repeal of the tax on marriage would encourage more marriages must analyze the question of whether people pay attention to tax law in deciding whether to marry.

Evaluating Countervailing Incentives

Economic dynamic analysis also rejects the assumption that actors will always respond to the economic incentives that law creates and that they know about. Analysis intended to play a large role in policy formation must consider whether countervailing incentives exist that may mitigate, or even nullify, a law's effect. For example, even if it turns out that engaged couples study tax law carefully before marrying, one would want to know if they have noneconomic motivations for marrying. It is possible that love and sexual desire may cancel out tax law's tendency to entice people to remain single.

Scenario Analysis

Since we cannot know the future, policymakers and analysts should, at least in making very important decisions, apply economic dynamic analysis to multiple scenarios. Accordingly, this book devotes some attention to the literature on scenario analysis and the role it played (or more precisely, did not play) in planning for the Iraq war and in other situations. Scenario analysis can usefully force us to confront and think through potential uncertainties and identify the most effective actions to address especially serious or especially likely consequences. Economic dynamic analysis frequently can employ scenario analysis.

The Public Choice Component: Empowerment Analysis

Economic dynamic analysis incorporates and extends public choice theory. Public choice theory posits that policymakers tend to respond to well-organized interest groups.[9] Thus, it offers a description of the world that tends to reinforce

---

[8] See generally Herbert A. Simon, "Rational Choice and the Structure of the Environment," in *Models of Man: Social and Rational* 261, 270–271 (1957).

[9] See generally Daniel A. Farber and Philip P. Frickey, "The Jurisprudence of Public Choice," 65 *Texas L. Rev.* 873 (1987); Amartya K. Sen, *Collective Choice and Social Welfare* (1970);

a skeptical view of government.[10] It provides no account of how groups become powerful and well organized. Any such account would recognize that law plays a role in empowering some groups and disempowering others.

Economic dynamic analysis includes noticing whom new laws might empower and disempower. This empowerment analysis can help predict implementation difficulties, as one can expect powerful groups to influence implementation of laws tending to frustrate their ambitions. Too often, legal analysis of law's effects ignores power differentials. Empowerment analysis can also help us understand potential opportunities. For example, it may make sense to make disempowerment of fossil fuel industries and empowerment of renewable energy companies and utilities keen on nuclear power a conscious goal of climate disruption policy. In this way, insights derived from public choice theory, hitherto used primarily to describe influences on policy, can help us analyze new laws' effects and craft policies changing our future direction.

Because economies produce new winners and losers as some businesses disappear and others prosper, the nature and identity of powerful groups can change over time. For that reason, we should not treat losing out to today's powerful special interests as inevitable. Instead, policymakers should disempower or work around the moment's special interest obstacles.

Other Economic Tools to Support Economic Dynamic Analysis

Economics employs fairly sophisticated tools (such as game theory) to think about economic incentives, and law and economics scholarship has begun to follow economists' lead in this. This book addresses the potential role of these more sophisticated tools in contributing to economic dynamic analysis. But a tension arises between tools designed to reduce a problem to a form amenable to mathematical modeling and the need for realism that the economic dynamic theory demands. Some forms of economic analysis that illuminate academic problems may prove useless or worse if policymakers take them too seriously, but some forms of economic analysis may prove helpful.

Economic dynamic analysis provides a method for characterizing the future and the likely effects of possible policy options by studying the shape and nature of change over time. It primarily seeks to describe the nature of future consequences qualitatively, employing quantitative analysis either not at all

Kenneth Arrow, *Social Choice and Individual Values* (1963); James M. Buchanan and Gordon Tullock, *The Calculus of Consent: Logical Foundations of Constitutional Democracy* (1962).

[10] *See* Jerry L. Mashaw and David L. Harfst, *The Struggle for Auto Safety* (1990); Mark Kelman, "On Democracy-Bashing: A Skeptical Look at the Theoretical and 'Empirical' Practice of the Social Choice Movement," 74 *Va. L. Rev.* 199 (1988).

or in a modest (and often limited) way to avoid blinding us to systemic risks through bland and misleading quantification of costs and benefits.

Accordingly, economic dynamic theory refocuses inquiry by demanding attention to the shape of change over time. It emphasizes avoidance of systemic risk as a normative goal. And it demands economic dynamic analysis, a systematic way of considering how law might shape the future. Economic dynamic analysis, in turn, involves the following elements, as summarized in this section

1) Analysis of incentives' effects through the lens of bounded rationality
2) Analysis of countervailing incentives
3) Use of scenario analysis for especially important decisions
4) Use of empowerment analysis

In addition, it can make use of economic tools like game theory. It also demands an increase in legal precision as a core element.

For the most part, I leave discussion of possible objections and qualifications to the economic dynamic theory to chapters 4 (Economic Dynamic Theory) and 12 (Conclusion), but several key points merit brief mention here even if they need subsequent elaboration. The economic dynamic approach recognizes that some actions chosen to avoid systemic risks have negative collateral effects that require evaluation. For example, nuclear power chosen to help avoid climate disruption might present a risk of a catastrophic accident, even if it proves efficacious for addressing climate disruption.

Economic dynamic analysis can help identify qualitative factors that should influence evaluation of how to address collateral negatives once governments abandon the goal of static optimization, as they should. Dollar values of costs and benefits do not prove terribly helpful in evaluating what to do about avoiding systemic risks that will profoundly alter macroeconomic conditions. Often, the goals of fostering long-term economic development and avoiding systemic risk are in harmony. For example, minimizing fossil fuel use will help us avoid an economic crisis when the fuels run out, while avoiding climate disruption's systemic risks. Maximizing energy conservation often pays for itself, and current investments in alternative fuels greatly increase our chances of avoiding future economic collapse and sustaining economic development. Yet a tension often exists between maximizing development and minimizing systemic risks. Although it follows that we should evaluate collateral negatives, economic dynamic analysis, not CBA, offers the appropriate tool for doing this, because analysts cannot predict the magnitude of economic collapse (if systemic risks are not avoided) or of economic development (if systemic risks are avoided in ways that hinder investment and development).

The book's first part provides three foundational chapters developing the economic dynamic theory and the background to it (chapters 2 through 4), with a fourth chapter (Chapter 5) on financial regulation illustrating this theory's potential to generate good policy analysis. The second part offers chapters on specific areas of law demonstrating that many sophisticated analysts in a variety of areas already implicitly employ an economic dynamic approach or some of its elements, and suggests ways in which more conscious use of this approach may usefully shape future decisions and analysis. These chapters address the law of contract, property, intellectual property, national security, antitrust, and climate disruption. The book closes with a chapter summarizing the economic dynamic theory's value, scope and limits, drawing on the insights obtained in Part Two.

The first part begins with a chapter on neoclassical law and economics. This chapter introduces the concept of allocative efficiency and the key assumptions undergirding the neoclassical approach. This chapter shows that mainstream law and economics is static, even though cutting-edge economics is not. It defines efficiency with reference to a fixed technological state, thereby rendering its findings of questionable relevance to conditions where technological states may change – that is, to understanding the future. It also shows that CBA, the form of analysis neoclassical law and economics focuses on, tends to dangerously ignore serious but unquantifiable risks. This chapter also explains how these concepts, developed as descriptive tools for understanding markets, came to dominate policy analysis prior to the 2008 crash, an influence that continues to exist to a significant degree even today.

A chapter on the financial crisis of 2008 follows. This chapter emphasizes the neoclassical law and economics worldview's role in setting the stage for this debacle. It did this primarily by encouraging deregulation. But the chapter also explains how financial models that failed to account for the possibility of a change in the shape of change over time, namely a nationwide fall in the value of housing prices, contributed to the failure to account for systemic risk.

The book's most important chapter, the one developing the economic dynamic theory, comes next. It develops and defends the theory sketched above, with appropriate caveats and answers to some possible objections.

The first part closes with a chapter on financial regulation, showing how the economic dynamic theory helps analyze the question of how to avoid future financial crises. It contrasts two models of containing risk. One model views the role of government as correcting market failure by supplying information that enables market actors to protect themselves from risks. The other model, which the Glass-Steagall Act exemplifies, envisions more systematic containment of risk through government limits on market structure. This chapter shows that an economic dynamic approach supports more emphasis on structural reform and an economic dynamic analysis can contribute to evaluating specific structural reform proposals. It also shows that some of finance scholars' most illuminating and prescient work, which predicted the financial crisis, relied upon an economic dynamic approach.

The book's second part demonstrates the theory's application to a variety of areas of law. By doing this it demonstrates the theory's generality, thereby extending the work accomplished in my previous book, *The Economic Dynamics of Environmental Law* (MIT Press, 2003), which applied an earlier version of this theory primarily to the area its title suggested.

Because of common law's foundational status in the United States and many other countries, the second part begins with two chapters (chapters 6 and 7) on the common law's economic dynamics. This context provides the theory with its greatest challenges, both because scholars usually think of the common law as retrospective and because neoclassical law and economics has enjoyed especially great influence over common law scholarship. These chapters show that one can view contract and property as providing a foundation for economic growth and that their relationship with efficiency proves more problematic than previously recognized.

Part Two starts with a chapter on contract (Chapter 6), which scholars think of as the quintessential example of a subject where neoclassical law and economics must provide the right theory for understanding the area. After all, contracts provide the foundation for markets, the primary subject economists study. This chapter shows that while neoclassical economics does usefully explain people's reasons for reaching contracts, the economic dynamic theory provides a better explanation of why courts enforce them.

The second common law chapter, Chapter 7, addresses property, another foundation for markets, since ownership of property creates the need for purchases. This chapter first shows how property law and economics scholarship has overwhelmingly focused on trying to figure out how to choose between property and liability rules – that is, rules requiring damage awards or injunctions – to facilitate efficient transactions. This chapter then discusses how the economic dynamic theory helps us explore the reasons that a key expectation of the traditional theory of property's law and economics, that parties to nuisance cases will usually bargain around inefficient results, has seldom, if ever, come to pass. This chapter, following several property law theorists, argues for a richer view of property law, seeing it as more than just a prerequisite to efficient bargains. In particular, some of the most interesting property problems arise from efforts to cope with change over time in ways that establish an appropriate macroeconomic framework for economic growth and, occasionally, for avoiding systemic risks. While property law often provides stability, this chapter shows that economic dynamic theory still helps us select the most important problems needing study and illuminates our approach to those problems.

Chapter 8, on intellectual property, provides a bridge between private and public law. The traditional law and economics story of intellectual property, often associated with Harold Demsetz, posits that innovators underinvest in innovation; they therefore require strong and broad property rights in all manner of creative work in order to make innovation's costs worth the benefits. Most prominent intellectual property scholars have expressed grave doubts about this theory, and many of them provide an implicit economic dynamic critique of this pro-property rights picture. Over time, innovation generates spillover effects that benefit society, because innovations provide information that produces further innovation. Therefore, the proper approach to intellectual property rights balances the need to create adequate incentives for innovation against the need to allow innovations to spread and develop. This approach to change over time leads many leading intellectual property scholars to complain about too much intellectual property and to recommend limits on the commoditization of intellectual work. This chapter shows that this approach involves an economic dynamic analysis of the shape of change over time conforming to this book's theory.

Chapter 9 addresses antitrust – an area where neoclassical economics in general, and law and economics' preeminent scholar, Richard Posner, in particular, have enjoyed a large influence. This chapter explains how neoclassical law and economics' skepticism about government regulation has supported a narrowing of antitrust law's scope and vigor. It then shows how an economic dynamic approach can yield much wiser antitrust policy. It shows that an empowerment analysis and an emphasis on dynamic factors suggest the need for much more vigorous antitrust policy, both to limit the systemic risks that some large firms create for the economy as a whole and to preserve economic opportunities for most Americans.

The next chapter (Chapter 10) addresses an area where one might expect neoclassical law and economics to have no influence: national security. Yet in recent years, some proponents of law and economics have advocated the use of CBA to choose and prioritize among security measures. This approach has not caught on, because most of the important variables defy quantification.

Another favorite neoclassical law and economics reform, privatization, has made more significant inroads on national security policy. We have outsourced important national security functions in Iraq and elsewhere, sometimes with disastrous results.

While no economic theory solves all national security problems, the economic dynamic theory has something to contribute even here. The economic dynamic theory focuses us on lengthening our time horizons and thinking through problems strategically, emphasizing analysis of efficacy rather than optimality. This chapter emphasizes the value of scenario analysis, which has long played a role in careful military thinking. It also contains detailed analysis showing how questions that appear to present tradeoffs requiring CBA turn out to involve mostly questions of efficacy requiring economic dynamic analysis. This chapter shows that an economic dynamic approach aids analysis of privatization, treatment of detainees, and decisions about when and how to go to war.

Chapter 11 uses the climate disruption problem as an example of neoclassical economic failure and shows how an economic dynamic theory reveals a better approach. U.S. policy conforms roughly to the suggestion of William Nordhaus's CBA, which purported to show that the costs of reasonably vigorous action to protect the climate outweighed the likely benefits to the United States. This analysis undervalued benefits by neglecting nonquantifiable impacts of climate disruption and through the choice of assumptions that favored doing nothing. Recently, however, some leading experts on climate disruption economics have begun to realize that the most important features of climate disruption science are not the quantitative predictions of the climate disruption models, but rather the potential for catastrophic feedbacks that defy quantification. They have, therefore, begun expressing doubt about the neoclassical approach to this issue.

Chapter 11 shows that an economic dynamic approach influences how much of the world approaches the climate disruption problem. This approach takes systemic risk very seriously. It also recognizes that the costs and benefits of taking action are themselves dynamic and unpredictable. The focus on systemic risk and economic dynamics helps us choose goals for programs addressing climate disruption and more critically analyze the role of market mechanisms, such as emissions trading, in such efforts.

The book closes with a conclusion bringing together the lessons of the chapters showing the theory's applicability to a variety of areas of both public and common law. It focuses on elucidating the theory's scope and limits, but also considers some possible objections to the theory best addressed after seeing it in action. The economic dynamic theory sheds light on a host of practical and theoretical issues in an impressively broad range of areas. But like any legal theory, it cannot address every important aspect of law. Nevertheless, the economic dynamic theory helpfully describes important changes in the law and provides useful guidance to thinking carefully about future reforms.

We too often develop law as if the past tells us what to do about the future. While thinking about the future in ways that confront rather than wish away uncertainty presents serious challenges, this book shows that doing so is both vital and, with the adoption of economic dynamic theory, possible.

Economic dynamic theory puts both law and economics in their proper places. Governments need to employ economic dynamic analysis to avoid systemic risks while providing basic institutional support for economic development. We should view government not as a master resource allocator, but as a useful check on systemic risk and a source of basic stability. While markets can make fine-grained adjustments enhancing efficiency, market actors can, and often do, create colossal problems of unquantifiable magnitude and scope. Wise laws will flow from careful analysis of future scenarios, not calculation of known costs and benefits.

PART ONE

2

Neoclassical Law and Economics

Neoclassical law and economics applies a few of the concepts economists use to describe markets as norms to evaluate policy and law. This chapter explains the basic microeconomic concepts underlying neoclassical law and economics, describes the deployment of those concepts by legal scholars advancing a deregulatory agenda, and discusses the influence of all this on policymakers. These concepts played a key role in an era of deregulation capped by the financial crises of 2008.[1]

NEOCLASSICAL ECONOMIC CONCEPTS

Economists employ a vast array of concepts to inform our understanding of markets. A small subset of these concepts forms the foundation for neoclassical law and economics. This subset comes from the realm of neoclassical microeconomics, which uses concepts describing individual transactions under conditions of perfect competition to study how individual parts of the economy allocate resources. Microeconomic concepts inform our understanding of a wide variety of transactions and form the basis for economic models employed by financial institutions, which, as we shall see, played a role in the 2008 crises.

By contrast, neoclassical law and economics pays little attention to macroeconomics. Macroeconomics, however, focuses on the field's most important questions, such as how to encourage economic growth and avoid a depression.

Microeconomic analysis focuses on evaluating economic transactions' allocative efficiency. Economists consider transactions efficient when their costs equal their benefits. Economists assume that consumers purchasing goods do so on the basis of their "preferences." Thus, the prices consumers

---

[1] *See* Joseph E. Stiglitz, *Freefall: America, Free Markets, and the Sinking of the World Economy*, xvi–xvii (2010) (accusing many economists of providing "the intellectual armor that the policymakers invoked in the movement toward deregulation").

offer to pay presumably reveal their preferences. A transaction occurs only when the price a consumer is willing to pay equals or exceeds the price the seller is willing to accept. Since this kind of bargain would occur only if both sides expect it will make them better off, economists consider such a transaction *Pareto efficient*, a term used to describe a transaction that benefits both parties.

Of course, transactions only reflect parties' *expectations*; products and services sometimes disappoint consumers. Neoclassical economics assumes that all parties have perfect information, which suggests that the future will conform to prior expectations. Thus, the perfect information assumption makes time and disappointment with market transactions disappear. It suggests elimination of the possibility that a transaction that looked good at the time will later turn out to have made the purchaser worse off, thereby assuming away lemon vehicle problems and similar common experiences with markets. And it assumes that actors in markets use this perfect information rationally to pursue the actors' own ends. The rational actor and perfect information assumptions generate the conclusion that transactions in perfectly competitive markets will generally prove Pareto efficient and enhance consumer welfare, defined in terms of preference satisfaction.

I often refer to allocative efficiency as static, because economists frequently define an allocatively efficient transaction as one that balances costs and benefits for a particular technological state. When technologies change, so can the costs of producing products and even their value to consumers; for example, a typewriter may be very valuable to a consumer in a world with no word processing, but as soon as word processing comes onto the scene the value of a typewriter sharply declines. But the standard efficiency definition excludes this sort of change from consideration.

Economists, of course, know that perfect information and unchanging technology do not characterize the world in which we live. Indeed, two economists, Joseph Stiglitz and Sanford Grossman, won the Nobel Prize for showing that financial markets depend on imperfect information for their very existence.[2] An investor can sell shares to somebody else because that other person believes the stock will go up, even though the seller believes it will go down. In a world of perfect information, they would both share the same beliefs about the stock's future earnings and therefore would have no reason to trade. Economists also know that people do not always act rationally in the economic sense. They often assume perfect information, rational actors, and unchanging

---

[2] *See* Sanford J. Grossman & Joseph E. Stiglitz, "On the Impossibility of Informationally Efficient Markets," 70 *Am. Econ. Rev.* 393 (1980).

technology as a modeling convenience; such assumptions make it much easier to mathematically model economic life than do more complex assumptions. Nevertheless, these core neoclassical assumptions provided influential arguments that markets were "efficient and self-regulating."[3]

I hasten to add that economists sometimes relax these assumptions in order to examine problems they associate with changing technology or imperfect information. So, for example, economists studying economic growth do not focus much on allocative efficiency, but instead seek to develop models of the economy that identify factors that contribute to economic growth.[4] The most dynamic and sophisticated models in the field, however, have met with some resistance within economics, both because of the complexity of the mathematics involved and because complicated models do not always produce the smooth, ordered results associated with simpler models.[5] Economists more readily accept modeling of "dynamic efficiency" – efficiency over a long time period. But the unpredictability of technological change makes modeling of dynamic efficiency unreliable.

Economists also study decision making under conditions of uncertainty. But they typically do so by assuming that we know the probabilities of predicted occurrences. When this assumption does not hold (that is, quite often) economists have more difficulty developing models that track reality. Models not tracking reality perfectly may prove illuminating or very misleading, depending on the extent and importance of the deviations.

Finally, the field of macroeconomics rejects key assumptions at the core of neoclassical microeconomics. Economists studying macroeconomics generally recognize that irrational or poorly informed transactions can become common, causing bubbles or an economic collapse. Indeed, much of macroeconomics involves trying to figure out how to keep "irrational exuberance" from creating bubbles that must collapse and how to keep irrational fear from debilitating economies. Although, in principle, understanding how economic actors operate at a micro level should aid understanding of macro-level impacts, those employing neoclassical economic assumptions in conducting microeconomic analysis choose assumptions at war with those of many students of macroeconomics.[6] Hence, economics as a whole recognizes

---

[3] See Stiglitz, supra note 1, at xx.

[4] See David Warsh, Knowledge and the Wealth Of Nations (2006) (discussing the intellectual history of economic growth models); Charles Jones, An Introduction to Economic Growth (1998).

[5] See Warsh, supra note 4, at 156–57, 195–202.

[6] See David Colander et al., "The Financial Crisis and the Systemic Failure of Academic Economics," in Lessons From the Financial Crisis: Causes, Consequences, and Our Economic

irrationality, poor information, instability, and uncertainty, even if the neoclassical microeconomic core of it often ignores all of this.[7]

Macroeconomics reflects an understanding that the economy basically
relies on trust and does not assume that perfect information and rational
actors have done away with the need for institutions to help generate trust.
Law, of course, plays a large role in creating that trust.

In spite of the existence of these dynamic elements in economics itself, law
and economics usually focuses on the most fundamental and simple elements
of neoclassical law and economics: the summation of known costs and benefits
to evaluate the efficiency of laws and policies under static conditions. Dynamic
efficiency, economic growth models, bubbles, depression, and systemic risk
play a very limited (albeit growing) role in law and economics, even though
they do play a role in some areas of economics itself.

The Growth of Neoclassical Law and Economics

While economists' main business involves describing markets, legal scholars focus more often on critically evaluating law and policy. Law and economics arose primarily from efforts by legal scholars to adapt economic concepts intended to describe markets into tools for evaluating the desirability of
laws and policies.

Law and economics has treated allocative efficiency as a key goal for law
and policy. Most people use the term *efficiency* to describe the best means
of meeting some predetermined goal, rather than as a concept relevant to
determining goals. So, for example, one can ask if bicycling offers the most
efficient means of getting to work. The answer to this question may hinge on
which variable one wants to maximize. If one wants to get to work in the least
costly way, then bicycling proves efficient. Economists describe this sense of
efficiency as cost-effectiveness, not allocative efficiency. One may instead seek
the quickest way to get to work, in which case a car might provide the answer to
an efficiency puzzle. But ordinary people do not use the term *efficiency* when
they are asking themselves where they want to work – that is, what goals they
have. Goal selection involves introspection and value choice. Economists,
however – and, by extension, law and economics – use the term *efficiency*

Future 427, 428–31 (Robert W. Kolb, ed., 2010) (claiming that modern economics has "neglected
and . . . supressed" the study of crisis phenomena in favor of models built upon the rational
expectations of a single agent).

[7] *See* Stiglitz, *supra* note 1, at 16 (pointing out the inconsistency between the IMF belief that
markets are efficient and self-correcting and its support for "massive government assistance" to
prevent "contagion" after a crisis occurs).

precisely to guide decisions about goals, such as the decision about where to work, at least when using the term *efficiency* as shorthand for allocative efficiency.

Legal scholars establishing and operating within this tradition of allocative efficiency as a goal-setting mechanism have typically treated government decisions, whether judicial, administrative, or legislative, as resource allocation decisions and evaluated such decisions' allocative efficiency by asking whether those decisions' benefits equal (or outweigh) their costs.[8] This emphasis on balances between costs and benefits implies a focus on, and a transformation of, law's goals. Thus, environmental law ceases to involve a decision about how to protect against environmental harms, but becomes instead a decision about what quantity of environmental benefits to purchase. Similarly, the law of financial regulation ceases to function as a means of avoiding a depression, and instead becomes thought of as a product of balancing a proposed regulation's benefits against its costs. Counterterrorism similarly ceases to focus on how to effectively combat terrorism, but instead becomes a calculation about how much money we should spend per life spared by a particular counterterrorism measure.

Law and economics scholars have argued that judicial decisions in a variety of fields implicitly adopt an efficiency norm. They also argue or suggest that law's primary goal should not be justice, fairness, or avoidance of disaster, but rather allocative economic efficiency. This focus on goal transformation became explicit in the work of its most important founder, Richard Posner, when he argued that wealth enhancement constitutes a major goal of legal systems and that the value of this goal justifies giving primacy, or at least significant attention, to the allocative efficiency goal.[9] More recently, Steven Shavell and Louis Kaplow, two Harvard law professors, have gone further, arguing that an efficiency goal should govern law because all theories of justice and fairness prove incoherent.[10]

Legal academics' explicit emphasis on efficiency as a normative goal for policy distinguishes their work from that of most economists. Although economists

---

[8] *See* Susan Rose-Ackerman, "Putting Cost-Benefit Analysis in its Place: Rethinking Regulatory Review," 65 *U. Miami L. Rev.* 335 (2011) (characterizing CBA as based on an analogy between government decision making and corporate decisions about how to choose investments maximizing net gains).

[9] *See* Richard A. Posner, "The Value of Wealth: A Comment on Dworkin and Kronman," 9 *J. Legal Stud.* 243, 244 (1980); Richard A. Posner, "The Ethical and Political Basis of the Efficiency Norm in Common Law Adjudication," 8 *Hofstra L. Rev.* 487 (1980). *Cf.* Richard A. Posner, "Wealth Maximization Revisited," 2 *Notre Dame J. L. Ethics & Pub. Pol'y* 85, 90 (1985) (characterizing wealth maximization as a "reasonable" goal for society).

[10] *See* Louis Kaplow & Steven M. Shavell, "Fairness versus Welfare," 114 *Harv. L. Rev.* 961 (2001).

tend to like efficiency, they use the concept primarily as a useful tool for describing markets. A significant number of economists evaluate policies' efficiency as well, but they typically do not claim any sort of normative primacy for efficiency, instead regarding efficiency as the attribute of policy that economists are best equipped to evaluate. Although Richard Posner has echoed the economists' approach to this at least once, suggesting that there is nothing wrong with Congress selecting an inefficient measure justified on other grounds, the central thrust of his work and that of many other leading law and economics scholars involves justifying a leading role for allocative efficiency in shaping law and policy. Thus, legal academics in the field of law and economics, rather than economists without legal training or orientation, deserve the lion's share of the credit or blame for the academic trend favoring static efficiency as an overriding policy goal.

Yet many legal scholars and philosophers have resisted this redefinition of law's traditional goals. Mark Sagoff, a philosopher, has argued that thinking of legal decision making as a resource allocation decision involves a category mistake.[11] He sees lawmaking as a process reflecting debate about what sort of society we should view as desirable, rather than as an aggregation of citizens' existing "preferences" as expressed in markets. He envisions civic debate informing and changing people's desires, and believes that citizens' desires for society often diverge in significant ways from their individual "preferences," as expressed in purchase decisions. For example, a wealthy individual may have a preference for a tax deduction for interest on the mortgage for a vacation home. This same individual, however, may oppose such tax benefits politically on the grounds that other social priorities merit more funding. Others have questioned the notion that wealth enhancement should constitute society's primary goal, sometimes defending various forms of justice and fairness not well captured by the efficiency rubric.[12]

My previous work on economic dynamics questions the importance of economic efficiency to wealth enhancement, arguing that wealth enhancement depends on frequently inefficient creativity and growth to a much greater extent than efficient satisfaction of existing preferences.[13] Other scholars before me have made similar points, relying on an economic literature generally attributing most economic growth to technological change.[14] This view has

---

[11] See Mark Sagoff, *The Economy of the Earth* (1988).

[12] See, e.g., Jules L. Coleman, "Efficiency, Utility, and Wealth Maximization," 8 *Hofstra L. Rev.* 509 (1980); Ronald M. Dworkin, "Is Wealth a Value?," 9 *J. Legal Stud.* 191 (1980).

[13] See David M. Driesen, *The Economic Dynamics of Environmental Law* 4 (2003).

[14] See Michael Carrier, *Innovation for the 21st Century: Harnessing the Power of Intellectual Property and Antitrust Law* 31–33 (2009); Robert Ashford, "The Socio-Economic Foundation of

begun to influence law and economics. In particular, Robert Cooter and Aaron Edlin argue in a recent paper that innovation matters so much more to economic growth than static efficiency that law should focus on maximizing innovation, rather than trading off innovation and static efficiency, at least as long as we think future generations' welfare matters as much as or more than our own.[15] A key economic underpinning for this argument, which harkens back to the work of the economic growth economist Paul Rohmer, involves the recognition that very small increases in economic growth generate huge increases in GDP over long time horizons.[16] And Cooter and Edlin argue, in a manner consistent with economic dynamic theory's emphasis on focusing on change over time, that no good reason justifies discounting future utility. Hence, even assuming that wealth enhancement by itself constitutes an important normative goal for law, it does not necessarily follow that we should make allocative efficiency a central goal for law, as neoclassical law and economics has.

The adoption of this efficiency goal has also made many legal scholars advocates of increased use of cost-benefit analysis (CBA) in regulatory decision making. This form of analysis seeks to identify allocatively efficient action by quantifying and monetizing all costs and benefits of a given decision. Application of CBA to regulation usually requires analysts to assign a dollar value to such things as a lost human life, an illness, or the loss of an ecosystem. The foremost advocates of this approach, Cass Sunstein, Matthew Adler, and Eric Posner, have some qualms about a pure preference-based concept of allocative efficiency as the sole guide for policy, but advance a suite of arguments in favor of CBA, which nonetheless echo the predominant themes in neoclassical law and economics.[17] Matthew Adler and Eric Posner see CBA as supporting decisions enhancing "overall well-being," a concept similar to, but not identical to, welfare enhancement in neoclassical law and economics. Cass Sunstein tends

Corporate Law and Corporate Social Responsibility and Binary Economics, Fiduciary Duties, and Corporate Social Responsibility: Comprehending Corporate Wealth Maximization and Distribution for Stockholders, Stakeholders, and Society," 76 *Tulane L. Rev.* 1187, 1200–1201 (2002) (pointing out that neoclassical marginal analysis offers a theory of efficiency, not a theory of wealth maximization, which depends upon sometimes discontinuous technological advances); Robert Ashford, "Socioeconomics and Professional Responsibilities in Teaching Law-Related Economic Issues," 41 *San Diego L. Rev.* 133, 150–52 (2004) (pointing out that neoclassical efficiency theory is not a theory of general growth or wealth maximization).

[15] See Robert Cooter & Aaron Edlin, *Maximizing Growth versus Static Efficiency or Distribution* (2011); *see also* Robert Cooter & Aaron Edlin, *Law and Growth Economics: A Framework for Research* (2011).

[16] *See* Cooter & Edlin, *Maximizing Growth, supra* note 15, at 6; Carrier, *supra* note 14, at 32.

[17] *See* Matthew D. Adler & Eric A. Posner, *New Foundations of Cost-Benefit Analysis* (2006); Cass R. Sunstein, *Risk and Reason: Safety, Law, and the Environment* (2002).

to see CBA as advancing regulatory rationality, thereby echoing the folk beliefs of many economists, who tend to divide the world between those carrying out CBA and those practicing wholly irrational politics. This belief in CBA as both the soul of rationality and its sole analytical manifestation is utterly naïve, as CBA always includes value choices and is always, when used in real-world decision making, subject to political manipulation. Furthermore, other forms of analysis rationally serve other values.[18]

Experts on government regulation have expressed skepticism about CBA, primarily on pragmatic grounds. Many scholars, for example, have pointed out that we cannot quantify many important consequences of regulation.[19] Tom McGarity points out that scientifically honest risk assessment of the environmental consequences most amenable to quantification produces huge ranges of estimates, which make results depend on rather arbitrary choices about which values to use.[20] No scholars seriously dispute this, but generalists often support CBA in spite of this problem. Lisa Heinzerling and Frank Ackerman have criticized CBA because of the unreliability of the methodologies employed to monetize benefits and these methodologies' dependence upon unacceptable value choices.[21]

Most defenders of CBA have responded by saying that if a problem with methodologies exists, economists should improve them, thus implicitly raising the question of how much improvement is possible. More recently, Douglas Kysar has questioned the emphasis on CBA as crowding out the space for normative judgment and moral responsibility that must form a part of regulatory decision making.[22]

For purposes of understanding economic dynamic theory, CBA's static nature looms as its most important attribute. First, it tends to focus on what can

---

[18] *See, e.g.*, David M. Driesen, "Distributing the Costs of Environmental, Health and Safety Protection: The Feasibility Principle, Cost-Benefit Analysis, and Regulatory Reform," 32 *B. C. Envtl. Aff. L. Rev.* 1 (2005); David M. Driesen, "Two Cheers for Feasible Regulation: A Modest Response to Masur & Posner", 35 *Harv. Envtl. L. Rev.* 313 (2011); *cf.* Jonathan Masur & Eric Posner, Against Feasibility Analysis, 77 *U. Chi. L. Rev.* 657 (2010).

[19] Thomas O. McGarity, "A Cost-Benefit State," 50 *Admin. L. Rev.* 7, 13 (1998) (describing the lack of testing vehicles for ecological or health risks); Masur & Posner, *supra* note 18, at 671, 674, 682 (discussing the agencies' inability to quantify non-cancer health risks in the rules they used for their case studies); Ellen K. Silbergeld, "The Risks of Comparing Risks," 3 *N.Y.U. Envtl. L. J.* 405, 413–414 (1995).

[20] *See, e.g.*, Thomas O. McGarity, "Professor Sunstein's Fuzzy Math," 90 *Geo. L. J.* 2341 (2002); McGarity, *supra* note 19.

[21] *See* Frank Ackerman & Lisa Heinzerling, *Priceless: On Knowing the Price of Everything and the Value of Nothing* (2004).

[22] *See* Douglas Kysar, *Regulating from Nowhere: Environmental Law and the Search for Objectivity* (2010).

be quantified. As Lawrence Tribe pointed out long ago, CBA tends to give short shrift to soft variables – those that do not lend themselves to quantification.[23] Academic advocates of CBA all say that policymakers should take nonquantified factors into account. In spite of this, CBA tends to shift the focus from the important to the quantifiable. While these two things can overlap, subsequent chapters will show that surprisingly often some, or even all, of the most important attributes of a problem resist quantification. This shift of focus toward the quantifiable may attract policymakers who like synoptic answers to questions. Understanding important qualitative factors can require real knowledge of a subject, while dollar values for costs and benefits appear to convey solid neutral information that anybody can understand, even if they depend upon quite arbitrary and limited calculations.

CBA also places emphasis on past experience, rather than future change. For example, in estimating the cost of cleaning up pollution, regulators typically rely on past market prices for the technologies they expect private parties to use to clean up. This approach does not take into account a very frequent experience with regulation: a drop in price occasioned by innovation or simply competition among vendors of pollution control devices once a regulation creates demand for clean technology. Regulators frequently do not take future price drops into account because they cannot predict the extent of the price drop. This does not mean that CBA is necessarily bad; it just means that it tends to be static. CBA draws attention away from the possibility that the future might differ from the past.

Most academics working in the tradition of neoclassical law and economics have favored deregulation. Richard Posner's work, for example, has almost always pointed toward regulating less, rather than more.[24] Thus, law and economics scholars have been at the forefront of arguments for less vigorous anti-trust regulation, deregulation of enterprises previously thought of as natural monopolies requiring price regulation, less regulation of financial markets, abandonment of overly protective approaches to environmental regulation, and a variety of privatization solutions. Subsequent chapters will detail some of the particulars. Law and economics scholars tend to justify these results on the grounds that the costs of strict regulation outweigh the benefits. In many cases, they reached this conclusion with no actual CBA, but by emphasizing potential perverse consequences of regulation and then suggesting that the

---

[23] *See* Laurence A. Tribe, "Trial by Mathematics: Precision and Ritual in the Legal Process," 84 *Harv. L. Rev.* 1329 (1971).

[24] *See* David Campbell, "The End of Posnerian Law and Economics," 73 *Modern L. Rev.* 305 (2010) (reviewing Richard A. Posner, *A Failure of Capitalism: The Crisis of 2008 and the Descent into Depression* (2009)).

costs must outweigh the benefits. Resort to this approach frequently proved necessary, because the most important features of the problems they analyzed defeated quantification.

Law and economics scholars also assumed that private actors would rationally make perfectly informed decisions that would remedy a host of problems that academics and policymakers had hitherto thought of as justifications for government regulation. A faith in private ordering permeates this literature, with the basic assumptions of neoclassical economics being used to make government regulation appear unnecessary. Conversely, this literature recognizes that government regulation sometimes has negative "unintended consequences." The insistence on CBA and efficiency provided a framework that allowed for ad hoc arguments against regulation based on unrealistic neoclassical assumptions, but often without the economically rigorous modeling the assumptions were designed to facilitate.

Neoclassical law and economics has exerted enormous influence on the academy. Many scholars have singled out Richard Posner, the founding father of the movement, as the most important legal scholar of the late twentieth century (and the first part of this one). His influence emanates not only from the power of his ideas, but also from his extraordinary skill as a writer and his legendary productivity. In addition, he has applied the concepts of neoclassical law and economics that he helped establish to a wide variety of areas of law. Also, while Posner's oeuvre is remarkably one-sided in the results he advocates, his analysis usually appears fairly even-handed, because he habitually considers the most prominent arguments against his position and usually has something cogent to say about them. Neoclassical law and economics utterly dominates teaching and scholarship in a wide variety of areas, and has some influence in almost all domains of law. Perhaps more importantly, this work has provided the intellectual underpinning for big changes in the role of the state in the late twentieth century.

Policy Influence

Although some law and economics scholars have testified before Congress or otherwise influenced policy, politicians, corporations, and conservative think tanks constitute the major proponents of neoclassical law and economics in the policy realm. The politicians, corporations, and conservative think tanks using neoclassical law and economics to influence policy often adopted less nuanced deregulatory arguments than the best law and economics scholars. In the policy realm itself, neoclassical law and economics began to have an impact even in the 1970s, but grew enormously influential with the election of

Ronald Reagan in the United States and Margaret Thatcher in Britain. These leaders did not employ a subtle approach.[25] They simply glorified individual action and markets, and echoed the Chicago school of economics, which portrayed government as "the problem" rather than as part of the solution.[26] Reagan promised to get the government "off the backs" of private companies that generated real wealth.

Of course, the private companies whose backs government had supposedly been riding supported the idea of deregulation. They did this not only in their own lobbying, but also by funding conservative think tanks devoted to glorifying markets and demonizing government. Throughout the late twentieth century, the Heritage Foundation, the Cato Institute, and a host of other organizations devoted to "markets" and "freedom" supported deregulation as the key to freeing markets to solve our most pressing problems. These think tanks and their industry supporters produced all sorts of anecdotal arguments about government regulation's unintended consequences. They consistently opposed government regulation as doing more harm than good. They also called for tax cuts in order to "starve the beast" – that is, to make the government dysfunctional.

In implementing and justifying efforts to deregulate, conservative politicians and their allies drew heavily on the teachings of neoclassical law and economics. Ronald Reagan, for example, promulgated an executive order designed to "reduce the burdens of . . . regulation."[27] He proposed to do this by mandating use of neoclassical law and economics' favorite analytical technique, CBA. In a move strikingly embracing the view that all regulation is about resource allocation, rather than protection, he authorized the federal Office of Management and Budget (OMB) to oversee implementation of the executive order. Historically, OMB employed economists to make budgetary decisions always thought of as carrying out resource allocation. By giving an office of economists within a budget office influence over government regulation, Reagan implicitly embraced the view that regulation was about resource allocation, not prevention of harms.

Relying on this CBA-based framework, OMB's regulatory office carried out a decades-long campaign to eliminate or weaken government regulation. I have shown elsewhere that OMB, which administers these executive orders,

---

[25] See, e.g., Daniel Yergin & Joseph Stanislaw, The Commanding Heights: The Battle for the World Economy 74–106, 342 (2002) (discussing the influence of neoclassical economic ideology on Margaret Thatcher and Ronald Reagan).

[26] See id. at 343 (stating that "Chicago economists . . . argued that government was the problem, not the solution.").

[27] E.O. 12291 (1981) (preamble).

uses CBA as a means of establishing the legitimacy of interventions weakening
or curtailing regulation on a variety of grounds congruent with free market
glorification rather than solely as an analytical guide to policy. OMB has
recommended weakening government regulation even when CBA suggests
that government agencies should strengthen it.[28] And many of its recommendations to weaken government regulation do not flow from CBA. Instead,
they reflect concerns about excessive burdens (even when the benefits justify
them),[29] assumptions that regulations must always have serious unintended
consequences,[30] love of flexibility in regulation,[31] an attitude favoring free
trade,[32] and zeal for states' rights.[33] In short, OMB regularly prefers to have
agencies craft regulations that reduce interference with markets even when
CBA indicates that stronger regulation would prove optimal. OMB also regularly supports weakening regulations when government agencies, for quite
understandable reasons, cannot quantify any of the relevant benefits, so that
CBA cannot influence a regulation's outcome.[34] CBA legitimizes OMB's
continued effort to weaken regulations, but does not control OMB's reform
recommendations.[35] Thus, in the policy world, neoclassical law and economic
thinking has helped legitimize specific reforms that its analytical methods
would not justify.

Although neoclassical law and economics' influence became enormous
during the Reagan and Thatcher era, its influence did not end when those
pioneers left office, but continued throughout the late twentieth century and
continues to a remarkable degree even today, and not only through OMB.
Indeed, in the United States, the influence of neoclassical law and economics
arguably increased in the late 1990s and the early twenty-first century. Politicians and their consultants actively sought to translate neoclassical law and
economics' precepts into language the public could understand and accept.
Thus, a prominent Republican political consultant, Frank Luntz, advised

[28] *See* David M. Driesen, "Is Cost-Benefit Analysis Neutral?," 77 *U. Colo. L. Rev.* 335, 369–70
(2006).

[29] *See, e.g.,* id. at 370 n. 207, 383.

[30] *See, e.g.,* id. at 373.

[31] *See, e.g.,* id. at 371–72 (discussing OMB's insistence that air pollution regulations not change
the array of snowmobile models currently produced).

[32] *See, e.g.,* id. at 376 (discussing OMB's effort to weaken economically trivial requirements
governing FAA certification of foreign aircraft repair stations).

[33] *See, e.g.,* id. at 374 n. 236.

[34] *See* id. at 376–78.

[35] *Cf.* id. at 372–75 (examining cases where CBA proved important to OMB's recommendations,
and finding that OMB's position regularly preferred low benefits estimates and declined to
give weight to substantial unquantified benefits).

Republican politicians not to explicitly endorse CBA, as this was a concept of "corporations," not individuals.[36] Instead, he suggested, politicians should translate their support for CBA and allocative efficiency into non-technical language by saying that we needed to avoid regulation that does "more harm than good." Political campaigns aimed at liberating the public from too much government proved remarkably successful during much of this period, as the public elected a solidly Republican Congress in 1994, in a campaign relying heavily on deregulatory precepts, and elected George W. Bush, a staunch opponent of just about all government regulation, as president twice.[37] Nor did the climate of ideas that the neoclassical law and economic agenda helped support leave Democratic politicians untouched. President Bill Clinton, for example, promulgated an executive order on CBA that closely resembled that of Ronald Reagan, and many Democrats became more skeptical of government regulation in the late twentieth century than they were in the 1970s or early 1980s.

It is difficult to exaggerate the influence that this glorification of markets and demonizing of government regulation had on policy. During this period, governments privatized garbage collection, prison administration, intelligence gathering, some provision of basic education, and numerous other government functions. Governments deregulated formerly regulated industries, such as telecommunications, airlines,[38] and electric utilities.

In areas where deregulators could not simply privatize, they relied on "market-based" approaches wherever they could. Thus, for instance, environmental policy shifted from a reliance on performance standards telling individual facility owners how much pollution to eliminate to an approach that created markets in emission reductions. The United Kingdom auctioned off broadcast spectrum, which it had hitherto distributed through administrative decisions.

Obtaining sufficient political support for new regulatory initiatives became virtually impossible in this climate, at least in the United States. The United States had hitherto been a world leader in addressing major environmental problems, but refused to take meaningful action addressing the most serious

---

[36] *See* Robert Luntz, *Straight Talk, The Environment: A Cleaner, Safer, Healthier America* 131 (2002) http://www.ewg.org/briefings/luntzmemo/pdf/luntzresearch_environment.pdf.

[37] President Bush, however, supported climate disruption regulation during his first presidential campaign, so his antiregulatory character may not have been obvious to the electorate in his first presidential election.

[38] Airline deregulation preceded Ronald Reagan. *See* Yergin & Stanislaw, *supra* note 25, at 355–58. On the other hand, it set the stage for later deregulatory reforms. *See id.* at 359–67, 372–74.

environmental problem that the world has ever faced, that of global climate disruption. Similarly, as credit derivative markets took off, thereby potentially spreading formerly isolated risks throughout the economy, the federal government deliberately decided to leave them unregulated, trusting that market participants would adequately address their dangers as rational actors eager to reduce their own risks.

This list only contains illustrative examples of how neoclassical law and economics supported deregulatory reforms. (More will follow in Part Two.) Few areas of law remained untouched by the neoclassical law and economics push toward deregulation.

All these cases involve the influence of the skepticism toward regulation and the enthusiasm for markets that permeate law and economics scholarship. Many deregulatory reforms reflect even more specific law and economics influence, either adopting reforms specifically advocated by law and economics scholars (e.g., CBA, emissions trading), or receiving substantial support from those using specific neoclassical law and economics concepts as part of the justification for reform.

At this point, I do not attempt to sort out the useful from the dangerous or useless reforms (although I will have something to say on this in later chapters). Nor does this chapter necessarily blame law and economics scholars for all of the dangerous government failures that did occur. My only point here is that the neoclassical law and economics framework proved enormously influential and supported deregulation.

Law and economics gained this influence by making static allocative efficiency into a highly respected goal and CBA into a highly respected method for achieving that goal. It also gained strength through policymakers treating neoclassical assumptions about markets – their tendency toward efficiency, their rationality, and their ability to respond optimally to information – as if they were actually truths. Finally, the law and economics movement benefited from the support of powerful corporations seeking independence from pesky government regulation.

Recent Trends in Law and Economics

My description of *neoclassical* law and economics focuses on its core elements and does not purport to describe all of law and economics. While in its early years, a very simplistic version of neoclassical law and economics dominated law and economics discourse, law and economics has become richer in recent years. I doubt that this expanded discourse has obtained anything like the level of influence the earlier simpler version did, but it merits discussion for several reasons. First, some of the new developments provide building blocks for the economic dynamics of law. Second, I want to avoid implying that my effort to describe neoclassical law and economics encompasses all of law and economics.

Institutional law and economics has increased its influence in the legal academy in recent years. That influence has always been present but seems to have picked up steam of late.[39] This school of thought shares the neoclassical economic goal of equilibrium and static allocative efficiency, but it approaches that goal in a much more evenhanded and sophisticated way than neoclassical law and economics. Neoclassical law and economics scholars often reached results favoring privatization simply by identifying inefficiencies, or potential inefficiencies, in government policies. Neil Komesar pointed out that both markets and governments have imperfections, and that sound institutional choice, therefore, arises from comparing the flaws of each to see which is worse.[40] In doing this, he built on similar insights from the founders of institutional economics.

By contrast, neoclassical economics usually assumes zero transaction costs even though one of the movement's founders, Ronald Coase, devoted much of his career to arguing that transaction costs – such as the costs of negotiating, monitoring, and enforcing a contract – matter a lot. A host of privatization arguments combine careful attention to inefficiencies in government, what one might call public transaction costs, with the complete neglect of private transaction costs generated in market transactions, a neglect greatly facilitated by the neoclassical habit of assuming that these costs do not exist.[41] When scholars operating within the neoclassical law and economics tradition mentioned that transaction costs existed, they often did so in order to recommend elimination of some government regulation creating them.[42] Economic dynamic theory builds on institutional economics' insights.

Legal scholars have often employed the techniques of game theory to evaluate legal rules.[43] These techniques aim to predict how various actors will respond to rules. Although this approach has generated some well-respected

---

[39] *See generally* James Hackney, *Under Cover of Science* 60–79 (2007) (discussing institutional economics' influence on legal scholars in the early twentieth century).

[40] *See* Neil K. Komesar, *Imperfect Alternatives: Choosing Institutions in Law, Economics, and Public Policy* (1994). *See also* David M. Driesen & Shubha Ghosh, "The Functions of Transaction Costs: Rethinking Transaction Cost Minimization in a World of Friction," 47 *Ariz. L. Rev.* 61 (2005).

[41] *See* Driesen & Ghosh, *supra* note 40, at 75–76, 106.

[42] *See id.* at 74–82 (reviewing examples).

[43] *See* Eric Talley, "Interdisciplinary Gap Filling: Game Theory and the Law," 22 *Law & Soc. Inquiry* 1055 (1997).

work, it has not gained the prominence in the legal academy, and certainly not in the policy realm, of the more simplistic law and economics based on simply characterizing rules as efficient or not based on the analysts' assumptions about costs and benefits. Game theory typically shares and therefore reinforces the neoclassical assumption of a rational actor, but it tends to generate predictions about behavior that analysts can use for broader purposes than just the pursuit of an efficiency goal.

Of special importance to economic dynamic theory's emphasis on the goal of avoiding systemic risk, the attack on the World Trade Center and growing evidence of climate disruption's gravity led both Cass Sunstein and Richard Posner to write books applying law and economics to catastrophes prior to the financial crises.[44] Both of them find that CBA works poorly in these cases, because of the difficulties of quantifying the likelihood and magnitude of catastrophic events. Nevertheless, they both endorse use of CBA, not as a complete guide to decision-making, but as a tool adding useful information. Martin Weitzman, Eric Posner, and Jonathan Masur, however, have expressed doubts about the utility of CBA of climate disruption for a variety of reasons, including, especially for Weitzman, the problem of a nonquantifiable possibility of an enormous catastrophe stemming from runaway warming.[45] Chapter 11 will address this debate in the climate disruption context, but for present purposes it will suffice to note that all perceptive analysts recognize that a serious problem with quantifying the benefits associated with the avoidance of catastrophic risks at least lessens CBA's utility, but only some of them recommend abandoning it because of these difficulties.

CONCLUSION

The foregoing has established the following points. First, neoclassical economics itself creates a flattering picture of markets and often makes allocative efficiency a focal point of analysis. Second, law and economics took the most fundamental and simple concepts of neoclassical economics and used them to elevate the role of efficiency and admiration of markets in policy-making. Third, these arguments helped support a movement of corporations,

---

[44] See Richard A. Posner, *Catastrophe: Risk and Response* (2004); Cass R. Sunstein, *Worst-Case Scenarios* (2007).
[45] See Jonathan Masur & Eric Posner, "Climate Regulation and the Limits of Cost-Benefit Analysis," 99 *Cal. L. Rev.* 1557 (2011); Martin L. Weitzman, "On Modeling and Interpreting the Economics of Catastrophic Climate Change," 91 *Rev. Econ. & Statistics* 1 (2009); Martin L. Weitzman, "A Review on the Economics of Climate Change," 45 *J. Econ. Lit.* 703 (2007).

conservative think tanks, and many politicians to privatize former government functions, roll back regulation, and reshape any remaining law.

This book concerns itself with the theory of law and economics – in other words, with the question of how law should address economic concerns. It does not attempt to tell economists what they should model or how, although policy arguments sometimes influence economists' thinking about that sort of thing. This book tries to figure out which concepts should most heavily influence government, with an emphasis on economic concepts. So far, I have shown only that the concepts neoclassical law and economics has put forward have played a role in supporting significant policy changes in recent decades.

3

The Economic Collapse of 2008

Neoclassical law and economics played a major role in creating the economic collapse of 2008. The faith it inspired in the market's capacity to regulate itself led to the shredding of government regulation that almost surely would have prevented a collapse. Neoclassical economics also supported the practices within financial institutions that created the crises, by encouraging decision makers within these institutions to believe that they could adequately manage risk by relying on mathematical models to guide their decisions. We avoided the full potential impact of the crises only because government, when facing the prospect of a global depression, abandoned a neoclassical law and economics approach in favor of an economic dynamic policy.

The erosion of structural financial regulation made the subprime lending debacle that precipitated the 2008 financial crises possible. In response to the Great Depression, Congress passed the Glass-Steagall Act in 1933. This act erected a wall between commercial banks, which issue mortgages and other loans to consumers, and the investment banks, which underwrite securities.[1] The history of securities involvement weakening commercial banks' asset base led to passage of the act, rather than concern about deficient mortgage lending leading to the collapse of securities, which occurred in 2008. But Congress also expressed concern that a bank involved in issuing securities might make unsound loans in order to aid its sale of securities, as they did prior to the crises.[2] Congress also found some evidence that banks had used their trust departments to unload undesirable securities.[3] Congress deliberately chose to sacrifice economic efficiency and competition in order to reduce systemic risks by separating commercial and investment banking as completely as

---

[1] See Securities Industry Ass'n v. Board of Governors, 468 U.S. 137, 144–45 (1984).
[2] Id. at 146–47.
[3] Id. at 147.

36

possible.[4] Although a sector of the economy could conceivably collapse under Glass-Steagall, the structural separation of sectors would likely limit the damage. Deposit insurance for commercial banks and strict regulation also greatly diminished the likelihood of the entire commercial banking sector collapsing.

The ideological climate of the 1980s led the regulatory agencies implementing the Glass-Steagall Act to erode this structural separation of commercial and investment banking. Developments in economic theory tending to glorify markets powerfully contributed to this erosion. In the 1970s and 1980s, economists studying finance formulated and refined the "efficient market hypothesis." The most prevalent versions of this hypothesis maintain that share prices, after a short period of time, reflect all available information. The hypothesis supports a view of investors as rational actors processing all publicly available information. Although a few scholars doubted the hypothesis' significance or even validity even then, for the most part economists and law and economics scholars accepted it as an empirically verified truth. The efficient market hypothesis pushed aside the Keynesian view of markets as prone to wild vacillations from time to time, and cast doubt on the need for regulation, especially structural regulation.[5]

The ensuing erosion of Glass-Steagall paved the way for the expansion of securitization of loans that led to the debacle.[6] In particular, Lehman Brothers, Bear Sterns, Merrill Lynch, Citibank, and Goldman Sachs – large financial institutions that would later play a key role in the subprime lending debacle – persuaded the Federal Reserve Board to allow bank holding companies to both originate and securitize mortgages (within certain limits). In 1989, the U.S. Second Circuit Court of Appeals upheld the erosion of the separation between commercial and investment banking that made this possible.[7] The key regulatory decision expressed doubt that securitization would create incentives for making unsound loans, thereby reflecting faith in the ability of free-market actors to police themselves.[8] This decision to tear down the wall separating origination of mortgages from securitization, while important to the subsequent economic crises (since it led to a large volume of securitization and lending), constitutes but one of many regulatory decisions of that era eroding

---

[4] Id. at 147–48.

[5] *See* James Hackney, "On Markets and Regulation: Richard Posner's Conservative Pragmatist Evolution," 3 *Law & Fin. Markets Rev.* 539, 540 (November 2009) (book review).

[6] *See* Kurt Eggert, "The Great Collapse: How Securitization Caused the Subprime Meltdown," 41 *Conn. L. Rev.* 1259 (2009).

[7] *See Securities Industry Ass'n v. Clarke*, 885 F.2d 1034, 1042 (2nd Cir. 1989).

[8] Id. at 1046.

the traditional separation between commercial and investment banking put in place in response to the Depression.

By 1999, this erosion had gone so far that it contributed to Glass-Steagall's demise. At that time, Congress, with the support of President Bill Clinton and only a handful of dissenting votes, repealed Glass-Steagall outright. The judicial and administrative erosion had permitted the growth of banking practices that blurred the distinction between commercial and investment banking. Globalization also created competitive pressures encouraging the growth of large interconnected institutions carrying out both commercial and investment functions. In this context, almost nobody objected to casting aside a major structural reform designed to avoid having the collapse of one financial sector destroy another.

The antecedents of the economic crises also involved innovations in mortgage lending that increased lenders' fees and earnings while increasing borrowers' risks. These innovations included the introduction and extensive marketing of adjustable-rate mortgages, which charge a low introductory teaser interest rate, but reset later on to a higher rate correlated with an index.[9] Neither the buyer nor the seller can accurately predict what this higher rate will be (especially not most buyers) and variability increases the risk that the lender and buyer may underestimate a loan's costs and therefore the buyers' capacity to repay.[10] Government facilitated adjustable-rate mortgages, passing the 1982 Garn-St. Germain Depository Institutions Act, which authorized state-chartered banks to offer variable rate mortgages as part of President Reagan's "comprehensive program of financial deregulation."[11] The year before, the Comptroller of the Currency had authorized national banks to issue variable-rate mortgages.[12]

The most important of the mortgage lending innovations involved the introduction and increased use of subprime loans, loans to borrowers who could not qualify for conventional loans. In the past, buyers generally had to pay 20 percent of the value of the house they wished to purchase as a down payment and convince the lender that they could afford to pay back the loan at a stable rate of interest over a long term, often thirty years. If the buyer looked as if he or she might default, the commercial bank underwriting the mortgage would simply refuse to make the loan. Subprime lenders, however, targeted borrowers not eligible for conventional loans.

[9] *See* Kathleen C. Engel & Patricia A. McCoy, *The Subprime Virus: Reckless Credit, Regulatory Failure, and Next Steps* 16 (2011).
[10] *Cf.* id. at 197 (discussing the inadequacy of disclosure requirements for some ARMs).
[11] Simon Johnson & James Kwak, 13 *Bankers: The Wall Street Takeover and the Next Financial Meltdown* 72 (2010).
[12] Id.

Financial models predicated on neoclassical economic precepts helped convince the largest institutions in the banking sector to participate in and greatly expand subprime lending, often by selling adjustable-rate mortgages to these poorly qualified borrowers.[13] The models generated estimates of the risks of subprime lending that made them appear manageable. Using the most recent data readily available, these models would estimate the expected default rate for subprime loans. The models assumed that the future would closely resemble the past, a decidedly non-dynamic assumption typical of any CBA in neoclassical economics.[14] Using the assumption that a small minority of the low-income borrowers trying to pay off subprime loans would default, these models made it possible to estimate the interest rate that banks must charge to ensure a reasonable rate of return, even assuming that some defaults occurred. This subprime mortgage rate must exceed the interest rate for prime borrowers, since the interest rate must rise to compensate the recipient of the loan proceeds for subprime loans' increased risk of default.

If one cast aside complex economic modeling exercises and relied on just a simple understanding of the basic economics at work, one could see instantly that this approach would increase mortgage lending's overall riskiness. Low-income buyers were entering the market in greater numbers than before and instead of receiving cheaper loans designed to make it possible for them to actually pay in spite of their low incomes, they received more expensive loans than high-income borrowers. The models diverted attention from readily understandable basic problems by creating a false confidence that society knew how to manage the risks it was creating.[15]

Financial institutions not only increased their participation in issuing subprime loans, they also securitized loans themselves. Two government-sponsored enterprises (GSEs) created to provide liquidity to housing markets during the depression, Freddie Mac and Fannie Mae, pioneered securitization in the 1970s.[16] Private financial institutions competed with them vigorously in the early twenty-first century, partially by including subprime loans that did not meet the GSE's underwriting standards.[17] Expanded securitization also

[13] *See* Kathleen C. Engel & Patricia A. McCoy, "A Tale of Three Markets: The Law and Economics of Predatory Lending," 80 *Tex. L. Rev.* 1255, 1284–85 (2002).

[14] Arthur E. Wilmarth, Jr., "The Transformation of the U.S. Financial Services Industry, 1975–2000: Competition, Consolidation, and Increased Risks," 2002 *Ill. L. Rev.* 215, 343–44 (discussing assumptions about volatility in the Black-Sholes model resembling past volatility as creating the "potential for serious error").

[15] *See* id. at 345–46 (discussing how financial models cause greater losses during extreme events because they focus risk managers on the "probability of loss" thereby diverting attention from the "potential magnitude of loss" under adverse conditions).

[16] *See* Ingrid Gould Ellen, John Napier Tye, & Mark A. Willis, *Improving U.S. Housing Finance Through Reform of Fannie Mae and Freddie MAC: Assessing the Options* 2 (2010).

[17] Id. at 4.

created a predictable and unhealthy economic dynamic. When a lender holds the loan it makes, it will suffer the consequences of default, which creates an incentive to make sure that the buyer can pay and that the collateral, the property that a bank might seize and sell in the event of a default, has enough value to justify the loan. If the banker making and holding the loan operates within the community where the property and borrower are located, it is well positioned to get all the information necessary to make this assessment well. Securitization changes the incentives. If the lender can sell the mortgage to investors, it will not suffer the consequences of default, and therefore need not concern itself too much with the loan's quality.

Securitization took off in the years preceding 2008, with issuers creating increasingly complex financial products that included mortgages, with some subprime loans in the mix, and selling them, for a fee, to investors around the world. These products included collateral mortgage obligations (CMOs), bundles of securities based on groups of mortgages, and collateral debt obligations (CDOs), bundles of securities based on different types of loans that sometimes included mortgage loans in the mix. (Since one might think of CMOs as a type of CDO, I will refer to both as CDOs.) Furthermore, financial firms sold derivatives based on these securities, basically bets on the future of these securities.

Financial firms designed their CDOs to serve several purposes, none of them having the slightest social utility. The first purpose was simply to multiply the number of financial products financial institutions could sell and thereby multiply fees.[18] A second purpose was to allow financial institutions to sell risks to investors that would otherwise boost their requirements to hold capital reserves – in other words, to evade regulation.[19] A third purpose was to allow the use of "special purpose entities" to facilitate off-shore tax evasion.[20] A fourth purpose was to reduce the amount of scrutiny investors would give before purchasing loans.[21] Prior to the development of the more sophisticated investment vehicles, purchasers of a mortgage could examine detailed information for each loan they would purchase. By creating vast pools of loans,

---

[18] Arthur E. Wilmarth, Jr., "The Dark Side of Universal Banking: Conglomerates and the Origins of the Subprime Financial Crises," 41 *Conn. L. Rev.* 966, 995 (2009) (describing the model of originating loans to distribute them through CDOs as maximizing fees). Certain technical features of CDOs, such as the dicing of them into tranches with varying risk characteristics, also made the fees high. *See* Gillian Tett, *Fool's Gold: How the Bold Dream of a Small Tribe at J.P. Morgan Was Corrupted by Wall Street Greed and Unleashed Catastrophe* 52–53 (2009).

[19] Tett, id. at 45.

[20] Id. at 54.

[21] *Cf.* Wilmarth, *supra* note 18, at 995 (describing the transfer of risk to investors as a goal of the originate to distribute model); Eggert, *supra* note 6, at 1268 (pointing out that it was the CDO that made it "almost impossible" to trace the mortgages generating the value in CDOs).

dicing them into finely engineered CDOs, and using abstract statistical models to evaluate CDOs' risks, the creators of these securities reduced the amount of knowledge investors had about each component of the investment, thereby increasing the risk of errors. This reduction in information costs increased risks and hurt investors, but served the purpose of allowing mass production of financial products that could multiply fees.

Faith in the financial models used in creating these securities led the ratings agencies to assign high ratings to many of these products, even when they included some subprime loans in the mix. The financial models helped convince large financial institutions, like Merrill Lynch, Bear Sterns, and Lehman Brothers, to participate heavily in securitizing, and in some cases issuing, subprime loans. Many large financial firms purchased subprime lenders to secure a source of origination for the loans they securitized, thus making the lunatic fringe of consumer lending a central part of the establishment.[22]

All this securitization changed lending's economic dynamics. Securitization increased the supply of funds available for making mortgages, as investors around the world purchased the newfangled, and apparently safe, products. This meant that lenders could earn fees by increasing the volume of mortgage lending with almost no limit, and without a great concern for quality. This led to a decline in underwriting standards.[23] Increasingly, lenders issued loans without verifying such basic information as employment and wage history. The industry even had a name for loans made based on false information about a borrower's capacity to pay: "liars' loans." Of course, this decline in underwriting standards increased the risk of defaults.

Although the literature on the financial crises provides strong support for the view that securitization contributed to a decline in underwriting standards, a few scholars seem to dissent.[24] Steven Schwarcz, for example, argues that the "liquidity glut" may have been a factor.[25] But securitization contributed to the liquidity glut. Even Schwarcz agrees, however, that securitization involves enough risk of moral hazard (the tendency of those immunized from risk's consequences to engage in risky behavior) to justify standards requiring originators

---

[22] *See* Partricia A. McCoy, Andrew D. Pavlov, & Susan M. Wachter, "Systemic Risk Through Securitization: The Result of Deregulation and Regulatory Failure," 41 *Conn. L. Rev.* 1329, 1354 (2009) (discussing Citibank's purchase of the "disreputable" subprime lender, Argent Mortgage, as an example of the "heavy inroads" of major banks into the low- and no-documentation loan business).

[23] *See* Wilmarth, *supra* note 14, at 1024–25 (discussing link among securitization, riskier loans, and lax underwriting); Eggert, *supra* note 6, at 1276–92 (reviewing the evidence regarding declines in underwriting standards and securitization).

[24] *See, e.g.,* Steven L. Schwarcz, The Future of Securitization, 41 *Conn. L. Rev.* 1313, 1318–21 (2009).

[25] Id. at 1319.

to keep some of the assets being securitized, so that they suffer consequences from lax underwriting.[26]

The financial models used to estimate the risks from CDOs and their derivatives, however, did not take the decline in underwriting standards into account. Financial models need data and have no way of dealing with critically important qualitative factors that have not generated data that analysts can feed into a model. Furthermore, the decline in underwriting standards appeared fairly late in the game, and the models were not completely up to date. Data take time to gather, so models cannot be up to date, and often key factors are qualitative and do not generate quantitative data at all.

The models also failed to anticipate the decline in housing prices that began to occur around 2007. It seemed to many observers that housing prices would rise forever, as they had experienced no serious nationwide decline since the 1930s. Nonetheless, a few economists predicted that housing prices would fall and disrupt mortgage markets. The financial modelers helping the industry estimate default risks had considered the possibility of localized declines in housing prices, but assumed that such a decline would not occur broadly across the entire country and therefore would not radically change the overall value of the securities. In this respect, these models, like all models predicting the future, provided very precise-looking guesswork.[27]

Dynamic factors such as the growing breadth of the securities markets and increasing speculative purchase of homes based on the housing bubble made twenty-first-century real estate markets more highly correlated than in the past. But using a quantitative model can divert attention from dynamic factors that make key assumptions in the model inaccurate.

Some of the people at J.P. Morgan who helped create the models and develop CDOs appreciated the model's limitations better than many model users did.[28] The J.P. Morgan crowd understood that a simultaneous decline in housing prices nationwide would create an unhealthy dynamic for CDOs based on mortgages.[29] They also understood that no reasonably recent data existed with which to model the likely extent of correlation of local real estate markets.[30] They therefore, after reluctantly participating in a few deals, initially kept J.P. Morgan out of mortgage-backed securitization (even though J.P. Morgan was a leader in derivatives generally).[31] This represents an application

---

[26] Id. at 1320.
[27] *See* Tett, *supra* note 18, at 64–69.
[28] *See* id.
[29] Id. at 68.
[30] Id. at 67.
[31] Id. at 69, 96, 103, 120.

of what might call the precautionary principle to finance, the idea that in the face of uncertainty one should usually avoid actions that might have serious negative consequences.

Competitive dynamics, however, made a cautious approach difficult to maintain. Competing financial institutions that became active in financing the Internet bubble realized enormous profits as a result.[32] Bubbles tend to generate attractive profits for those participating in the most dubious financial transactions. Competitors' profits placed enormous pressure on J.P. Morgan, which realized much less spectacular profits since it stayed away from some of the riskiest transactions, leading to two takeovers of the firm.[33] This dynamic suggests that market bubbles create pressures to follow the most profitable, and therefore the most dangerous, practices in the financial industry.[34]

The takeovers of J.P. Morgan exemplify a more widespread phenomenon generated by deregulation and the financial innovation it supported, the enormous growth in the size of the financial sector and its largest firms. Financial sector debt grew from $2.9 trillion, or 125 percent of GDP, in 1978, to more than $36 trillion, or 259 percent of GDP, in 2007.[35] These figures, striking as they are, exclude derivatives, which grew worldwide from near zero in 1978 to $33 trillion in 2008 – more than twice the U.S. GDP. Between 1980 and 2005, financial sector profits, which historically correlate well with profits in the economy as a whole, grew eightfold while firms serving the real economy did not even triple their profits.[36] Thus, the financial sector ceased to function as a mere adjunct of the real economy and became a dominant sector in its own right.

The largest financial institutions, freed from practically all regulatory structural restraints, became much bigger and more interconnected, both in absolute terms and relative to the size of the burgeoning financial sector. This bloating reflected both growth in the sector outpacing the real economy and a wave of frenetic mergers.[37] The ten largest bank holding companies held 26 percent of all bank assets and 17 percent of all deposits in 1990.[38] By 1999, their shares equaled 45 percent of all bank assets and 34 percent of all deposits.[39]

---

[32] Id. at 69, 76.

[33] Id. at 76–81, 103–104.

[34] *Accord* Jonathan R. Macey & James F. Holdcroft, Jr., "Failure Is an Option: An Ersatz-Antitrust Approach," 120 *Yale L. J.* 1368, 1383 (2011) (characterizing large banks as like "lemmings" because of their tendency to mimic each other's "bad bets").

[35] Johnson & Kwak, *supra* note 11, at 59.

[36] Id. at 60.

[37] Id. at 84–86.

[38] Id. at 85–86.

[39] Id.

The growth in economic concentration of the financial sector continued in the new century. Citibank and Travelers held $700 billion in assets in 1998 after their merger; their descendent, Citigroup, held $2.2 trillion in assets at the end of 2007 and had some relationship to an additional $1.1 trillion in off-balance-sheet assets.[40] Bank of America grew from $570 billion in assets to $1.7 trillion over roughly the same period.[41]

The sector's growing wealth generated increased political power. The sector became an ever-larger source of campaign contributions and invested $2.7 billion between 1999 and 2008 in lobbying to protect its interests.[42] The financial sectors' many hired guns usually found a receptive audience for their lobbying, as the overwhelming majority of those crafting the deregulatory financial policies of the late twentieth and early twenty-first centuries came from Wall Street. Of course, most of those with Wall Street backgrounds found the neoclassical law and economics' perspective natural, so faith in markets and disdain for regulation permeated the political establishment thoroughly.

When derivatives began to develop in earnest, representatives of the financial sector successfully urged their friends in government agencies to refrain from regulating derivatives, thereby allowing financial institutions to sell them privately without the transparency associated with stock exchanges. By this time, the financial institutions' power had become so great that they went beyond this regulatory victory and successfully lobbied Congress to pass a law prohibiting government agencies from ever regulating derivatives in the future. This decision reflected the dominant position the neoclassical law and economics notion that markets adequately regulate themselves had achieved among those in a position to regulate financial institutions.[43]

When housing prices declined and default rates began to rise, large financial institutions faced large exposure to the resulting risk, but figuring out the precise scope of this exposure had become impossible. The instruments securitizing the loans, the CDOs and derivatives based on them, had become too complex for the major players, let alone normal investors, to fully understand. And all of the derivatives had intertwined so many financial firms that the entire edifice began to crumble. This intertwining of risk was precisely, of course, the thing that Congress had designed Glass-Steagall to prevent.

---

[40] Id. at 86.

[41] Id. at 85–86.

[42] Sewall Chan, "Financial Crisis Was Avoidable, Commission Asserts," *New York Times*, A3 (January 26, 2011).

[43] Tett, *supra* note 18, at 29–40 (describing how true believers in self-regulating markets defeated regulation of derivatives).

In short order, major financial institutions such as Merrill Lynch, Lehman Brothers, Bear Sterns, and the American Insurance Group (AIG) basically collapsed and the entire economy began to slide toward depression.[44] In March 2008, Bear Sterns imploded and J.P. Morgan Chase purchased it for a pittance only after securing a guarantee that the New York Fed would pick up potential losses exceeding $1 billion.[45] On September 7, the government had to take over Fannie Mae and Freddie Mac and place them in a conservatorship – bankruptcy for GSEs.[46] Lehman Brothers went bankrupt when the Fed declined to bail it out later in September 2008.[47] The AIG's derivatives trades did it in, but the federal government kept it afloat to avoid a likely calamitous chain reaction.[48] Bank of America saved Merrill Lynch by purchasing it, only to find the subprime lending risk Merrill Lynch had incurred jeopardized Bank of America's survival.[49] Because of finance's globalization, the contagion spread overseas. For example, the Royal Bank of Scotland (RBS), while issuing statements minimizing its involvement in subprime lending, owned a division, Greenwich Capital Markets in Greenwich, Connecticut, that was a leader in securitizing mortgages, including securities with many subprime loans. Moreover, in 2007 (after the subprime lending sector already was in trouble) RBS acquired a Dutch bank, ABN Amro, which owned banks in the United States and was involved in subprime lending. The United Kingdom basically nationalized RBS in response to the crises.[50]

The U.S. federal government realized in 2008 that the collapse of large intertwined financial institutions threatened to bring down the whole economy. Clearly subprime lending and its securitization had created enormous systemic risk – that is, risk to the economy as a whole. Why had securitization, which many economists assume reduces risk, increased it? Basically, securitization had increased the volume of subprime lending. Since subprime lending is risky, increased volume implies increased risk. Also, the creation of derivatives meant that borrower defaults delivered losses not only to the holders of mortgages (including owners of mortgage-backed securities), but also to all of those who had bet on the securities' retaining or increasing their value.[51] Thus, derivatives multiplied the number of people and institutions facing losses from

---

[44] *See* Wilmarth, *supra* note 18, at 966–67.
[45] *See* Johnson & Kwak, *supra* note 11, at 158–59.
[46] Id. at 161.
[47] Id. at 162.
[48] Id. at 163.
[49] Id. at 168.
[50] *See* Wilmarth, *supra* note 18, at 1045.
[51] *See* id. at 970 (stating that large financial institutions "aggravated the risks of nonprime mortgages by creating multiple financial bets based" on them).

borrower defaults and multiplied the amount of risk (potential losses from a default) in the system exponentially.

These risks affected the big players in CDOs and their derivatives most seriously. But these big players purchased each others' securities and provided liquidity to much of the economy. So their fate became crucial to the economy as a whole. Thus, governments around the world faced a macroeconomic problem in 2008.

Richard Posner describes securitization as "reduc[ing] through diversification the risk of default."[52] This statement reflects modern portfolio theory's assertion that diversification reduces risk. Securitization itself, however, transfers risk; it does not diminish the amount of risk in the economy as a whole (as Posner seems to acknowledge).[53] Assume, for example, that a lender issues a subprime loan. That loan's riskiness depends on the borrower's financial status, housing prices, and prevailing interest rates (e.g., the risk of default will rise if an adjustable-rate mortgage resets at a higher rate than the borrower anticipates). Now the lender sells the loan to an investor, thus securitizing the loan. If the borrower's finances, the housing prices, and the interest rate remain the same, the risk is the same as it was before – neither more nor less. Now the bank that sold the loan has reduced its risk. But the risk to the investor who purchases the loan has increased. The overall economy experiences no change in the amount of risk when an originator sells a loan. This same analysis holds true for a more complex security bundling numerous mortgages. Securitization spreads, rather than diminishes, economywide risk.[54]

Posner's phrasing, even in a work that does recognize the financial crises' macroeconomic features, reflects neoclassical law and economics' fixation on microeconomics at the expense of emphasizing the dynamics influencing macroeconomics. From the transactional perspective at the heart of neoclassical law and economics, Posner's statement makes a lot of sense. After all, the bank selling the security does reduce its risk. Posner probably has something subtler in mind than this; perhaps the risk gets transferred to the actor most prepared to bear it, which economists treat as a form of risk reduction. Or perhaps he means that the risk of default from any one loan has become more widely shared, so that the risk from that default is less for any single actor.

[52] *See* Richard Posner, *A Failure of Capitalism: The Crises of '08 and the Descent into Depression* 55 (2009).
[53] *See* Wilmarth, *supra* note 18, at 985 (pointing out that "securitization permitted banks to transfer to investors much of the credit risk associated with securitized loans").
[54] *Cf.* David Colander et al., *The Financial Crisis and the Systemic Failure of Academic Economics*, Keil Working Paper No. 1489 12 (2009), ww.ifw-kiel.de (derivatives viewed "through the lens of general equilibrium models" appear to enhance efficiency, but this is an artifact of the model not an empirical fact).

Posner's characterization also can make sense if one embraces neoclassical assumptions about perfect information and rational actors under modern portfolio theory, which emphasizes reducing individual risk through diversification.[55] Perfectly informed rational actors would use these new financial tools to hedge their own risks from mortgage-backed securities. Thus, they might purchase a security allowing them to profit from continued payments and then use a derivative to bet that the securities' price will decline. This would diminish the risks from increased default rates for this rational actor. But for this bet on a price decline to occur somebody else must bet against the price decline, so the net effect is not a decrease in risk for the economy as a whole. The most prominent example of hedging helping one party at the expense of another without reducing overall risk in the economy involves Goldman Sachs, which bet, to some extent, on the decline in the subprime lending market and profited from those bets, but has been accused of duping its clients on the other side of the wager, who would experience reciprocal losses.

From an economywide perspective, however, the whole process had created a dynamic increasing risks to society as a whole, as Posner seems to recognize.[56] Hence, instruments designed to diminish some individuals' risk can generate enormous systemic risk threatening the well-being of millions of people.

Important systemic risks to the economy have roots in inevitably imperfect information and actions not wholly rational in the traditional economic sense.[57] Subprime lending losses, in and of themselves, might not sink any major economy, even though they can and did sink institutions relying on revenue from subprime lending for all, or almost all, of their revenue. Many subprime lenders went out of business in 2007 without destroying the economy as a whole. Losses turned into a crisis because of the economic dynamics of subprime losses at major financial institutions with wide-ranging and diverse activities.

These dynamics flow from the actions of economic actors in the face of inevitably incomplete information and substantial uncertainty about potentially serious threats. Once something is seriously amiss, many economic actors tend to avoid the transactions they see as risky. This avoidance behavior becomes especially virulent when the magnitude and scope of the risks have become impossible to determine. And that is what happened during the subprime crises. The value of the derivatives based on subprime loans and other

---

[55] *See* James R. Hackney, "The Enlightenment and the Financial Crises of 2008: An Intellectual History of Corporate Financial Theory," 54 *St. Louis U. L. J.* 1257, 1258 (2010).

[56] Id. (recognizing that securitization "spreads risk to ... otherwise ... safe markets").

[57] *See* Schwarcz, *supra* note 24, at 350 (stating that "in a panicked market investors may not act rationally").

assets were extremely difficult to properly calculate, because the financial instruments involved became too complex. Furthermore, it became difficult to know how much exposure various institutions had to the classes of assets investors had become concerned about. Accordingly trust declined, leading to a collapse of financial markets.[58]

Neoclassical law and economics' assumptions obviously could not help policymakers address the financial collapse. Government policymakers could not possibly quantify and weigh the costs and benefits of plausible policy responses, so instead they became dedicated (at least after Lehman Brothers' scary demise) to making sure that no major financial institution collapse, lest the economy slide into depression.[59] In making its commitment to financial institutions, government policymakers implicitly evaluated the situation's economic dynamics. They understood that the collapse of one institution could generate fear about another's fate, so that, like dominos, they all collapsed. They recognized that absent drastic action, liquidity would evaporate, and many businesses would have to shut down or at least scale back their operations for lack of capital. Hence, government actions at this time focused on minimizing budding systemic risks by reversing a negative economic dynamic.

This fundamental macroeconomic framework limited, but did not wholly determine, the choices government must make. For example, the United States' predominant strategy involved making massive loans to the largest financial institutions and receiving shares in return. By contrast, the United Kingdom virtually nationalized the Royal Bank of Scotland. Officials making these choices implicitly did so based on an analysis of what set of actions would best reduce fear in the market and avoid an economic dynamic leading to collapse. In doing so, they considered the advantages and disadvantages of nationalization, focusing on efficacy rather than balancing costs and benefits. Moreover, they could not possibly quantify nationalization's costs and benefits or those of bailouts even if they were of a mind to, since the benefits in particular defied quantification. The benefit of bailing out a bank should, in principle, equal the difference in losses from the economy absent nationalization from the losses that would ensue if banks were nationalized. But calculating either number was impossible. Hence, government made macroeconomic judgments based on the economic dynamics of the situation, not microeconomic judgments aimed at maximizing calculated net benefits.

---

[58] *See* Steven L. Schwarcz, "Keynote Address: The Case for a Market Liquidity Provider of Last Resort," 5 *NYU J. L. & Bus.* 346, 348 (2009) (citing a decline in confidence in financial institutions as the cause of the crises).

[59] Johnson & Kwak, *supra* note 11, at 167.

Policymakers also made some use of models and calculations, but not to measure the costs and benefits of policy to society as a whole. Thus, for example, the U.S. government employed stress tests, modeling large financial institutions' capacity to weather future economic downturns in order to evaluate whether they needed fresh infusions of capital after an initial round of bailouts. For the most part, stress tests reassured investors and led to an increase in confidence in the financial institutions, thereby helping to ameliorate the crises.

Hence, neoclassical law and economics set the stage for economic collapse by encouraging government deregulation and hubris among market actors. It proved utterly useless, however, when it came time to establish policy to address the financial crisis. Policymakers instead analyzed, in rudimentary terms, the economic dynamics they confronted and deployed a remedy designed to change the direction of change over time. Their decision to employ an economic dynamic approach almost surely saved the economy from an immediate long-term collapse.

By the time this book appears in print, we may know whether we have truly escaped a major depression or simply gained a temporary respite through the 2008 bailout. A slide back into depression after 2011 (if one materializes) will not prove the 2008 measures mistaken, but will instead reflect an ill-advised failure to take further steps to prevent a backsliding in the years immediately following the 2008 debacle.

The next chapter (Chapter 4) further develops the economic dynamic theory of law described in the introduction. Chapter 5 applies that theory to the subject of financial reform.

4

The Economic Dynamic Theory

The economic dynamic theory requires a focus on the shape of change over time. Its chief normative goal involves the avoidance of systemic risk without shutting down important opportunities for economic development. Finally, it employs economic dynamic analysis in order to identify systemic risks and proposals to avoid them or meet other legal goals. Accordingly, an economic dynamic approach implicates law's focus, goals, and methods; this chapter takes up each of these elements in turn. It then addresses a possible concern about the theory: the question of how this theory addresses the collateral negative consequences of measures chosen to avoid systemic risks. It closes by describing how widely recognized economic tools can aid economic dynamic analysis.

FOCUS ON THE SHAPE OF CHANGE OVER TIME

In Chapter 3 we saw that policymakers confronting a major financial crisis focused on the likely future direction of change over time – straight down. They saw their task not as achieving some perfect equilibrium or providing an ideal allocation of resources, but as changing the direction the economic dynamics pushed toward by stabilizing the economy to prevent a downward turn from metastasizing into a broad economic collapse.

This focus on the direction of change over time, though underappreciated, plays a fundamental role in our law, and not only in moments of such obvious crisis. Lawmakers create new law because they recognize that a serious problem requires a remedy. This often means that they see society headed down a self-destructive path and pass legislation or take other action to change that path's direction. Lawmakers sometimes seek to provide new opportunities as well. But often those goals merge. Avoiding future dangers opens up space to seize opportunities.

Subsequent chapters will show that this focus on change over time, although fairly obvious in the public law area, permeates the common law as well. The common law, we shall see, often provides a framework to manage change over time.

Path Dependence

The idea of focusing on the shape of change over time builds on the institutional economic concept of path dependence, which teaches us that past choices tend to constrain future decisions. We often enact laws because we see ourselves headed down a path that promises bad outcome and wish to change that path. We need to see the nature of the path we are on and envision what different paths might look like in order to make appropriate choices.

Embracing Normative Commitment

A commitment to focusing on change over time suggests that law involves choosing normative commitments.[1] Efforts to address climate disruption, the financial crisis, and terrorism, for example, reflect normative commitments to a healthy environment, a sound economy, and national security. Thus, current efforts to address climate disruption recognize that we currently march down a path fraught with dangers, such as massive ecological disturbance, increasingly violent natural disasters, and eventual depletion of fossil fuels. Those addressing climate disruption should aim to change our direction to one of conserving fossil fuel resources and minimizing climate disruption's impacts. Similarly, those crafting U.S. counterterrorism efforts foresee an increasingly violent world where horribly destructive attacks such as those that occurred on September 11 become common. The counterterrorism effort aims to put us on a path to a safer world, where such mass violence disappears.

Normative commitments exist at a fairly high degree of generality. I will have more to say later in this chapter and throughout the book about translating general commitments into specific government actions. But successful law starts with basic normative commitments like these, which help frame debates about specific actions and seek to change the direction of change over time.

Although it may seem obvious that such efforts to change the shape of change over time (and the vision of a better future such a focus implies) influences and should pervade law, the law and economics movement has spent the last several decades portraying law as an enterprise that does not – or at least should

[1] *Accord* Jed Rubenfeld, *Freedom and Time: A Theory of Constitutional Self-Government* (2001).

not – reshape our future. As Douglas Kysar points out, law and economics seems to deny the very idea of normative engagement.[2] Instead, it sees law as about satisfying individuals' current preferences. A focus on change over time implies a recognition that law must creatively shape preferences.[3] If satisfying existing preferences favors racial injustice, environmental destruction, or financial collapse, the focus on the shape of change over time suggests that policymakers ought not try to satisfy individual preferences, but should discuss what sort of society we hope to become. Although one can raise legitimate questions about the extent of law's capacity to reshape preferences,[4] it often comes into being because individuals pursuing their individual preferences have created serious problems that require remedies. Summing up preferences does not necessarily remedy problems that preferences create, so society should not necessarily address societal problems by summing up preferences. One can debate, for instance, whether society should address recreational drug use through legalization and treatment or through harsh penalties, but government would fail us if policymakers simply treated a preference for heroin as an element of a cost-benefit calculus, weighing the benefits of heroin use as shown by drug users' willingness to pay against whatever costs it imposes on society to formulate policy.

Regulators usually aim to advance some broad policy goal enjoying sufficient political support to indicate some alignment with citizens' political views, rather than to satisfy individual preferences for goods and services. Accordingly, regulatory regimes often reflect citizens' aspirations for the society as a whole, not just their preferences for benefits as individual consumers. As we saw in Chapter 2, the philosopher Mark Sagoff explains that citizens' collective ideals for society differ from an aggregate of their individual preferences as consumers. Moreover, he points out, each individual's own ideals for society, which many individuals may support at the ballot box and work toward promoting, may differ from each person's own individual preferences.[5]

Law creates a temporally extended commitment to a better future. Law is not like an individual purchase decision, a decision made according to an individual's preferences at a given moment. Instead, law involves a decision by

[2] Douglas A. Kysar, *Regulating from Nowhere: Environmental Law and the Search for Objectivity* (2010).
[3] *See* id. at 117.
[4] *See, e.g.*, Russell B. Korbkin & Thomas S. Ulen, "Law and Behavioral Science: Removing the Rationality Assumption from Law and Economics," 88 *Cal. L. Rev.* 1051, 1115–16 (2000) (describing the question of whether the law should change behavior rooted in habits, traditions, or addictions as controversial).
[5] *See* Mark Sagoff, *The Economy of the Earth* (1988).

the society as a whole about what rules to put in place. As such, every decision to enact a law, including a common law decision establishing precedent, governs the future, often for an extended period of time.

In putting forth a vision of law as embracing a set of normative commitments, I do not mean to deny that special interests often shape the law to their liking. But lawmakers should, and sometimes do, embrace normative commitments that make sense for society.

Hence, lawmakers must think about the nature of the changes they see occurring and anticipate occurring in the future. They cannot merely calculate; they must commit.

A Macroeconomic Perspective: Law as a Framework, Rather than a Resource Allocator

The view of law as shaping the future's general contours assigns it a broad role. Insofar as this role is economic, it is macroeconomic, not microeconomic. From this vantage point law does not function as a master allocator of resources, but provides a framework for avoiding economy-wide disasters and creating opportunities for economic development. In providing a framework that can preserve or help create economic opportunities, it resembles monetary policy. Monetary policy influences, but does not control resource allocation, providing a framework that influences the course of economic development. Even when the law has few directly observable impacts on output or employment, it typically has broad and temporally extended impacts that make macroeconomics a better analogue for law creation than microeconomic transactions.

Thus, for example, if the government uses its antitrust authority to break up a monopoly, it provides a framework for macroeconomic development, rather than determines resource allocation. By negating the existing market structure, trust-busting does prohibit a large actor from continuing to exist in its current form, but leaves to subsequent market decisions the question of how to allocate production resources among the remaining firms or future entrants. Of course, a consistent policy of breaking up extremely large entities will cause sensible market participants to decline to create monopolies or large oligopolies, thereby establishing a framework for resource allocation. Since producers can choose a variety of firm sizes and combinations consistent with a prohibition on monopoly or oligopoly, even a vigorous antitrust policy does not determine the specifics of market structure, let alone resource allocation within that market structure.

Similarly, when Great Depression-era reformers decided to separate commercial and investment banking, they did not determine how many loans banks would make, what they would pay their employees, or even what mix of transactions they would engage in within their designated spheres. Government did not make fine-grained allocation decisions; instead it provided a framework for private decisions allocating resources.

More fundamentally, governments define property rights. This definition of property rights facilitates transactions, but does not determine how market actors allocate resources.

Government regulation influences resource allocation more directly when it moves from regulating conduct or market structure to setting prices, as it has sometimes done in regulating industries thought of as natural monopolies, such as electric utilities, telephone companies, and airlines. Although this sort of regulation has often embraced some fairness concerns, efficient resource allocation serves as a major goal of these regimes, which seek to prevent natural monopolies from extracting exorbitant rents from consumers. The remedy of government-set prices providing a fair rate of return on capital roughly emulates efficient markets in areas where competitive markets would not normally arise. And the deregulation that ensued in regulated industries in the 1970s and 1980s likewise aimed at achieving allocative efficiency, as deregulatory reformers argued that competition under a different regulatory structure would allocate resources more efficiently than government regulators could through price controls. Even these regulatory and deregulatory decisions, however, involved an effort to shape the future, not just to serve existing preferences. Macroeconomic concerns about stifling innovation that might generate not just increased efficiencies, but also economic development, played a role in some of these deregulatory decisions; government officials wanted to open up room to create new preferences – such as, it turned out, a preference for cellular phones – not just serve the old ones. And an ideal of universal service, where rural communities obtain access to key services at reasonable prices, permeated both government rate making and the specifics of deregulatory regimes, even though an efficiency goal would dictate that rural consumers would have no service or pay exorbitant prices, since rural areas do not offer the economies of scale that lower the costs of providing services in densely populated regions.[6] Universal access policies implicitly involve a vision of a future of full national integration, embracing even remote

[6] See David M. Driesen, The Economic Dynamics of Environmental Law 206–07 (2003); Joseph Kearney & Thomas W. Merrill, "The Great Transformation of Regulated Industries Law," 98 Colum. L. Rev. 1323, 1347–48 (1997).

areas within the country. Thus, even price regulation pays attention to shaping our future, making efficiency one (albeit a major one) among several goals.

Outside the regulatory context, government makes some decisions that allocate resources directly, most obviously through government procurement decisions, spending programs, and taxation. Often, however, long-term macroeconomic concerns influence even these programs. For example, desire for increased economic growth motivated tax cuts in recent years. Similarly, many government expenditures seek to shape the future and reflect decisions about what sort of people we are. In an era when society views itself as deeply involved in providing basic economic security for individuals, robust welfare programs come into being. Great Society programs in the United States and social welfare programs in Europe aimed to prevent widespread poverty that portended potential social chaos. These programs involved a vision of a society in which all participated with an adequate resource base. Those who subsequently sought to limit social spending in the United States saw themselves as changing the country's character and future as well. Decrying growing dependence on government and the erosion of ideals of self-reliance important to having a productive people, conservatives sought to limit the nanny state. They envisioned an "ownership society," in which society reduced poverty and encouraged economic growth through greater individual productivity. For conservatives and liberals alike, macroeconomic concerns influence government policy about taxing and spending.

Even government procurement, where efficiency concerns should and often do play a major role, sometimes has transformative ambitions. Thus, many local governments purchase vehicles employing very clean fuel or other advanced technology in order to create an impetus to advance technological development contributing to future progress in reducing pollution. These clean fuel fleet programs involve deliberate decisions to pay more than necessary to provide transportation in order to realize a broader social goal over time. Nor can we explain clean fuel fleet programs merely as programs in which municipalities efficiently purchase some environmental benefits with their transportation dollars. Instead, these programs have government play a role in catalyzing the growth and development of clean technology over time. Nobody claims that these programs offer the most cost-effective approach to meeting immediate pollution reduction targets, but they do play a role in securing a better future. So even when government acts as a market participant rather than a regulator and therefore participates directly in resource allocation, it frequently does so with an eye on social or economic transformation over time, not merely satisfaction of existing preferences.

Thus, most government regulatory regimes address change over time by establishing a framework for realizing normative goals. With the possible and limited exception of now largely defunct price controls, government regulatory regimes are not primarily about static economic efficiency. Outside the regulatory context, macroeconomic motives frequently play a large role in tax policy and occasionally even in some government spending decisions. Accordingly, for most legal decisions, macroeconomic policy measures form a more appropriate analogy than microeconomic transactions.

The Relative Triviality of Equilibrium and Preferences

Recognizing law's role as a temporally extended enterprise for realizing normative commitments leads to a recognition of the triviality of the equilibrium goal at the heart of traditional law and economics. A law's costs and benefits will vary over time depending on how the activities it regulates change. Today's equilibrium will inevitably disappear tomorrow, implying that equilibrium is a transient, fleeting thing too trivial to serve as a major goal for law.

Chapter 2 explains that frequently inefficient innovation plays a much greater role in economic growth and wealth enhancement than static efficiency does. Innovation can drive changes that make old investments inefficient and cause costly and sometimes inefficient adjustments, even as it creates new wealth.

Consumers' individual preferences, as expressed in their purchase decisions, should enjoy no special pride of place in government policy. People daily express their preferences in markets for all sorts of goods and services. Yet the literature on happiness shows that past a certain minimum increased consumption does almost nothing to promote human happiness.[7] Thoughtful

---

[7] *See, e.g.*, Christine Jolls, "Dworkin's 'Living Well' and the Well-Being Revolution," 90 *B.U. L. Rev.* 641, 650–51 (2010) (finding "high income . . . spectacularly unimportant to . . . well-being"); John Bronsteen, Christopher Buccafusco, & Jonathan S. Masur, "Welfare as Happiness," 98 *Geo. L. J.* 1538, 1587 (2010) (characterizing "making people wealthier" or satisfying their preferences as "weak proxies for their experienced well-being"); Mark Sagoff, *Price, Principle, and the Environment* 102 (2004) (pointing out that "virtually all . . . empirical evidence" shows "no correlation" between preference satisfaction and well-being "after basic needs are met"); Ed Diener & Robert Biswas-Diener, "Will Money Increase Subjective Well-Being?: A Literature Review and Guide to Needed Research," 57 *Soc. Indicators Res.* 119 (2002); Robert H. Frank, *Luxury Fever: Why Money Fails to Satisfy in an Era of Success* 6 (1999) (arguing that after a certain threshold has been reached increases in material wealth do not correlate with increases in subjective well-being); Richard A. Easterlin, "Will Raising the Incomes of All Increase the Happiness of All?," 27 *J. Econ. Behav. Org.* 35 (1995). *Cf.* Matthew Adler & Eric A. Posner, "Happiness Research and CBA," 37 *J. Legal Stud.* 253 (2008) (arguing that happiness research does not undermine their case for CBA based on "laundered preferences").

scholars have been aware for some time of occasional disconnects between individual preferences and individual well-being and people's preferences, such as the hapless drug addict who brings misery upon himself when he satisfies his preference for drug use. The broad disconnect between consumption and happiness, however, poses a fundamental challenge to the whole idea of individual preference satisfaction as a major goal for government. Indeed, government provides a forum where society can solve long-term problems created in part by individuals' myopic pursuit of short-term preferences. This is not to say that government should forbid the pursuit of happiness, even when silly choices make it elusive. But government must deal with many of the negative consequences of socially counterproductive behavior (including productive behavior with negative by-products).

People have ample incentives to focus on their short-term impulses and desires. We form governments to create stable cooperation in solving long-term problems.

Thus, a focus on change over time reflects a more accurate and better view of government than the neoclassical framework. It recognizes that law creates a framework for effectuating normative commitments over an extended period of time. It does not generally try to make government imitate the perceived virtues of markets, as an aggregator or preferences and as an achiever of an elusive static equilibrium.

GOALS

The focus on the shape of change over time builds upon and fosters agreement about basic societal goals. Frequently, society can agree about what sorts of paths create threats to our long-term interests. Thus, widespread consensus exists that we wish to avoid terrorist attacks, environmental catastrophes, and economic collapse. More positively, society can frequently agree about what the general shape of desirable change over time looks like. We should pursue national security, a clean environment, and a sound economy. These points of agreement are extremely important, as they form the basis for moving forward in addressing serious problems. We can usefully evaluate actions in terms of whether they move society in the agreed-upon direction. Hence, the simple idea that government should move society in a desirable direction over time provides the basis for sound government.

That said, legitimate disagreements arise about the proper role of the state in every society, even though functional societies have significant shared goals. This implies some level of disagreement about what goals law should have and a lot of disagreement about the means of achieving those goals. Anxiety about

political disagreement about goals, even though this tends to be minor compared to disagreement about means, leads many technocrats (law professors
like myself and other policy professionals) to pretend they have abandoned
the whole project of normative engagement in favor of cost-benefit balancing.
Although at the end of the day this amounts to embracing a goal of short-term
economic efficiency (or some similar goal maximizing individual desires at
the moment) at the expense of long-term goals and equity, it gives an appearance of neutrality.[8] In this context, it will prove helpful to discuss the goals an
economic dynamic theory embraces.

Avoidance of Systemic Risk as a Major Minimum Goal

Institutional economics has something to say about how lawmakers should
formulate law's goals.[9] Douglas North points out that uncertainty about the
future often makes calculation of costs and benefits impossible, as it was when
policymakers confronted the financial crisis. In such situations, actors should
try to keep society's options open.[10] North thus favors a goal of providing scope
for creative endeavor and change. He calls his concept *adaptive efficiency*, a
locution suggesting a goal of keeping a society resilient enough to adapt to
changes in its environment (both physical and social).[11]

This adaptive efficiency objective suggests an overarching goal for society:
the avoidance of systemic risk. Economists typically define systemic risk in
terms of their preferred object of study, the economy, using it to describe
risks to the economy as a whole, or at least to a substantial portion of it.[12]
The economic definition highlights the problem of risk spilling over from
one institution to another, implicating confidence in the financial system as
a whole. Finally, economists and policymakers use the term to signal significant "macroeconomic effects," such as substantial reductions in output and

---

[8] Although economists and many policymakers and lawyers associate CBA with efficiency, the
  most thoughtful philosophical defense of CBA instead sees it as serving a goal of "overall well-
  being." *See* Matthew D. Adler & Eric A. Posner, *New Foundations of Cost-Benefit Analysis*
  (2006). Overall well-being refers primarily to an aggregate of individual desirves, but with some
  "laundering" of preferences to make sure that objectively bad preferences do not count.

[9] *See generally* Edward L. Rubin, "The New Legal Process, the Synthesis of Discourse, and
  the Microeconomic Analysis of Institutions," 109 *Harv. L. Rev.* 1393 (1996) (arguing for using
  institutional economic analysis to unite disparate legal academic discourses).

[10] *Accord* Cass R. Sunstein, *Worst-Case Scenarios* 9 (2007) (suggesting that we "maintain flexibility" when the probabilities of catastrophe are not known).

[11] Douglas C. North, *Institutions, Institutional Change, and Economic Performance* 81 (1990).

[12] *See* Stefan Gerlach, *Defining and Measuring Systemic Risk* 3–4 (November 23, 2009), available
  at http://www.europparl.europa.edu/activities/committees/studies.do?language=EN.

employment. The term, however, indicates more than that, as it addresses risks to systems generally, not just to economic systems. Hence, the concept of systemic risk encompasses risks to our planet's ecosystem, or a large portion of it, when these risks affect multiple resources at once, involve serious negative consequences, and impair fundamental natural systems. Similarly, the term includes risks that destroy the basis for social trust in a society, such as risks of war or other massive destruction destroying social or political systems. Thus, the goal of avoiding systemic risk properly applies to all our key systems.

The goal of avoiding systemic risk has a lot in common with the precautionary principle, but it operates at once more vigorously and more narrowly than the precautionary principle. The precautionary principle generally states that uncertainty shall not provide a basis for failing to take actions reducing risks.[13] As such, it applies to all significant risks, not just systemic risks, so that a goal of avoiding systemic risks functions more narrowly than the precautionary principle. Within its narrow domain, however, the goal of avoiding systemic risk operates more vigorously than the precautionary principle by creating an affirmative duty to reduce risk. By contrast, the precautionary principle just takes scientific uncertainty off the table as a reason for inaction, leaving open a variety of other reasons for inaction.

Broadly conceived to embrace multiple systems, not just the economy, avoidance of systemic risk constitutes a primary goal that underlies a lot of widely agreed-upon objectives and offers a vision of the minimum goals a state should seek to accomplish. We expect governments to prevent potential man-made catastrophes. This goal underlies financial reform, counterterrorism, and climate disruption policy. The concept of adaptive efficiency supports this goal, because systemic risks cut off opportunities for a society. An economic depression makes it very hard to have a productive economy and creates widespread poverty, thereby minimizing economic opportunity for many people. Widespread terrorism threatens the same sort of economic catastrophe, limits people's opportunities to engage in the world by making them fear participation in activities that might make them targets, and can create dissension and distrust within a society, which can lead to reduced freedom and diminished opportunities to work together toward common goals. Climate disruption can also cause economic catastrophe, disrupt food supplies, spread infectious diseases, destroy water supplies, and thereby undermine the minimum physical conditions for living an adequate life. These sorts of problems can greatly limit economic and social opportunities.

●

[13] *See* John Applegate, "Embracing a Precautionary Approach to Climate Change," in *Economic Thought and U.S. Climate Change Policy* 171–96 (David M. Driesen, ed., 2010).

Failing to avoid systemic risks also constrains collective choices in significant ways. A society facing a serious terrorism threat cannot provide as much freedom for its people as a society that has eliminated the threat. A society in a depression loses the opportunity to choose a laissez-faire policy that might maximize economic freedom, as such a policy cannot cure a depression. A society suffering from a climate catastrophe's effects cannot preserve its biodiversity, cannot use much of its land (for example, in increasingly large flood-prone areas), and must devote huge resources to disaster relief and public health measures. In short, systemic risks limit society's opportunities and, therefore, its capacity to adapt to changing conditions.

Identifying Significant Systemic Risks

The definition of systemic risk I have offered implies that the goal of avoiding systemic risks limits itself to avoiding very serious harms indeed. But economic dynamic theory adopts as a major societal goal avoidance of only "significant" systemic risks. Significance implies a focus on systemic risks that are reasonably likely or have unknown probabilities. Although government may choose at times to take small steps to avoid low-probability risks, this is not a major goal of economic dynamic theory.

Governments aiming to address significant systemic risks need to carefully study available information about the nature of risks we face, including the likelihood of them occurring, in order to separate systemic risks from ordinary risks and to make sure that serious efforts focus on significant risks. The differentiation of systemic risks from nonsystemic risks requires analysis of the dynamics of systems to see whether the evil examined produces the kinds of negative spillover effects undermining entire systems that characterize systemic risks. Analysis of dynamics also produces knowledge – albeit rarely quantifiable knowledge – about the likelihood of a risk becoming a systemic problem.[14] Chapters 10 and 11 will illustrate how we separate significant systemic risks from other kinds of risks.

Systemic Risk Avoidance versus Optimality

Although thoughtful commentators like Richard Posner recognize that catastrophic systemic risks provide a special challenge to law and economics,

---

[14] *See* Martin L. Weitzman, "On Modeling and Interpreting the Economics of Catastrophic Climate Change," 91 *Rev. Econ. & Statistics* 1 (2009); Martin L. Weitzman, "A Review of the Stern Review on the Economics of Climate Change," 45 *J. Econ. Lit.* 703 (2007).

economics tends to treat all risks alike and to see society's task as providing an optimal balance between costs and benefit. This perspective implies that policymakers should focus on the task of quantifying the risk at issue, systemic or not, in dollar terms in order to allow it to be weighed against costs incurred in its avoidance. Thus, if we know the probability of some catastrophic event occurring and we know its consequences reasonably well, economists will calculate a value by discounting the predicted event's value by the probability of its occurrence.[15]

There is something to be said for this approach, even in the case of catastrophic events, but not as much as many law and economics scholars believe. No man-made catastrophe destroys everything. Even nuclear war, which might destroy all human beings and many other life forms, would probably not shatter the earth itself. Catastrophes can have varying effects and therefore varying magnitudes. Therefore, even with a catastrophe, it is possible to ask questions about the magnitude of effects.

Although one can ask questions about the magnitude of potential catastrophes, one cannot answer them with reasonable precision. The dynamics that create catastrophes rule out reasonably reliable calculation of their magnitude, although we usually know enough about their nature to enable us to decide which risks constitute serious systemic risks. We might predict that terrorists will strike again, that burning fossil fuels will disrupt the climate, or that financial markets will collapse. This does not mean that we know how many people the terrorists will kill, how many humans and other living beings will perish as seas rise and violent storms and droughts afflict us, or how many will lose their jobs in a new depression.

Nor can we quantify the probability of a terrorist attack, a climate catastrophe, or an economic collapse. I will illustrate our inability to quantify systemic risks further in subsequent chapters. Thus, where systemic risk exists, we have to make avoiding the systemic risk the chief societal goal, rather than make a balance between the systemic risks and the costs of avoiding it the main goal.

Government decisionmakers may, of course, legitimately choose to pursue desirable changes over time where no systemic risk presents itself. The economic dynamic theory may not dictate particular goals in such cases, but the theory's focus on change over time asks policymakers to choose goals that make society better over time. And economic dynamic analysis, discussed next, applies to a variety of goals, even though I discuss it here primarily in the context of avoiding systemic risks. For example, policymakers can use economic

[15] *See* Sunstein, *supra* note 10, at 8.

dynamic analysis to help them select policies producing just outcomes that depend upon the consequences of government policies.

USING ECONOMIC DYNAMIC ANALYSIS TO CHOOSE THE MEANS
OF AVOIDING SYSTEMIC RISK

Generally, any analysis of law's consequences must include economic dynamic analysis because a law creates incentives, and its consequences depend on the responses to these incentives. This section develops the concept of economic dynamic analysis and explains how it can provide good answers to fundamental questions about how law influences the future.

Functions

Policymakers can use economic dynamic analysis to evaluate whether a measure, or a package of measures, will prove effective in avoiding systemic risk – the primary question one should address in crafting measures to address systemic risk. Policymakers can also employ economic dynamic analysis to a large number of related questions that arise when focusing on long-term trajectories. Analysts already use economic dynamic analysis to identify systemic risks in the first place. This same form of analysis can help identify whether a measure aimed at avoiding a systemic risk itself poses a systemic risk or creates other kinds of risks that one might avoid through the selection of alternative measures or approaches. One can use this form of analysis to try to anticipate whom law will empower, an important question for predicting law's ability to address a problem over time. Although economic dynamic analysis does not resolve all normative questions that society confronts in choosing how to avoid systemic risk or achieve other desirable changes over time, it does at least clarify the basic dimensions of the choices society must make, thereby facilitating thoughtful normative engagement and well-informed wise choices.

A Systematic Approach to Economic Incentives

The idea of the economic dynamic analysis of law develops and extends one of conventional law and economics' key insights – its recognition of economic incentives as important. Many legal scholars employ this insight routinely, frequently commenting on the incentives a particular law creates. Policymakers also frequently consider the incentives a law creates, as the tax on marriage example offered in the introduction suggests.

Yet academic lawyers' analysis of economic incentives frequently appears ad hoc. Typically, the "analysis" consists only of an observation that law X creates an incentive to do Y, with no analysis of whether Y will likely occur.

A good example of this tendency to substitute a mere observation for real analysis of economic dynamics comes from standard analysis of the practice of imposing stricter pollution control standards on new sources than we do on existing sources of pollution. Numerous commentators and policymakers have suggested that this differential in standards retards turnover of facilities by providing a disincentive to the creation of new pollution sources. Congress apparently thought about this disincentive problem, for it required the Environmental Protection Agency (EPA) to impose strict new source controls not just on new facilities, but also on modified facilities. Thus, facility owners cannot add capacity increasing emissions without adding state-of-the-art pollution controls. This implies that strict new source controls apply not only to new sources, but also to existing sources of pollution (when they upgrade). Until recently, analysts generally ignored the modification provisions in the Clean Air Act in analyzing new source review's incentives, thereby raising the risk of reaching erroneous conclusions.

Legal Precision
Economic dynamic analysis demands attention to legal detail, which conventional analysis of economic incentives often lacks. Richard Revesz and Jonathan Remy Nash's recent work on new source review exemplifies the benefits of this improvement in precision.[16] They do pay attention to the Clean Air Act's modification provisions and therefore reach more nuanced conclusions about the law's effects than other commentators. Simply put, if new source review applies both to new sources and to modifications, then it does not create incentives to choose modification of an existing source over construction of a new source.[17]

---

[16] *See* Richard Revesz & Jonathan Nash, "Grandfathering and Environmental Regulation: The Law And Economics of New Source Review," 101 *Nw. U. L. Rev.* 1677 (2007); *see also* Driesen, *supra* note 6, at 187–91.

[17] I have assumed for purposes of creating a simple illustration that EPA implements modification provisions in a straightforward manner. It does not. As a result, modification provisions often do not apply in situations where the literal language in the statute would indicate that they should. Of course, this implies that an economic dynamic analysis of the statute's effect as enacted might reach different conclusions from an analysis of EPA's implementation of the statute. But the fundamental point that economic dynamic analysis benefits from consideration of countervailing incentives does not depend on one's particular take on new source review.

Countervailing Incentives

Economic dynamic analysis also requires more complete analysis of incentives than legal scholars typically employ. Legal scholars usually focus only on the incentives a law creates. But other forces may create countervailing incentives. For example, the Clean Air Act new source review provisions create incentives to avoid modifying facilities or building new ones – that is, to keep old facilities running without modification. It does not follow that facility owners avoid updating or replacing their facilities. One must ask whether other laws or factors create countervailing incentives to update facilities. This inquiry must include analysis of such questions as whether equipment wears out and needs replacement and whether utilities face economic pressures to expand their capacity. Since equipment must wear out eventually, the answer to the first question alone implies that incentives to modify or replace facilities are stronger, at least in the long run, than the incentives to avoid all change, since running facilities with no change at all is physically impossible. And indeed, facility owners have renovated their facilities, avoiding required pollution control primarily through illegal avoidance of new source review requirements, which generated massive fines. In this example, the economic and physical incentives to renovate countervailed the law's incentive to leave facilities alone.

Bounded Rationality

Economic dynamic analysis also demands study of the likely response to economic incentives. Legal analysis implicitly relies on the neoclassical assumption that actors respond rationally to all pertinent information. This assumption, however, is known to be incorrect. A better approach to studying incentives' likely effects builds on the institutional economic concept of "bounded rationality."[18] Individuals and institutions pay attention to the incentives and information made relevant by their habits and routines, and ignore everything else. This implies that actors will not necessarily respond to all nominally relevant incentives. In order to figure out which incentives relevant actors will pay attention to, one must study the habits, routines, and tendencies of relevant institutions and individuals. One must also recognize that actors have limited time available for considering information. This latter observation becomes crucially important in a society in which access to information has become easier than ever, but the capacity and skill necessary to analyze information remains in short supply and may become scarcer than ever in the

---

[18] *See Organizational Theory: From Chester Barnard to The Present and Beyond* (Oliver Williamson, ed., 1995).

future.[19] Subsequent chapters will show that many perceptive scholars already take the concept of bounded rationality into account in analyzing economic incentives' effects, at least implicitly.[20]

The Public Choice Dimension: Empowerment Analysis

Economic dynamic analysis has a public choice dimension. Public choice theory posits that politicians have incentives to cater to large well-organized groups. As such, it reinforces neoclassical economics' tendency to favor deregulation, for it suggests that special interests will capture government, making wise regulation unlikely. The analysis of financial institutions' role in lobbying for deregulation presented in Chapter 3 matches what public choice theory would lead one to predict.

Yet we know that lawmaking sometimes does not conform to public choice theory's dictates. As Richard Revesz has pointed out, public choice theory cannot explain the existence of environmental law, which defends public interests at the expense of special interests.[21] It has become fashionable to speak of environmental groups as special interest groups. Yet environmental groups represent an interest in environmental quality that practically all citizens share – a general, not a special, interest. Public choice theory would lead to the conclusion that organizing those with such a broadly shared interest would prove much more difficult than organizing industries with a stake in any particular regulation, and, indeed, industry spends far more time and money on influencing environmental regulations than even the strongest environmental advocacy groups do. So environmental law does appear inconsistent with public choice theory.

More broadly, special interest influence seems to vary by country, even among democracies. So the extent of special interest influence must depend on some sets of conditions that vary with time and place. Special interests do not always win.

Surely law plays a role in empowering or disempowering special interests. Indeed, those enacting early U.S. antitrust laws aimed to reduce certain large corporations' influence, thereby empowering small business at the expense of

---

[19] *See generally* Nicholas Carr, *What the Internet is Doing to Our Brains: The Shallows* (2010).

[20] *See* Victoria Nourse & Gregory Shaffer, "Varieties of New Legal Realism: Can a New World Order Prompt a New Legal Theory?," 95 *Cornell L. Rev.* 61, 76–77 (2009) (suggesting that behavioral economists have successfully attacked rational actor models and that a behavioral approach is becoming the new mainstream analytical approach).

[21] *See* Richard L. Revesz, "Federalism and Environmental Regulation: A Public Choice Analysis," 115 *Harv. L. Rev.* 553, 571 (2001).

the trusts. By contrast, U.S. subsidies for fossil fuels have no doubt contributed to the fossil fuel industry's enormous wealth and power.

Economic dynamic analysis should include an evaluation of whom a proposed law would empower or disempower. When special interests become too powerful, they can lobby to thwart implementation or enforcement of laws. Thoughtful scholars have argued that this problem has influenced, and should influence, law's design.[22] This analysis can lead to laws designed to lessen special interest power, such as antitrust law and campaign finance reform. Or it can lead to avoidance strategies, as seen in President Obama's recent health care legislation, which accommodated health insurers' concerns in order to secure the passage of a reform. Either way, empowerment analysis should form part of economic dynamic analysis, especially when crafting legislation.

Scenario Analysis

Economic dynamic analysis of especially important decisions, such as a decision to enact a major legislative proposal, should incorporate scenario analysis.[23] This provides a way of thinking seriously about unpredictable risks.[24] Scenario analysis plays a prominent role in military planning, strategic planning in large businesses, and in government decision making abroad.

All these institutions face up to the fact that a mathematical model cannot predict the future, so careful analysis of several possibilities provides superior guidance for key decisions. Thus, scenario analysis focuses on understanding the variables that might influence the future and what various futures might look like. Although scenario analysis sometimes employs quantitative methods, its proponents emphasize identifying key causal relationships that could influence the future.

For purposes of avoiding systemic risk, such analysis should include some worst-case analysis.[25] An analysis of the key causal factors that might produce a catastrophe can better equip government to prevent or at least ameliorate such

---

[22] *See, e.g.,* Amy Sinden, "In Defense of Absolutes," 90 *Iowa L. Rev.* 1405 (2005) (arguing that concern about special interest influence justifies absolutism in the Endangered Species Act).

[23] *See generally* Daniel Farber, "Uncertainty," 99 *Geo. L. J.* 901, 933–34 (2011).

[24] *See* Richard B. Heydinger & Rene D. Zentner, *Multiple Scenario Analysis: Introducing Uncertainty into the Planning Process,* in *Applying Methods and Techniques of Futures Research,* 51, 51–52 (James L. Morrison, William L. Renfro, and Wayne I. Boucher, eds. 1983) (describing multiple scenario analysis as a way out of the "dilemma" of needing to plan for the future when no one forecast can be relied upon).

[25] *Accord* Peter Conti-Brown, "A Proposed Fat-Tail Risk Metric: Disclosures, Derivatives, and the Measurement of Financial Risk," 87 *Wash. U. L. Rev.* 1461 (2010) (proposing a particular method of analyzing the worst case to inform financial regulators and investors).

an event. The original interpretation of the National Environmental Policy Act included a requirement for worst-case analysis, but the executive branch and courts have subsequently eroded this requirement.[26] This erosion reflects the view that the government should not waste money studying unlikely scenarios. The study of a worst case, however, often serves as an important antidote to endemic tendencies toward hubris and overoptimism. Policymakers have an overwhelming tendency to imagine that their projects or continuation of a status quo trajectory that would prove difficult to disturb cannot possibly have a catastrophic outcome. By forcing policymakers to put their worst foot forward, worst-case analysis overcomes cognitive bias. Furthermore, often characterization of a worst case as a low-probability event reflects no actual study of a worst-case scenario and therefore has no scientific basis.[27] Often, scientists do not know the probabilities of various future events, so characterizations of worst cases as improbable often stem from the analyst's optimstic assumptions, not provable facts. Worst-case analysis forces analysts to critically examine their frequent assumption that a worst case must be unlikely and to learn about causal links that might cause or prevent a worst case from other experts. This will prevent them from assuming away the possibility of drastic consequences that society should take into account in making wise decisions. Society should assess potential worst cases, but temper its choice of remedies if a worse case appears unlikely after completing that assessment.

If resource constraints concern agencies engaged in economic dynamic analysis, scenario analysis can explore the causal chains leading to various outcomes and the general nature of outcomes, and eschew costly and very unreliable efforts to quantify the magnitude of possible consequences. Furthermore, the proposal to reserve scenario analysis for especially important decisions also takes information costs into account, as good scenario analysis can prove time consuming.

Subsequent chapters will show that U.S. neglect of scenario analysis has played a big role in its failure in Iraq and in addressing climate disruption, both of which have been subject to scenario analysis that top-level U.S. decision makers paid little attention to (although that is changing). Scenario analysis offers a much more realistic and useful approach to the problem of uncertainty than CBA based on probabilistic risk assessment.

Although it is easy to say that accidents can happen and nobody anticipates them, in fact, usually somebody does anticipate systemic risks (often

---

[26] *See* Farber, *supra* note 23, at 915.

[27] *Cf.* Richard A. Posner, *Catastrophe: Risk and Response* 49–50 (2004) (suggesting that the inability to attach probabilities to catastrophic climate change is a fundamental problem for Nordhaus's CBA of climate change).

through worst-case analysis focused on causal chains). We shall see in the next chapter that several scholars employing economic dynamic techniques foresaw the bursting of the housing bubble and its likely effects. Government, however, often fails to appreciate systemic risks because it does not regularly conduct economic dynamic analysis, even if it occasionally recognizes economic dynamics informally. It fails to protect us against systemic risks, partly because the belief that unregulated markets will adequately protect us has captivated many high-level government officials, and partly because when policymakers do think seriously about regulation, they too often focus on CBA rather than economic dynamics. One avoids systemic risks by seriously analyzing the dynamics that create them, not by pretending to measure the costs and benefits of particular actions as if every government decision has nothing more at stake than efficient resource allocation.

To summarize, economic dynamic analysis employs three core elements:

1) Studying the economic incentives law creates with careful attention to legal detail
2) Using the bounded rationality assumption to figure out which actors will pay attention to nominally applicable incentives and how they might respond
3) Considering whether countervailing incentives might counteract legal ones

It complements these three core elements with empowerment analysis and, for especially important large-scale measures, scenario analysis. This form of analysis provides a set of powerful tools for understanding law's implications and the problems it must confront.

ON EFFICACY AND COLLATERAL NEGATIVE CONSEQUENCES

Although society must make normative commitments, including the commitment to avoid systemic risk, it will confront choices in deciding how to fulfill these commitments. Economists tend to see this problem of means selection as a question of tradeoffs. Without denying that actions chosen to avoid systemic risks can have negative collateral consequences, an economic dynamic approach seeks to place the question of efficacy front and center. The question of efficacy focuses on whether a given measure (or a package of measures) helps substantially reduce the systemic risk of concern. It focuses on the cause-and-effect relationship between a contemplated measure and the risk it seeks to address. This section first argues for the centrality of efficacy and then discusses an economic dynamic approach to collateral negatives. It also includes comments on the role of CBA and other forms of economic analysis in an economic dynamic analysis.

Efficacy

Acceptance of the idea of law addressing change over time through normative commitments implies an emphasis on choosing the most efficacious way of achieving goals the society has agreed upon. If we have committed ourselves to some goal, when we go about choosing the means of fulfilling our commitments we focus first and foremost on evaluating how well various alternatives would work at effectuating our shared goals. We do not consider all the advantages and disadvantages of potential options anew. To do so would imply that we had made no normative commitment in the first place. Law and economics has confused policymakers by making them see tradeoffs everywhere, even though many key choices about how to address systemic risks implicate efficacy.

An example will help illustrate how problems often viewed as involving tradeoffs usually raise efficacy questions that economic dynamic analysis can help resolve. One can view decisions about whether to torture terror suspects as involving a tradeoff between national security and individual rights. But prominent military leaders have questioned this view. They see torture as fueling terrorism by providing propaganda opportunities aiding Al Qaeda's recruitment efforts.[28] This analysis would imply that torture does not provide the benefit of a reduced likelihood of terrorist attack, and therefore that there are no net deterrence benefits to be weighed against torture's costs. Policymakers cannot assess the problem of torture's potential downsides without assessing this argument. Many of our disputes about the means of achieving goals revolve not only around issues of tradeoffs, but also around questions of efficacy. Does invading Iraq combat or foment terrorism? Will President Obama's health care policy reduce or raise costs? Although collateral negative consequences can occur that require consideration, an emphasis on change over time implies greater emphasis on analyzing efficacy questions.

Because economic dynamic analysis focuses on evaluating how legal changes will actually influence conduct, it is well suited to evaluating questions of efficacy. These efficacy questions pervade government decision making and public discussion, but the lack of any analytical method for resolving them has

---

[28] Brief of *Amicus Curiae* of Former National Security Officials and Counterterrorism Experts in Support of Petitioner, *Ali Saleh Kahlah Al-Marri v. Daniel Spagone*, No. 08–368 (S. Ct. 2009).

converted them, at least in the United States, into almost theological matters, individually resolved by one's faith in government or markets instead of sound analysis, thereby dividing government officials into warring factions incapable of effective policymaking. Thus, economic dynamic theory's emphasis on efficacy provides an important tool for improving policymaking, especially in the United States.

Collateral Negative Consequences

At the same time, actions taken to avoid systemic risks can have serious negative consequences that society must consider. Hence, we must engage the question of how to take these negatives into account,[29] even though efficacy in avoiding systemic risks, which by definition are very serious, must remain the primary consideration.

We cannot forgo all risks, and the goal of avoiding systemic risks does not require such extreme caution. The concept of avoiding systemic risks does not require avoidance of all, or indeed any, individual risk. Readers should not make the error of confusing the goal of avoiding systemic risk with the goal of avoiding all harm.

Furthermore, Douglas North's concept of adaptive efficiency, which underlies the economic dynamic theory's goals, implies that we must choose options that allow a reasonably robust set of economic opportunities to remain as government takes actions needed to avoid systemic risks. The analysis that follows of how to deal with potential negative collateral consequences builds on this insight.

When measures taken to limit systemic risks present significant problems of their own, governments should consider a range of alternatives that hold promise of avoiding systemic risk, and economic dynamically analyze them for efficacy. It should then choose among efficacious measures that avoid undesirable consequences, if possible.

When no satisfactory alternative allows us to avoid undesirable consequences, policymakers should make value choices in choosing among measures minimizing systemic risks. For example, assume that torturing potential terrorists does not aid Al Qaeda's recruitment and sometimes elicits valuable information, so that torture helps avoid a significant national security risk but has collateral negative consequences with respect to human rights. We need a qualitative understanding of what is at stake in order to confront, rather than avoid, the key value choice involved. We conceive of terrorism as a threat to

---

[29] *See* Kip Viscusi, *Fatal Tradeoffs: Public and Private Responsibilities for Risk* (1995).

our national security, not just the cause of a set of deaths. Indeed, in terms of the numbers of deaths alone, terrorism has caused less damage in the United States than either air pollution or automobile accidents. Terrorism threatens stable democratic institutions, as terrorism can create a dynamic that leads to fear, repression, and government becoming the ruler of its citizens, rather than their servant. After all, terrorists cannot literally take away our freedom, which President Bush characterized them as attacking in statements made just after the 9/11 attacks, but the state can if it overreacts to terrorism. Hence, the real value choice implicates the question of what sorts of compromises in our democratic tradition effectively reduce national security risks without changing the character of the state so much that we no longer have a democratic state worthy of defense. We must decide whether torture constitutes a threat to the survival of what Philip Bobbitt calls "states of consent."[30] Hence, we must make discerning value judgments in order to properly decide how to take collateral negative consequences into account.

Lawmakers often take the disadvantages of laws' commitments into account by creating narrow exceptions to core commitments. For example, we outlaw murder, but we take the negative consequences of forbidding murder into account by making a very narrow exception to this rule permitting murder in self-defense. By keeping the exception narrow and normatively grounded in the need to preserve life, we reaffirm the life-affirming norm underlying our murder prohibition, even as we admit that this rule has disadvantages that society must account for. Lawmakers can use this technique to lessen or even wholly avoid negative consequences of rules designed to help us avoid systemic risk, provided that the exceptions do not seriously undermine the effort to avoid systemic risk.

Although these techniques of consideration of alternatives, exceptions, and value choices will probably enable us to make wise choices in almost all instances, it will help clarify the theory to discuss how far we should go to eliminate systemic risks. The toughest case one can imagine would arise if the only means of eliminating systemic risks created systemic risks of its own. Since one cannot measure the consequences of systemic risk reliably, one would have to resolve this conundrum by comparing, roughly, the probability of the risks. Perhaps the best example of this involves the question of whether to deploy nuclear power to address climate disruption, assuming that nuclear power does involve a significant risk of catastrophe because of the potential for operator error, natural disasters, or terrorist attacks. Now the core question here is not one of collateral negative consequences, but of efficacy. Disagreement

---

[30] *See* Philip Bobbitt, *Terror and Consent: The Wars of the 21st Century* 441 (2008).

exists about whether renewable energy can provide sufficient energy to displace fossil fuels without nuclear power. If renewable energy can provide sufficient energy to displace fossil fuels, then the question of whether to deploy nuclear power may be easy to resolve; one should not risk a nuclear catastrophe if safer methods exist to effectively address global climate disruption. But assume for the moment that those skeptical about renewable energy's prospects are correct, and that one cannot effectively address climate disruption without nuclear power. The correct economic dynamic question becomes: Which is more likely, a nuclear accident or very serious climate disruption? Almost any analyst would agree that serious climate disruption is much more likely than a nuclear accident, even though the probabilities cannot be reliably quantified (since nuclear accidents often come from unpredictable operator error or a natural catastrophe). We would then seek to regulate the nuclear alternative to minimize safety concerns, but allow nuclear power to go forward.

The next most difficult case would involve a situation in which avoiding a systemic risk involved cutting off an opportunity for economic development. We consider this because it would not do to create an economic catastrophe in order to avoid one. Thus, shutting down all industry would reduce a host of systemic risks, but we would not engage in this (even if we could) because of the economic dynamic theory's commitment to a reasonably robust set of economic opportunities.

Since systemic risk involves, by definition, a catastrophic outcome, society should be willing to pass on any particular economic opportunity if doing so does not create a catastrophe. This willingness to forgo any particular economic opportunity to allow a society to remain adaptively efficient recognizes the dynamic and fluid nature of economic growth, a corollary of the observation that law provides a framework for economic development rather than determining all investment decisions. If society forgoes a particular opportunity, it presumably frees up capital to pursue other opportunities. Absent some catastrophe, society tends to adapt to loss of some forms of economic development by creating others. For that reason, we need not risk catastrophes just to hold on to a particular economic opportunity.

That said, if several efficacious means of avoiding systemic risk exist, there is nothing wrong with making choices designed to minimize disruption of economic development. In choosing which economic development possibilities to curtail for the sake of avoiding systemic risk (if there are no choices maintaining all opportunities), society should prefer sustainable "economic development" to mere "economic growth." The economist Herman Daly distinguishes sustainable economic development from economic growth defined as mere increases in throughput, use of natural resources as inputs and as waste receptacles.[31] Economic growth so defined may deplete natural capital and pose great risks. In such cases, increases in wealth flowing from resource exploitation may prove a prelude to subsequent economic decline. By contrast, improvements in human knowledge and in techniques that increase human welfare can provide economic development without necessarily increasing resource exploitation. Thus, economic activities that meet human needs in a sustainable manner constitute forms of economic development, which this theory generally aims to foster rather than throttle. Herman Daly's conception of a distinction between economic growth and economic development has proven controversial, and it would take another book to fully engage this debate.[32] Fortunately, this conceptual point will matter only when avoiding systemic risks involves cutting off a very substantial economic growth opportunity, not in most cases.

If forced to choose among means of avoiding systemic risks, all of which cut off substantial economic development opportunities, policymakers must decide which opportunities to cut off. The literature on human happiness demonstrates that increases in human consumption beyond a bare minimum does little to advance happiness. Hence, we should give priority to maintaining economic growth opportunities that meet basic human needs.

In general, a normative commitment to avoiding systemic risk does not allow us to eschew efforts to limit serious systemic risks merely because well-chosen measures taken to avoid it have some cost or lessen efficiency. The economic dynamic perspective assumes that the economy will innovate and make up for increased costs and lost efficiencies, but it cannot adapt to a catastrophic event in ways that avoid serious welfare declines. Economic dynamic theory does not treat measures or programs as mere transactions to be evaluated through marginal analysis of tradeoffs between costs and benefits. Instead, it views decisions about policy programs and measures as raising questions about how to wisely avoid systemic risks. Wisdom does require some consideration of collateral negative consequences, but it does not demand viewing everything as a valueless optimization exercise.

RELATIONSHIP TO OTHER ECONOMIC TOOLS

Clearly, the economic dynamic theory envisions analysis of law and policy as consisting of something different from an economic analysis of a market. It

---

[31] *See* Herman E. Daly, *Beyond Growth: The Economics of Sustainable Development* (1996); Herman E. Daly, *Sustainable Development: An Impossibility Theorem, in* Valuing the Earth (Herman E. Daly & Kenneth N. Townsend, eds., 1992).

[32] *See, e.g.,* Geoffrey M. Heal, *Valuing the Future: Economic Theory and Sustainability* (1998).

takes into account the proper function of law in avoiding systemic risk, fostering change over time, and embodying a long-term commitment to normative choices. That said, economic dynamic analysis relies on familiar techniques of analyzing the incentives legal rules might create; it just does so in a systematic manner. It also can make use of a number of economic tools. Examination of its relationship to some specific economic tools follows.

CBA's Dependence on Prior Economic Dynamic Analysis

A choice to conduct economic dynamic analysis does not rule out CBA. Indeed, economic dynamic analysis stands as a prerequisite to CBA. If a policymaker wants to attempt to quantify torture's costs and benefits, he or she must consider the argument that torture will aid Al Qaeda recruitment efforts. This would require economic dynamic analysis, assessing the likelihood that Al Qaeda, as a boundedly rational actor (even for a barely rational actor, some bounds exist) would notice this incentive and whether any countervailing incentive might lead Al Qaeda to refrain from using U.S. torture as a propaganda tool. Of course, the cost–benefit analyst would have to do more than just employ expert knowledge to understand Al Qaeda well enough to answer these questions. If the analyst concluded that torture would aid recruitment, he or she would have to venture away from somewhat predictable matters into the type of guesswork most well qualified experts will want to avoid, predicting how many new recruits U.S. torture would add and how much incremental destruction (deaths, injuries, property damage, etc.) the new recruits would cause. More generally, since CBA concerns itself with the consequences of government decisions that establish a framework for private resource allocation decisions, analysts conducting CBA must systematically consider precisely how private actors will respond to the incentives the framework creates. Absent employment of economic dynamic analysis, this crucial first step of predicting what private actors will do will likely miss the boat. Analysts cannot comprehensively assess the costs and benefits of private actions incentivized by law if they cannot predict what private actors will do.

CBA as a Potential Underminer of Norms

Although economic dynamic analysis stands as a prerequisite for CBA, the economic dynamic theory does not envision economic dynamic analysis as a mere first step in conducting CBA. On the contrary, in many cases, it should substitute for CBA.

This chapter has already hinted at the primary reason for this. If one accepts the idea of society making normative commitments in law, which seems the heart of the enterprise, then CBA seems inapposite, or at least of limited value. If every decision becomes an effort to decide what action to take all things considered (and valued in dollar terms), it implies that at every moment we ignore prior societal commitments. This denies the essence of law. We do not permit a particular murder when an unusually worthless victim and an especially sadistic perpetrator make that murder's benefits outweigh its costs. An evaluation of the benefits of murder to the perpetrator or the overall value of the victim's life would deny that law embodies a moral commitment to life. We enact laws embodying normative commitments, even with exceptions taking negative collateral consequences into account, in order to influence future actions. Most statutes envision a series of implementing administrative and/or judicial decisions. Administrators and judges then should conform their decisions to the policies in the statutes without reconsidering the policies' value. An agency may, from time to time, review statutes in order to recommend revisions, and a court may likewise appropriately comment on the need for more specific legislation on a matter before the court. But the decisions themselves should conform to prior normative commitments. Similarly, to the extent that common law precedents reflect a chosen normative commitment, those commitments should generally guide future decisions.

Normatively, CBA tends to focus on an efficiency objective, which I have argued is not the right primary objective for government policy. Law should substantively commit society to avoiding systemic risk and taking other actions that have a positive effect on change over time. CBA tends to undermine normative goals and reinforce policymakers' tendency to obsess about the costs of departures from a status quo baseline that often reflects multiple actors' unwise decisions.

CBA's Technical Limits

Chapter 1 already argued that CBA becomes either impossible or dangerously misleading in cases where large systemic risks loom. Catastrophic consequences tend to reflect complex dynamics generating significant uncertainties that defy reasonably reliable quantification, making scenario analysis a much better approach to grappling with uncertainty. Subsequent chapters will demonstrate this point in particular contexts and explore CBA's technical limits in some detail, but it is worth at this point elaborating a little on what these limitations mean.

The proposition that governments should take the disadvantages of its actions aimed at avoiding systemic risk into account (which this chapter embraces) does not imply that CBA should guide one's actions. CBA involves a particular choice about how to weigh advantages and disadvantages – through the quantification of dollar values with a view toward equating costs and benefits at the margin. People and societies consider the disadvantages of generally desirable courses of action all the time without using this particular approach, as my treatment of exceptions, value choices, and qualitative judgment illustrated. Hence, CBA can prove impossible or misleading and one can evaluate collateral negative consequences without it.

A More Modest Continued Role for CBA

This does not mean that economic dynamic analysis should always substitute for, instead of supplement and inform, CBA. If a law actually makes efficient balances between costs and benefits its primary goal, it is hard to see how one can avoid CBA, notwithstanding its many weaknesses. Also, for open-ended policymaking, such as some broad legislative decisions, CBA's assumptions may get the skeptical scrutiny they deserve and CBA may become one input among many. In such a context, CBA may usefully contribute to the decision-making process without necessarily commanding more attention than it merits. In administrative and judicial contexts, conversely, CBA often raises serious risks of technocratic pretension displacing valid collective normative value choices.[33]

Other Forms of Economic Analysis: Game Theory and Economic Growth Modeling

Even if one accepts the economic dynamic perspective – an emphasis on the general shape of change over time in lieu of an emphasis on the immediate costs and benefits of departure form a privileged status quo – questions remain about the role of economic analysis, as economists sometimes employ much more dynamic forms of analysis than CBA. These alternative forms of analysis may form part of an economic dynamic analysis.

Although not a central part of neoclassical law and economics, some legal academics and economists have employed game theory in policymaking

---

[33] *See* David M. Driesen, "The Societal Cost of Environmental Regulation: Beyond Administrative Cost-Benefit Analysis," 24 *Ecology L. Q.* 545, 608–10 (1997) for elaboration and defense of this point.

contexts. Game theory seeks to predict actors' strategic responses to incentives, and therefore seems quite relevant to analysis of law's economic dynamics. An inconsistency with economic dynamic theory, however, arises from modelers' tendency to use rational market actor assumptions, rather than more realistic assumptions about bounded rationality, to make their models tractable.[34] Because sophisticated game theorists recognize that these assumptions can prove problematic in the policymaking context, many of them do not recommend game theory as a tool for policy formation.[35]

Game theorists who argue for its use in policy analysis relax rational actor assumptions and explore bounded rationality, thereby making their analysis useful as a component of economic dynamic analysis. For example, Fritz Sharpf argues that to make game theory useful for analysis of law and policy, game theorists must develop empirically accurate descriptions of relevant actors' basic self-interest, normative role orientation, and sense of identity.[36] Of course, this amounts to a decision to employ an empirically accurate, though simplified, model of bounded rationality in order to analyze law. Thus, forms of game theory employing bounded rationality assumptions may usefully play a role in refining economic dynamic analysis. Of course, a reasonably complete economic dynamic analysis demands supplementing this with analysis of countervailing incentives, the public choice element, and attention to legal detail.

Economists have also experimented with economic growth models. Employment of economic growth models comports with the macroeconomic emphasis of economic dynamic theory. These models, however, have generated controversy within the economics profession itself.[37] The principal controversies revolve around disputes between those who favor simplifying assumptions in order to produce tractable mathematical outcomes and those, such as Paul Rohmer, who would employ rather more complex assumptions about growth to better track reality.[38] Policymakers should always treat these models' predictions with a few hundred grains of salt, as economists have not been able to predict the magnitude, or even the direction, of growth with any

34 Fritz W. Scharpf, *Games Real Actors Play: Actor-Centered Institutionalism in Policy Research* 6 (1999) (discussing the reluctance to depart from rational actor assumptions, because of the complexity of modeling real behavior).

35 Id. at 5–6 (discussing game theorists' reluctance to claim that game theory applies to policy actions because of the large number of actors and the limits of rational actor assumptions).

36 Id. at 64–65.

37 See David Warsh, *Knowledge and the Wealth of Nations* 153, 156–57, 225 (2006) (discussing some of the controversies).

38 See id. at 199 (discussing how less dynamic models purchase mathematical profundity at the expense of dynamic realism).

regularity. They can become sources of great error and hubris if used in CBA leading to a single result. One can, however, use economic growth models in scenario analysis to creatively explore the effects of possible future scenarios on policy. This sort of use of economic growth models, in which the modelers highlight their models' assumptions and subject the models to sensitivity analysis, and policymakers do not treat model results as truths, may provide useful guidance to policymakers.

More generally, mathematical modeling of scenarios can play a useful role in suggesting whether a potential risk can prove serious under various assumptions. This sort of exercise may help identify both systemic risks and potential remedies. The use of multiple scenarios, although expensive in this context, can help ameliorate the tendency to treat a mathematical result as a reasonably precise and reliable prediction of outcomes, and give policymakers some sense of what the nature and magnitude of the risks might turn out to be.

Hence, economic dynamic analysis can help evaluate various policies' potential to avoid systemic risk. The analysis involves a systematic study of economic incentives' likely influence on relevant individuals and firms in a world of uncertainty, important power relations, and multiple contingencies. Economic dynamic analysis substitutes pragmatic engagement with an uncertain future for a process of assuming away key information in order to arrive at neat synoptic conclusions.

CONCLUSION

An economic dynamic approach focuses on change over time to avoid systemic risk using economic dynamic analysis. It offers a pragmatic approach to help government provide a set of normative commitments and strategically wise actions to create a framework for shaping a brighter future.

5

Financial Regulation

The economic dynamic approach provides useful guidance for reforming financial regulation and has informed the work of some of the most perceptive scholars studying financial markets and their regulation. Economic dynamic considerations, we shall see, suggest that policymakers should consider structural reforms much more seriously than they have so far.

This book uses the term *financial regulation* broadly to include the regulation of financial institutions, such as banks, and securities regulation. Although historically these areas of regulation have been distinct, in light of the intermingling of traditional banking and underwriting securities a broad definition of financial regulation has become appropriate.

This chapter first examines economic dynamic analysis' role in predicting the financial crisis. It turns out that several scholars employing either economic dynamic analysis or some of its constituents predicted the crisis. The fact that some analysts employing economic dynamic analysis anticipated the financial crisis does not prove that this approach will always succeed at predicting the future. It does suggest, however, for reasons I will explain, that economic dynamic analysis increases policymakers' ability to recognize signs of potential future trouble, thereby increasing the odds of adopting wise policy avoiding systemic risk.

This chapter then discusses a model of financial regulation based on information disclosure. It explains that some of the most cogent criticism of the disclosure model implicitly employs economic dynamic analysis.

The chapter's third part argues that an economic dynamic approach tends to favor structural reform, which has a long history in financial regulation but has fallen into disfavor with the ascendancy of neoclassical law and economics. This chapter closes by showing how economic dynamic analysis can help evaluate several structural reforms that might help us avoid a future financial crisis.

ECONOMIC DYNAMIC ANALYSIS AND THE PREDICTION OF CRISIS

As many other commentators have noted, a handful of economists anticipated the economic collapse of 2008. None of these prescient economists employed a mathematical model in the neoclassical tradition in the papers predicting the crisis. Nouriel Roubini, as was widely noted, made his prediction in a paper presented to the International Monetary Fund (IMF), where it received an unfavorable reception because it did not appear as a mathematical model.[1] Roubini's thinking drew on information about historical experience in a large number of developing countries, including past modeling exercises.[2] Dean Baker likewise predicted the crisis using some back-of-the-envelope calculations, not a formal mathematical model.[3] He simply observed that fundamentals, such as the rate of population and wage increases, could not explain the run-up in housing prices then occurring. He also considered the lack of a comparable price increase in rental housing the "best evidence" that economic fundamentals could not explain the run-up in housing prices. Therefore, he reasoned, the housing price increase must be a bubble, which would end badly absent policy intervention.

Both Roubini and Baker focused on the fundamental economic dynamics of the problem at hand, drawing on macroeconomic experience with bubbles, not microeconomics. They focused on the causal factors that might produce systemic risks, as economic dynamic analysis should.

Roubini's analysis focused on financial markets' economic dynamics. He predicted widespread mortgage defaults, the unraveling of trillions of dollars of mortgage-backed securities, and a freeze-up of the global financial system. He later predicted, correctly, that at least one major Wall Street investment firm would go belly up. Not every Roubini prediction came to pass, but enough of what he predicted occurred that he became regarded, in the words of IMF economist Prakash Loungani, as a "prophet."

Dean Baker's analysis asked an exceedingly simple causal question: What could be causing the rapid rise in housing prices he was observing in major housing markets? Furthermore, he analyzed the relationship of the housing market to the economy as a whole, and suggested that a housing market crash could destabilize the entire economy, because consumers' perception of their own wealth and their borrowing depend heavily upon rising housing prices.

---

[1] *See* Stephen Mihm, "Dr. Doom," *New York Times Magazine* (August 15, 2008).

[2] *See generally* Nouriel Roubini & Brad Sester, *Bailouts or Bail-ins? Responding to Financial Crisis in Emerging Economies* (2004).

[3] Dean Baker, "The Menace of an Unchecked Bubble," in *The Economists' Voice*, at www.bepress.com/ev (March 2006).

Hence, he implicitly recognized a dynamic that would make a sudden decline in housing prices a potential cause of a more widespread economic problem.

Students of boom and bust cycles have long understood that bubbles tend to lead to crashes. This understanding of market dynamics, however, stands in tension with neoclassical economic theory's standard assumptions. As one of the leading writers on bubbles, Charles Kindelberger, remarked, proponents of neoclassical economics tend to dismiss conventional descriptions of the dynamics of bubbles as inconsistent with economics' fundamental assumptions.[4] The most fundamental assumption that students of the history of boom and bust cycles question is the assumption of rationality. Although it is possible, albeit perhaps a stretch, to describe fevered speculation followed by panic as rational *individual* behavior based on the information and predictions available to investors, the cumulative result is irrational, utterly unresponsive to fundamental reality.[5] Kindelberger found the dismissal of history by economists rejecting the history of bubbles and crashes "infuriating" and argued that "it is time that economics accepts reality."[6]

Neither Roubini nor Baker engaged in economic dynamic analysis of law, as neither analyzed the incentives law creates for relevant actors. They did, however, analyze the economic dynamics of the housing markets.[7] Thus, they used economic dynamic analysis to identify systemic risks.

Less widely noted than the handful of prescient economists who looked at the fundamental economic dynamics and predicted the crisis, the legal scholar Arthur E. Wilmarth, Jr. provided a cogent analysis of the economic dynamics of the financial markets' increased riskiness in 2002.[8] His analysis examined the incentives law creates for a wide range of relevant individuals and institutions. This analysis signaled, even better than Roubini and Baker, the true dimensions of the eventual economic collapse, as Wilmarth correctly anticipated that it might well implicate the insurance industry as well as the banks.[9] He explained that the repeal of Glass-Steagall (and its erosion prior to

---

[4] *See* Charles Kindelberger, *Manias, Panics and Crashes: A History of Financial Crisis* xiii (1989). *Cf.* Lynn A. Stout, "Why the Law Hates Speculators: Regulation and Private Ordering in the Market for OTC Derivatives," 48 *Duke L. J.* 701, 755–56 (1999) (examining the tension between bubbles and the predominant microeconomic theories).

[5] Kindelberger, *supra* note 4, at xii, 243.

[6] Id. at xiii.

[7] *See* Joseph E. Stiglitz, *Freefall: America, Free Markets, and the Sinking of the World Economy* 18–19 (2010) (noting that all those who predicted the financial crises were "Keynsians," who did not believe in self-correcting markets).

[8] Arthur E. Wilmarth Jr., "The Transformation of the U.S. Financial Services Industry, 1975–2000: Competition, Consolidation, and Increased Risks," 2002 *U. Ill L. Rev.* 215.

[9] Id. at 414–28.

that) had led to a wave of mergers and consolidation as financial firms of all
stripes (including insurance companies) had sought "too-big-to-fail" status. By
that, he meant that firms sought to become so large that the federal government
would have to bail them out if they seemed likely to fail, in order to prevent
an economic collapse. The combination of declining profits in the wake of
increased competition following the Glass-Steagall Act's decline and repeal
led, according to Wilmarth's writing in 2002, to large institutions behaving in
an increasingly risky manner. He cited expanded subprime lending and its
securitization as prime examples of this increasingly risky behavior.[10]

Wilmarth thus analyzed the economic incentives deregulation had created
in detail and recognized that it had made the system more vulnerable to
widespread failure. This underscores an important point about the value and
limits of economic dynamic analysis. Economic dynamic analysis can succeed in providing a predicate for wise policy even without squarely predicting
a crisis' dimensions or its timing. For example, Lynn Stout warned as early as
1999 that derivatives markets might give rise to a speculative bubble harming
"the economy as a whole."[11] Her analysis relies heavily on analyzing the incentives facing investors in light of bounded rationality and imperfect information.
The ideologically successful economic models had emphasized derivatives'
role in making markets more efficient by allowing rational actors to hedge risk
or to use arbitrage to make prices better reflect available information, in keeping with the efficient market hypothesis.[12] Stout, however, noted that often
investors have incomplete and differing information about the value of assets
at the base of derivatives trades.[13] She developed a model of bounded rationality, explaining that differing views may persist in some kinds of markets in
spite of some potential for learning to narrow differing expectations.[14] In keeping with economic dynamic theory, her theory emphasizes uncertainty about
future price movements, as distinguished from probabilistic risk.[15] She con-
ducts an economic dynamic analysis showing that traders speculating on the
basis of heterogeneous expectations cannot possibly realize net gains, but must,
because of transaction costs, incur net losses.[16] More importantly, she explains
in economic dynamic terms how these speculative trades can produce asset
bubbles and subsequent crashes.[17] Her economic dynamic analysis enables

---

[10] Id. at 392–407.
[11] *See* Stout, *supra* note 4, at 709 (emphasis in original).
[12] Id. at 735–740.
[13] *See* id. at 741–42.
[14] *See* id. at 747–51.
[15] *See* id. at 743–44.
[16] *See* id. at 745–46.
[17] *See* id. at 753–62.

her to spot serious risks of rampant speculation and to perceive the need for a remedy.[18]

It would be too much to claim that economic dynamic analysis provides a crystal ball that would necessarily predict a pending crisis, in spite of several economic analysts' now vindicated prophecies. But if one studies a worst case as part of scenario analysis and carefully examines the fundamental structural dynamics, as these analysts did, a competent analysis probably could identify large systemic risks that would warrant a remedy in advance of a crisis. Unfortunately, the dominance of neoclassical approaches made such much-needed analysis both scarce and unheeded prior to 2008, and perhaps even today.

In pointing out the conspicuous absence of a mathematical model among the work of the prescient, I do not mean to deny the possibility of mathematically expressed prescience or to claim that eschewing math ensures prescience. But if an analyst spends a lot of time refining a mathematical model, then he or she has less time available to look at facts and put together a big picture. Furthermore, an analyst studying empirical data in order to create a mathematical model will probably look at data sets useful for modeling, not necessarily those most useful for understanding the fundamental economic dynamics. Finally, as many economists recognize, mathematical models usually assume that the future will resemble the recent past, which helps explain conventional economics' miserable record at predicting recessions.[19] It is probably not a coincidence that the papers predicting a crisis or explaining the economic dynamics making the financial markets extremely risky did not employ mathematical models.

Of course, I have argued that an economic dynamic analysis does more than help us understand problems; it also helps craft appropriate policy responses. Now that we all know that a financial crisis occurred, governments around the world still wrestle with the question: What should the remedy be? We shall see that an economic dynamic approach leads to the idea that we should take structural remedies more seriously than we have in the recent past, and that a disclosure model may not prove adequate.

NEOCLASSICAL LAW AND ECONOMICS AND THE DISCLOSURE MODEL

The disclosure model of regulation has dominated U.S. securities law. This model assumes that markets perform efficiently as long as market actors

---

[18] *See id.* at 777–79 (arguing that reviving the common law rule against enforcing derivatives contracts will discourage derivatives speculation while preserving room for hedging and arbitrage). *See also* GAO, *Financial Derivatives: Actions Needed to Protect the Financial System* (1994) (suggesting that derivatives pose a threat to the financial system because the systemically important institutions dominate the trade).

[19] Mihm, *supra* note 1.

receive adequate information. Since market actors do not always receive adequate information, securities law has mandated disclosure of information that
investors need. Thus, issuers of securities must reveal risks facing the business
selling shares and stockbrokers must disclose material facts to investors.[20] Economics treats inadequate information as a market failure, thereby suggesting
that adequate information disclosure suffices to secure an efficient financial
market.

The disclosure model of regulation implicitly embraces the microeconomic
goal of efficiency.[21] A poorly informed investor may pay too much for securities
or sell securities at too low a price. If this investor has done so, he or she will
have engaged in an inefficient transaction. But inefficient transactions do not
necessarily constitute a serious macroeconomic threat. To be sure, overoptimism about securities' prospects can fuel a bubble, and widespread excessive
pessimism can spur a collapse. But the disclosure model operates more commonly to level the playing field between those with access to information
about a company and investors who lack such access absent a mechanism to
create disclosure. Securities experts generally think this an important function
at all times, not just when herd behavior creates risks of financial crisis, in part
because of the efficiency model.

The disclosure model, however, has not escaped criticism from neoclassical
law and economics scholars. Several of them have argued that unregulated
markets will produce adequate information because investors will demand
needed information, thereby creating sufficient incentives for securities issuers
and brokers to provide it.[22] They therefore oppose *mandatory* disclosure.[23]
Thus, faith in market actors' capacity to self-regulate has led to rather radical
financial deregulation proposals.

While these scholars claim that mandatory disclosure laws require too much
of financial firms, others suggest that they require too little. Steven Schwarcz,
for example, implicitly uses a partial economic dynamic analysis to call the
disclosure model's sufficiency into question.[24] Recall that the economic

[20] *See* John C. Coffee, Jr., "Market Failure and the Economic Case for a Mandatory Disclosure
System," 70 *Va. L. Rev.* 717 (1984).
[21] *See generally* Lynn A. Stout, "Are Securities Markets Costly Casinos?: Disagreement, Market
Failure, and Securities Regulation," 81 *Va. L. Rev.* 611, 648–50 (1995) (describing the efficient
market hypothesis as an article of faith in legal circles of the 1970s and 1980s).
[22] *See, e.g.,* Richard A. Posner, *The Economic Analysis of Law* 332 (2nd ed. 1977).
[23] *See* Frank H. Easterbrook & Daniel R. Fischel, "Mandatory Disclosure and the Protection
of Investors," 70 *Va. L. Rev.* 669, 682 (1984); *cf.* Gregg A. Jarrell, "The Economic Effects of
Federal Regulation of the Market for New Security Issues," 24 *J. L. & Econ.* 613 (1981); G.
J. Benston, "Required Disclosure and the Stock Market: An Evaluation of the Securities and
Exchange Act of 1932," 63 *Am. Econ. Rev.* 132 (1973).
[24] Steven L. Schwarcz, "Rethinking the Disclosure Paradigm in a World of Complexity," 2004
U. Ill. L. Rev. 1.

dynamic approach assumes that actors have limited capacity to consider potentially relevant information. Accordingly, economic dynamic analysis demands
that scholars address rationality limits. Schwarcz implicitly analyzes investors'
limits in questioning the disclosure model's adequacy.

Schwarcz pointed out long before the financial crisis that some securities
had become so complicated that even sophisticated investors have difficulty
understanding them. He argues that once securities reach a certain level of
complexity, a disclosure model proves insufficient. This critique certainly
applies to the derivatives at the heart of the financial crisis. Schwarcz's analysis
strongly suggests that even perfect information's existence and disclosure do not
necessarily create a well-functioning market. More importantly, for purposes of
illustrating the economic dynamic analysis' utility, he reaches this conclusion
by analyzing the limits of investors' information processing capabilities. Thus,
he employs a bounded rationality framework to analyze financial regulation's
effects. Having concluded that a disclosure model does not suffice for complex
transactions, he considers various types of structural reforms. Schwarcz's work
again illustrates that our most perceptive scholars of financial regulation tend
to gravitate toward economic dynamic analysis.[25]

Congress passed a financial reform bill, the Dodd-Frank Act, more than
a year after the 2008 crash. It relies heavily on a disclosure reform, namely
consigning speculative trading in derivatives to a clearinghouse to improve
transparency.[26] Schwarcz's analysis raises questions about this disclosure
reform's sufficiency. If the clearinghouse registration requirement produces
only information disclosure, but the information remains too complex for
investors to digest, then it may not have the desired effect of adequately limiting speculative derivatives trading.[27]

ECONOMIC DYNAMICS AND STRUCTURAL REFORM

Structural financial regulation goes beyond requiring the mere disclosure of
information. It may prohibit certain types of transactions altogether or, more
commonly, prohibit particular actors from engaging in specific transaction
types that might create conflicts of interest. The Securities and Exchange

---

[25] *Cf.* John C. Coffee, Jr., "Systemic Risk After Dodd-Frank: Contingent Capital and the Need
for Regulatory Strategies Beyond Oversight," 111 *Colum. L. Rev.* 795, 822–23 (2011) (pointing out
that bounded rationality suggests that both private market actors and regulators can misperceive
risks and therefore "one needs failsafe remedies").

[26] *See* Lynn A. Stout, "Derivatives and the Legal Origin of the 2008 Credit Crisis," 1 *Harv. Bus.
L. Rev.* 1, 33–35 (2011).

[27] *Cf.* id. at 35–36 (discussing the issue of whether the government will allow loopholes in
Dodd-Frank to gut the registration requirements).

Commission (SEC) possesses authority to regulate financial structure, but it seldom uses this authority.[28] Structural regulation, however, dominated the approach to bank regulation throughout the period of stable economic growth in the mid-twentieth century. A key Depression-era reform mentioned previously, the separation of commercial and investment banking, exemplifies the structural model. It prohibits specific transactions, or, to be more precise, specific transactions by parties thought unsuitable. Thus, under the regime prevailing until the 1970s, commercial banks could offer mortgages, but investment banks could not. Similarly, investment banks could underwrite securities, but commercial banks could not. These restrictions reflected a belief that a single actor's engagement in both types of action simultaneously creates unacceptable conflicts of interest. Furthermore, these restrictions serve an economic dynamic purpose, namely separation of sectors, which should prevent one sector's problems from infecting another sector, thereby substantially lowering systemic risks to the economy as a whole.

Minimum capital requirements provide another example of structural financial regulation. Both international and domestic laws generally require that banks set aside a certain minimum amount of capital in order to provide assurance that they can pay their debts. These capital set-asides reduce the likelihood of a bank run, thus countering a potential negative economic dynamic. Capital set-aside requirements provide an inchoate limit on the number and types of transactions of bank may engage in. In essence, they demand that banks engage in only the transactions they can afford to engage in. In the aftermath of the financial crisis, countries have sought to strengthen these requirements. But questions remain about their adequacy.

Structural financial regulation, unlike mere demands for disclosure, embraces economic dynamic goals. Structural regulation seeks to limit systemic risks, such as the risk of an economic collapse.[29] It embraces macroeconomic aims, and does not direct itself especially to the efficiency of individual transactions.

Furthermore, instead of assuming that rational actors will use perfect information to make the market work smoothly, structural regulation reflects a recognition that market actors can engage in dangerous behavior, creating a dynamic of bubbles and crashes. As we saw in Chapter 3, actors in the financial sector often respond to developments around them, not with cool, individual rationality, but with a marked tendency to follow the herd by emulating the

---

[28] *See* Walter Werner, "The SEC as a Market Regulator," 70 *Va. L. Rev.* 755 (1984).
[29] *Cf.* Stout, *supra* note 26, at 35–36 (arguing that Dodd-Frank's disclosure requirements for speculative derivatives trades have the potential to stem systemic risk).

behavior of successful firms in their industry. This tendency was particularly evident in the spread of dubious subprime lending practices across the industry and the intense pressures that success in making money with that practice placed on more conservative institutions to "loosen up." This herdlike tendency reflects a form of bounded rationality.[30] The incentive not to miss out on opportunities that peers profitably exploit provides a powerful incentive that people in the financial industry usually respond to. For those in a go-go climate (a prevalent climate during bubbles), the possibility of appearing behind the times appears much more dangerous than the risk of losing money if something unexpectedly goes wrong.

The emphasis on conflicts of interest found in structural reform laws reflects a recognition that actors respond to the incentives facing them. Conflicts of interest create incentives to cheat one set of actors in order to serve the interests of another. Structural regulation limiting conflicts of interests reflects an economic dynamic emphasis on considering economic incentives seriously and comprehensively.

In short, structural reforms generally reflect a recognition of market actors as humans prone to all sorts of mistakes and, at times, chicanery. Markets do not consist of rational actors smoothly processing perfect information to arrive at efficient results.

Smart structural reforms, then, reflect consideration of the economic incentives facing market actors aimed at understanding how actors will respond to market opportunities that could produce problems under bounded rationality constraints. Such reforms should account for the time and knowledge constraints facing investors and borrowers. They should account for the tendency toward hubris of people in the financial industry. In short, they should reflect careful study of the bounds limiting the rationality of people and institutions actually shaping markets.

Remarkably, in the wake of the financial crisis policymakers have on the whole given structural reform short shrift.[31] The Dodd-Frank Act mandates only minimal structural reform.[32] Much of the act, rather than ordering specific structural changes in financial markets, sets the stage for allowing government agencies to become more effective by consolidating regulatory authority

---

[30] *See generally* Coffee, *supra* note 25.

[31] *Cf.* Rosa M. Lastra & Geoffrey Wood, "The Crises of 2007–2009: Nature, Causes, and Reactions," 13 J. *Int'l Econ. L.* 531, 549 (2010) (pointing out that the provision in the Dodd-Frank Act prohibiting banks from engaging in proprietary trades constitutes a "limited" structural rule).

[32] *See generally* Arthur E. Wilmarth, Jr., "The Dodd-Frank Act: A Flawed and Inadequate Response to the Too-Big-to-Fail Problem," 89 *Oregon L. Rev.* 951 (2011).

and limiting opportunities for regulatory arbitrage.[33] In the past, numerous state and federal agencies shared authority over financial services regulation. The patchwork of regulatory authority created an economic dynamic favoring deregulation, as some companies could, in effect, choose their regulator and therefore flee uncongenial regulation. This situation, of course, put immense pressure on regulators to remain lax, which they generally did. Dodd-Frank, however, does not end all opportunities for regulatory arbitrage.[34] Furthermore, Dodd-Frank makes the Federal Reserve, an agency with a poor track record as a regulator and limited resources, the primary regulator of large conglomerates.[35]

Dodd-Frank embraces some potentially significant structural reforms, but few analysts think it goes far enough. It sets minimal capital set-aside requirements for large financial conglomerates.[36] It remains to be seen whether the Federal Reserve will have the will to go beyond these rather weak minimum standards in the face of pressure from regulated entities.[37] Dodd-Frank also generally seeks to prevent new mergers allowing one firm to control more than 10 percent of deposits in the United States.[38] But this rule contains important exceptions and did not break up the Bank of America, which held more than 10 percent of U.S. deposits when Congress enacted Dodd-Frank.[39]

Instead of embracing major structural reform removing existing systemic risk from the economy in short order, the Dodd-Frank Act establishes a procedure for dealing with systemic risks mostly when it is too late. It does this by establishing a procedure authorizing, but not specifically requiring, liquidation of a troubled firm.[40] It also forbids the use of taxpayer funds to bail out a failing firm.[41] Most analysts look at this reform through an economic dynamic lens and find it inadequate.[42] Once a too-big-to-fail firm gets in trouble, regulators will understand that its failure will likely set off a chain reaction like that

---

[33] *See* Elizabeth F. Brown, "The New Laws and Regulations for Financial Conglomerates: Will They Better Manage the Risks than the Previous Ones," 60 *Am. U. L. Rev.* 1339, 1389–1402 (2011) (describing the many provisions designed to consolidate regulatory authority and limit regulatory arbitrage).

[34] *See id.* at 1397–1400 (describing some of the remaining loopholes).

[35] *See id.* at 1400–02.

[36] *See id.* at 1403–05.

[37] *See id.*

[38] *See id.* at 1409–10.

[39] *See id.* at 1411. *See also* Wilmarth, *supra* note 32, at 990–92 (discussing this cap and a similar cap, with similar loopholes, for liabilities).

[40] *See* Brown, *supra* note 33, at 1410.

[41] *See id.*

[42] *See, e.g.,* Jonathan R. Macey & James F. Holdcroft, Jr., "Failure is an Option: An Ersatz-Antitrust Approach," 120 *Yale L. J.* 1368 (2011).

exemplified by space debris in Chapter 1, leading to an economic collapse. They therefore will likely not vote to liquidate such a firm, even if plans are in place for that express purpose.[43] Many analysts also conclude that the same pressures will lead regulators to evade the supposed prohibition on bailouts.[44]

Dodd-Frank failed to embrace structural reforms that many economists and others recommend to protect us from systemic risks. I do not intend to build a case for any particular package of reforms here. But I do intend to discuss how economic dynamic analysis would help guide consideration of such reforms.

The most obvious structural reform, prohibition of securitization of mortgages, received almost no serious discussion.[45] Instead, one heard that we do not want to "throw the baby out with the bathwater," a vague suggestion that such a reform would be too radical to seriously contemplate. Yet, mortgage markets worked very well for some forty years without substantial mortgage securitization. Since securitization of mortgages played such a prominent role in spreading the economic decline to so many sectors in practically all nations, one would think that the question of whether we should abandon it would receive more serious study than it has.

One reason that this question has received so little attention is that the efficient market hypothesis suggests to some policymakers and analysts that these transactions' existence proves their goodness, even though it does not state any proposition quite that broad.[46] In other words, mortgage derivatives must provide some value or nobody would bother with them.

That kind of argument deserves special skepticism in the world of finance. Transactions may exist because they generate fees, provide means of evading regulation, and prey on innocent investors, as Paul Krugman has pointed out.[47] During the period prior to the financial crisis, the over-the-counter market in which derivatives were traded grew to nine times the size of global economic output.[48] That sort of size indicates that the financial sector has grown too

---

43 *See* Adam J. Levitan, "In Defense of Bailouts," 99 *Geo. L. J.* 435, 439 (2011); Wilmarth, *supra* note 32, at 1005.

44 *See, e.g.*, Macey & Holdcroft, *supra* note 42, at 1389–90; Brown, *supra* note 33, at 1413 (pointing to use of taxpayer funds to assist receivers of liquidated firms); Wilmarth, *supra* note 32, at 956, 993–1006 (pointing to funds that might be used to creatively evade the prohibition on using "taxpayer funds"); Cheryl D. Block, "Measuring the True Cost of Government Bailout," 88 *Wash. U. L. Rev.* 149, 224 (2010).

45 *Cf.* Wilmarth, *supra* note 32, at 1030–34 (discussing the Lincoln amendment, which, as passed, potentially puts pressure on major banks to spin off some of their derivatives operations).

46 *See* Stout, *supra* note 4, at 735–40 (explaining how the models undergirding the efficient market hypothesis lead "contemporary scholars and policymakers to view speculation as beneficial").

47 *See* Paul Krugman, *The Return of Depression Economics and the Crisis of 2008* (2009).

48 Jee Lee, *Restructuring Financial Regulation* 4 (April 3, 2010), available at http://ssrn.com/abstract=1645351.

large to be simply performing a socially productive role of efficiently allocating capital to its best use.[49] More generally, the relationship of finance to efficient allocation of capital is often tenuous, as illustrated so well in Lynn Stout's work. Her economic dynamic analysis shows in detail why speculative derivatives trading benefits neither traders (at least not on average) nor society.[50]

Financial markets can, dare I say it, create socially useless speculation. The economics of asymmetric information shows that, at least in the short run, the perfect market hypothesis cannot be right. In light of that, we cannot just assume that a transaction must reflect efficient and flawless information processing. Indeed, the history of bubbles shows that markets give rise not only to minor deviations from perfections, but to gross errors and miscalculations. One should not rule out the possibility that certain types of derivatives might give rise to a great deal of useless speculation.

Markets can, however, create socially useful speculation. The dot-com bubble, the run-up in share prices for companies seeking to create value with the Internet, occurred shortly after Amazon.com got started and helped finance a lot of innovation, at least at startups, some of it quite worthwhile. Sometimes, inefficient losses are the price we must pay to finance increased productivity. But analysts should not cavalierly dismiss the possibility of useless transactions.

Moreover, a moment's reflection will reveal that showing securitization has a socially productive role does not suffice to justify its existence.[51] If securitization creates substantial systemic risks, such as the prospect of the collapse of the economy, then the existence of some benefit from securitization does not justify the practice. Rather, if securitization creates a substantial systemic risk, one should generally disallow it even if it has some social value. We should seriously consider allowing it only if getting rid of it would eliminate a crucial opportunity for economic development for which no good substitute exists.

An economic dynamic approach demands serious attention to several questions. First of all, one must analyze securitization's contribution to the systemic risks that manifested themselves during the financial crisis to evaluate whether securitization increases systemic risk. Chapter 3 showed that some very competent analysts have concluded that securitization contributed to the erosion of lending standards, and obviously securitization spreads risk. This increase and spreading of risk converted a United States housing sector financial

---

[49] *See* Stout, *supra* note 26.

[50] *See* Stout, *supra* note 4, at 751–64. *See also* Stout, *supra* note 21 (arguing that stock markets do not aid efficient allocation of capital to existing firms).

[51] *Cf.* Stout, *supra* note 26, at 31–36 (arguing that Dodd-Frank's clearinghouse provisions, if properly implemented, should prevent derivatives from creating speculative bubbles).

setback into a global debacle,[52] which strongly suggests that securitization creates serious systemic risks. In any event, this question would have to be analyzed by looking at the dynamics of markets with and without securitization.

Another systemic risk stems from securitization's role in complicating the aftermath of a housing market crisis.[53] Absent securitization, housing markets have mechanisms for realizing adaptive efficiencies. That is, they have ways of responding to a potential crisis to reduce its impact. If homeowners cannot pay their mortgages because of job losses or a decline in housing prices, banks will often forgo some profit and reduce the borrower's loan payment. Obviously, these workouts benefit homeowners by allowing them to keep their houses. These sorts of workouts, however, also can benefit banks, because foreclosure can prove more expensive than losing out on some amount of anticipated loan payments. More importantly, workouts may make the economy resilient, able to adjust to housing shocks without a collapse. Flooding a real estate market with foreclosed houses and casting homeowners out of their homes does not help an economy. In the aftermath of the financial crisis, we discovered that securitization had made these sorts of workouts just about impossible to achieve. The diffusion of mortgage ownership through securitization had apparently made it very difficult to obtain agreement from all of a mortgage's "owners" in order to allow a workout to occur. Thus, securitization enhances systemic risk by defeating an important adaptive efficiency mechanism otherwise available to cope with a potential crisis.

After analyzing whether securitization creates significant systemic risk, one must ask whether securitization provides important opportunities for economic development. Securitization increases the number of investors able to participate in financing the purchase of real estate. Accordingly, the economic dynamics would suggest that it lowers the cost of capital. This lowering of the cost of capital makes it easier for homeowners to afford to purchase a home. This in turn probably increases construction of new homes.

Dean Baker's analysis, however, suggests that we should regard increased home construction not as economic development, but as unsustainable economic growth. For the increase in housing starts did not reflect increases in real wages or population growth, but simply increased debt created by a vast supply of cheap capital. If so, we should be loath to continue securitization on economic development grounds.

---

[52] *See, e.g.* Stiglitz, *supra* note 7, at 8 (arguing that the complexity of derivatives increased risk and information asymmetry).

[53] I want to thank David Goldstein for pointing out the relevance of this problem to my thesis.

Economic dynamic analysis' focus on an array of alternatives in order to facilitate risk avoidance without losing economic opportunities could, however, come into play here. If one wants to encourage broader home ownership, ways of doing that exist that pose less economic risk.[54] For example, one might tax the purchase of second homes or mortgages financing second homes in order to subsidize lower interest rates for low-income homebuyers. This sort of reform provides a more sustainable approach to financing homeownership, as it adjusts to, rather than wishes away, the problem of low-income borrowers' weak economic capacity.

At this point, readers accustomed to the neoclassical economic perspective may find it difficult to distinguish economic dynamics from standard CBA. Although economic dynamic analysis can take both the advantages and disadvantages of economic arrangements or proposed policy changes into account, it does not do so by quantifying costs and benefits. The costs of securitization cannot be quantified, because the likelihood and magnitude of a crash caused by the increase in systemic risk stemming from securitization resists responsible quantification. Without ruling out the possibility of some quantitative analysis entering the picture, economic dynamic analysis requires qualitative judgment, including an imaginative exploration of alternatives that might be possible if energy now devoted to CBA gets employed to think of alternatives.

Since we had robust economic development without securitization, it seems likely that securitization is not fundamental to a sound economy. It most likely provides some additional economic boost that might well be worth giving up for the sake of financial stability. If one concluded, however, that securitization was crucial for economic development (probably a weak conclusion in light of the possibility of less risky alternatives), then one could consider how to keep it while protecting against its systemic risks.[55]

The economic dynamic analysis provided in Chapter 3 suggests several important structural reforms that might contain systemic risk. First, issuers might be permitted to securitize only a part of a loan, not all of it. They would retain a sufficient interest in a loan performing well to provide powerful incentives to ensure quality loans. This represents an application of the idea of providing exceptions to rules to address negative collateral consequences of policy decisions presented in Chapter 4, in this case through an exception to the rule permitting securitization of mortgages. This responds

---

[54] *Cf.* Stiglitz, *supra* note 7, at 5–6 (pointing out that Wall Street never developed a "good mortgage product for consumers" but focused on approaches raising fees).

[55] *Cf.* Stout, *supra* note 26, at 33–36 (advocating milder reform because of the potential for some types of derivatives trades to enhance efficiency).

to the fundamental economic dynamics discussed earlier. This reform might allow securitization to exist without creating incentives to reduce underwriting standards.

A second reform might involve restoring adaptive efficiency to the system. One way to do this would be to allow the issuer to retain rights to perform workouts when a risk of default seems imminent. To be effective, such a rule should forbid lawsuits by owners of securities and other intermediaries over workouts.

All these reforms, of course, would make securitization less attractive to potential issuers than it would be otherwise. But if securitization provides substantial economic value to consumers, then it should survive all these reforms. If it does not, that would be a sign that securitization provides no fundamental economic value; it gets more capital simply by increasing risk. If it only does that, then we should welcome its demise. Although we do not like to throw out babies with bathwater, we should not hesitate to drown monsters before they grow too large.

We should apply economic dynamic analysis to another structural reform that several economists have recommended – the breakup of large financial institutions.[56] Wilmarth's economic dynamic analysis suggests that too-big-to-fail institutions engage in risky transactions because their leaders know that the government will have to bail them out if things go wrong to prevent an economic collapse. Even without engaging in excessively risky transactions, allowing any institution to exist whose collapse could endanger the entire economy involves a great deal of systemic risk, as any institution can collapse because of mistakes by its leaders or employees.

Although a reasonably robust financial system is important to economic development, economic development ultimately depends more on the real economy than on a marvelously innovative and hyperevolved financial system. There is little reason to think that a few large institutions provide for significantly more economic development than a large number of small institutions. Hence, the economic dynamic case for breaking up too-big-to-fail firms seems quite strong.[57]

Supporters of huge financial firms argue that these firms enjoy economies of scale that make their operations more efficient than those of smaller firms. Many analysts who have studied banks doubt these assertions, with most studies

---

[56] *See, e.g.,* Stiglitz, *supra* note 7, at 167 (saying that banks too big to fail should be broken up). *Cf.* Wilmarth, *supra* note 32, at 1055 (noting that the Senate rejected a proposal with maximum size limits by a 2-to-1 margin).

[57] *See generally* James A. Fanto, "'Breaking up is Hard to Do': Should Financial Conglomerates by Dismantled?," 79 *U. Cinn. L. Rev.* 553 (2010).

finding that banks achieve economies of scale with just fifty to one hundred million dollars in deposits.[58] And evidence suggests that large financial firms can be very difficult to manage properly.[59] But for purposes of economic dynamic analysis, the efficiency assertion is of secondary importance. If some short-term efficiency is lost in making an economy economically sustainable, then we should give it up in hopes that some of the new small firms realize efficiencies that we have not anticipated.

Dodd-Frank authorizes a financial review board to order divestiture of assets to address systemic risks.[60] But it imposes a set of stringent procedural requirements that, in combination with the political difficulty of the task, virtually ensures that it will never use this authority to prevent a crisis.[61] Hence, Dodd-Frank failed to embrace a key structural form likely to significantly limit systemic risk.

Economic dynamic analysis can apply to more modest reforms as well. One reform worth considering involves adjustable-rate mortgages. Perhaps the time has come to abolish these (another structural alternative). An economic dynamic analysis of this reform would ask whether borrowers fully understand these loans and whether lenders tend to offer them too freely. This involves some understanding of how borrowers and lenders deal with the uncertainty of a loan that will reset at a higher rate later. If adjustable-rate loans act as vehicles for loans based on wishful thinking, the borrower imagining that the loan will not reset too high or that his or her wages will increase in order to afford the reset, with a lender hoping that that the increase in housing value will protect the bank if anything goes wrong, then perhaps they are dangerous.

Here, however, the analyst of economic dynamics might have to consider whether abolishing these loans would create countervailing systemic risks. Regulators approved these loans in the 1970s after a long period when lenders made only fixed-rate housing loans. At the time, the regulators saw

---

[58] *See* Peter C. Carstensen, "Public Policy Toward Interstate Bank Mergers: The Case for Concern," 49 *Ohio State L. J.* 1397, 1404 (1989). *Cf.* Robert DeYoung, Douglas D. Evanoff, & Phillip Molyneux, "Mergers and Acquisitions of Financial Institutions: A Review of the Post-2000 Literature," 36 *J. Fin. Serv. Res.* 87, 90–91 (2009) (finding a great deal of skepticism toward bank efficiency claims in the 1980s and 1990s, but more receptivity since 2000); Simon H. Kwan & James A. Wilcox, "Hidden Cost Reductions in Banks Mergers: Accounting for More Productive Banks," 19 *Res. Fin.* 109 (2002) (finding evidence of efficiencies after making adjustments for merger accounting rules). The financial crisis of 2008, however, casts doubts on the permanence of efficiency gains observed in these later studies.

[59] *See* Chapter 9, *infra*, note 87 and accompanying text.

[60] *See* Wilmarth, *supra* note 32, at 1024.

[61] *See id.* at 1024–25 (pointing out that the Federal Reserve Board has never used similar authority under the Bank Holding Act, even though it lacks the procedural impediments in Dodd-Frank).

adjustable-rate mortgages as a means of decreasing the risk of bank defaults that a high-interest-rate environment created. One would want to examine adjustable-rate mortgages' economic dynamics in the low-interest-rate environment prevalent today to gauge whether they now play an important role in ensuring bank survival. If not, perhaps it is time to abolish them, leaving open the possibility of reintroducing them in a high-interest-rate environment.

Richard Posner, in a book on the financial crisis published just after the collapse, argued against structural reform by saying that we needed time to study the costs and benefits and for passions to cool. But the problem with studying costs and benefits is more fundamental than that. Policymakers will never have sufficient "information" (as he calls the guesses in CBA) to measure structural reforms' costs and benefits. Hence, a demand to await the provision of this information amounts to a call for preserving a failed status quo indefinitely. An economic dynamic approach, however, offers a rational way forward.

The notion that reform should await the cooling of passions suggests a worldview uninformed by the most rudimentary empowerment analysis of the world we actually live in. We saw in Chapter 3 that owners of large financial institutions have employed lobbyists to create the financially dangerous conditions that gave rise to this crisis and to preserve them.[62] They give large campaign contributions to ensure that Congressmen protect their interests at the expense of everybody else and have, as of this writing, prevented major structural reform. The public, which has at times acted as a powerful countervailing force, more typically engages in reform efforts sporadically, if at all. If we consider reforms when public passion and engagement reach a zenith, rational reform serving the public's interest might get a serious hearing. Otherwise, the steady zealous advocacy of hired guns for special interests will almost surely prevail.

The public choice aspect of economic dynamic theory probably also supports structural reform, especially the breakup of large financial institutions.[63] I suspect that an economic dynamic analysis would show that large institutions with diverse operations that cannot be seriously harmed without crippling the economy will tend to lobby to keep all financial regulation minimal, especially at times when we need robust regulation (that is, during a bubble delivering profits prior to a collapse).[64] Breaking up financial conglomerates would not

---

[62] *Accord* Stiglitz, *supra* note 7, at 9–10 (pointing out that the financial industry paid to defeat regulation).

[63] *See* Macey & Holdcroft, Jr., *supra* note 42.

[64] *Cf.* Wilmarth, *supra* note 32, at 1011–12 (discussing the sources of "capture" of financial regulation analysts have pointed to and Dodd-Frank's dependence on sound exercise of regulatory discretion).

end lobbying, but would create smaller firms in place of the too-big-to-fail institutions. Smaller firms with narrower missions may compete with each other in ways that give them diverse interests, making it possible for even delegated authority to occasionally serve public interests. The early opposition of some firms to erosion of the wall between commercial and investment banking illustrates how diverse smaller interests can sometimes oppose deregulation. Ideology was probably as important as special-interest lobbying in getting the erosion process under way. Hence, the breakup of large firms may be important in creating a disparate array of economic incentives among firms, such that rational future regulation becomes possible.[65] We shall see that this theme, that big firms can undermine rational democratic governance, played a major role in early antitrust law. Chapter 9 will consider what the public choice dimension of economic dynamics has to say about this older antitrust tradition.

CONCLUSION

Economic dynamic analysis provides a fruitful way of analyzing financial reform. It has more capacity to anticipate systemic risk than traditional neo-classical CBA. And it aids serious consideration of very significant structural reform, which has received too little attention in policymaking circles to date.

---

[65] *See* Macey & Holdcroft, *supra* note 42, at 1382–83.

PART TWO

6

Contract Law's Inefficiency

Neoclassical economic theory seems to aptly characterize contract law's essence. Contracts enable two parties to reach a mutually beneficial agreement, thereby facilitating economically efficient transactions.

This chapter examines an alternative hypothesis – that contract law is about enforcing some inefficient bargains in order to provide enough security to enable people to cooperate over fairly long periods of time. On this account, contract law manages change over time, rather than achieves static efficiency.[1]

The traditional account explains why parties make contracts – because they anticipate benefits exceeding the costs of carrying out their bargain.[2] Yet the neoclassical account does not explain the *law* of contracts, which, except in narrow circumstances, coerces involuntary performance or payment of damages later on, when one party no longer agrees to perform. The breaching party presumably has determined that performance does not provide benefits exceeding that party's costs. If a mutual agreement indicating an efficient contract continued to exist, probably nobody would need to enforce the contract. The law of contracts exists because often something changes after the parties

---

[1] I have developed this argument at greater length elsewhere. See David M. Driesen, "Contract Law's Inefficiency," 6 *Va. L. & Bus. Rev.* 302 (2011). See *generally* Patrick Atiyah, "Contracts, Promises and the Law of Obligations," 94 *L.Q. Rev* 193, 196 (1978) (noting that "contracts have a chronology," since performance comes after agreement). The term "static efficiency" highlights a key feature of standard definitions of economic efficiency – their assumption of a given technological state. *See* David M. Driesen, *The Economic Dynamics of Environmental Law* 4 (2003) (noting that "economists define allocative efficiency in terms of matching supply and demand for a given technological state").

[2] In saying that the traditional account explains why parties make contracts, I do not mean to suggest that it constitutes a complete explanation of contracting behavior. *Cf.* Ian R. Macneil, "Relational Contract Theory: Challenges and Queries," 94 Nw. *U. L. Rev.* 877, 878–83 (2000) (describing a contract as an ongoing relationship among people rather than as a plan for a discrete transaction).

sign a contract, making the contemplated performance inefficient. Hence, contract *law* is largely about enforcing inefficient agreements in order to manage change over time – in other words, the economic dynamics involved in carrying out a bargain.[3]

Viewed this way, contract law continues to perform an economic function. But the principal function becomes the provision of a stable macroeconomic environment conducive to stable cooperation and economic growth. This macroeconomic environment often facilitates efficient contracting, but courts properly sacrifice efficiency in the case before them in order to preserve a stable environment for experimentation, cooperation, and economic growth.

An emphasis on economic dynamics and macroeconomics also helps explain the exceptions to the general rule that courts enforce inefficient contracts. In particular, traditional efficiency-based accounts cannot explain the courts' emphasis on unusual circumstances as a prerequisite to discharge of contractual obligations on grounds of impracticability or impossibility. An account that views contract law not as ensuring efficiency, but as providing a stable environment for parties to cooperate over long periods of time, provides a more convincing explanation of these excuse doctrines.[4]

Because contract law manages change over time rather than ensures efficiency, analysts should employ economic dynamic analysis of contract law as an analytical tool. I show that Ian Ayres and Robert Gertner have, in fact, employed economic dynamic analysis in their seminal work on default rules in contract and corporate law.[5]

This chapter begins with an explanation of how the neoclassical model explains voluntary contracts. The second part explains and defends the hypothesis that contract law requires enforcement of inefficient bargains. The third part explains why enforcement of inefficient bargains serves important economic purposes. The fourth part explains how an emphasis on change over time and macroeconomics helps justify case law on the excuse doctrines. The fifth part closes with a call for an economic dynamic approach to contract law and a description of how leading scholars have tacitly begun to employ this approach.

---

[3] *Cf.* Melvin A Eisenberg, "Why There Is no Law of Relational Contracts," 94 *Nw. U. L. Rev.* 805, 807 (2000) (claiming that classical contract law was "static" in that it focused on a single instant of time instead of an ongoing relationship).

[4] *Cf.* Richard Speidel, "The Characteristics and Challenges of Relational Contracts," 94 *Nw. U. L. Rev.* 823, 824 (2000) (describing long-term cooperative relationships as hallmarks of "relational contracts").

[5] *See generally* Ian Ayres & Robert Gertner, "Filling Gaps in Incomplete Contracts: An Economic Theory of Default Rules," 99 *Yale L. J.* 87 (1989).

EFFICIENT CONTRACTING

The neoclassical economic model provides a very satisfying explanation of why parties enter into contracts. Parties enter into contracts voluntarily. Accordingly, each party to the contract must anticipate that carrying out the deal embedded in the contract will provide benefits to herself exceeding her costs.[6]

For example, suppose a homeowner offers to pay a painter $5,000 to paint her house. The homeowner must anticipate that the value of the benefit she receives, a new paint job, will equal or exceed the $5,000 cost she will incur if the painter accepts her offer. Similarly, if the painter accepts this offer, then he must anticipate that the $5,000 benefit he will receive will exceed the cost he incurs in painting the house – the value of the time spent doing the work and the cost of supplies. Economists define exchanges generating benefits exceeding costs for both parties as efficient, in the sense of being a "Pareto optimal" exchange.[7]

Pareto efficiency has special normative appeal precisely because it brings benefits to both parties to an exchange, and parties make contracts to realize that sort of efficiency. Accordingly, my analysis of contract law's inefficiency will define efficiency in terms of Pareto optimality. I will, however, address contract law's relationship to Kaldor-Hicks efficiency – the definition of a transaction as efficient when one's party's gains could, in principle, allow that party to fully compensate any person who suffered losses from the transaction[8] – later in this chapter. Kaldor-Hicks efficiency proves problematic normatively, because it does not require the party gaining from a transaction to compensate the other party for his or her losses, but it continues to play a major role in law and economics.[9]

The most fundamental models of markets build on this idea of Pareto efficient contracting. Neoclassical economics assumes that the homeowner expects a certain utility from her new paint job. Let us say that this utility equals $7,000. It follows that she will voluntarily pay any amount up to $7,000

---

[6] *See* Richard A. Posner, *Economic Analysis of Law* 11 (2nd ed. 1977) (stating that a voluntary transaction occurs when both parties expect it to make them better off).

[7] *See* Robert Birmingham, "Breach of Contract, Damage Measures, and Economic Efficiency," 24 *Rutgers L. Rev.* 273, 278–80 (1970) (explaining Pareto optimality and defending it as a normative goal).

[8] *See* E. J. Mishan, *Cost-Benefit Analysis* 162 (1982) (defining Kaldor-Hicks efficiency in terms of the capacity to compensate losers, whether or not compensation actually occurs).

[9] *See* David M. Driesen, "The Societal Cost of Environmental Regulation: Beyond Administrative Cost-Benefit Analysis," 24 *Ecology L. Q.* 545, 580 (1997) (pointing out that because Kaldor-Hicks efficiency lacks Pareto optimality's "attractive consensual" feature, it is less normatively attractive).

for the paint job. She would prefer to pay as little as possible, of course, but she will pay any amount up to $7,000, but not one penny more. The painter's utility will equal the payment for the paint job. The painter, however, will incur costs in realizing this utility. Suppose that the painter expects that he will need to devote $3,000 worth of his time on the job and to spend $1,000 on supplies. He will be willing to undertake the job for any amount exceeding his $4,000 cost. The painter will prefer to get paid as much as possible, but any amount over $4,000 provides sufficient utility to justify the cost.

In this case, the parties will agree on a paint job costing between $4,000 and $7,000. Any deal in that range will provide an efficient exchange, making both parties better off. And, of course, this basic model applies to all kinds of contracts, not just painting contracts. People make deals because their expected utility functions overlap.

The explanation above uses the words "anticipate" and "expect" a lot, for a reason. People contract in order to try to realize an exchange in the future, and they do so based on their expectations for the future.[10]

We can extend this simple model temporally to explain a little more fully when a contract will likely produce voluntary compliance without formal invocation of law. Assume that the parties agree at time t_1 to a $5,000 paint job to be performed at a later time, t_2. Suppose nothing changes between t_1 and t_2. It is likely that the parties will perform their contract in this case.[11] The transaction agreed to at t_1 because it appeared efficient remains mutually advantageous at t_2, so the parties will likely perform.[12]

In most instances, neither party has a need to resort to contract law when the mutually advantageous deal at t_1 remains mutually advantageous at t_2.[13] The law's coercive force is not needed because performance is generally in both parties' interest. Just as their self-interest adequately motivated voluntary

---

[10] *See* Charles J. Goetz & Robert E. Scott, "Enforcing Promises: An Examination of the Basis of Contract," 89 *Yale L. J.* 1261, 1266–67 (1980) (insisting on a conceptual distinction "between the promise itself and the future benefit it foretells").

[11] *See* Alan O. Sykes, "The Doctrine of Commercial Impracticability in a Second-Best World," 19 *J. Legal Stud.* 43, 53 (1990) (constructing a model based on the assumption that sellers will not breach when the cost of performance is less than the contract payment).

[12] *Cf.* Posner, *supra* note 6, at 65 (stating that the exchange process operates reliably in "many cases . . . , especially where the exchange is simultaneous" the parties "fully and correctly apprehend" the exchange's costs and benefits).

[13] I do not mean to suggest that these are the only cases where contracting parties are likely to self-enforce. *See* Alan Schwartz & Robert E. Scott, "Contract Theory and the Limits of Contract Law," 113 *Yale L. J.* 541, 546 (2003) (pointing out that parties will self-enforce when the losses are less than the stream of future benefits from a series of future contracts or less than the value of reputational damage from a breach).

contracting at t_1, it should subsequently prove adequate to motivate voluntary performance at t_2, at least in most cases.[14]

Inefficient Contract Law

A variation on this simple temporal model can explain why parties sometimes resort to contract law, rather than rely solely upon voluntary fulfillment of promises. Suppose that the painter's cost rises between t_1 and t_2, so that at t_2 it exceeds the $5,000 the homeowner has promised to pay for the paint job. This could occur because the painter underestimated the amount of time the job requires (a fairly common problem with contracting for paint jobs or construction) or because the cost of paint rose. At this point, the painter has an interest in not painting the house, because the cost of the job outweighs the benefit (a $5,000 payment). Because it is not in his interests to complete the job, he may fail to perform.[15]

Economically speaking, exchange can also become inefficient because new opportunities arise. For example, suppose that at t_1 our painter agrees to paint the house in our earlier example for $5,000 at t_2. Before t_2 occurs, a second homeowner offers our painter $10,000 to paint his house at t_2. Assume no flexibility about timing in either case. If the painter fulfills the original contract, he will incur a $5,000 opportunity cost, the difference between the $10,000 forgone opportunity and the $5,000 earned under the original contract. Neoclassical economics treats lost opportunities as equivalent to losses, so this implies a $5,000 loss. It has now become inefficient for the painter to fulfill the contract.[16]

If the painter does not paint the house, the homeowner may sue to compel performance. The purpose of contract law, of course, is to compel performance of a contract when promised performance does not occur. Law is about compulsion, always, even if the compulsion follows voluntary agreement.[17] A court enforcing a contract will compel the breaching party to perform or pay

---

[14] *See generally* Karl N. Llewellyn, "What Price Contract?: An Essay in Perspective," 40 *Yale L J.* 704, 718 (1931) (noting how seldom law directly touches any case where performance has occurred).

[15] *See* Goetz & Scott, *supra* note 10, at 1273 (characterizing a new event making contractual performance a losing proposition as a "regret contingency").

[16] *See* Posner, *supra* note 6, at 89–90 (using a different hypothetical to illustrate the desirability from an efficiency standpoint of allowing parties to breach contracts when a better opportunity arises).

[17] *See* Llewellyn, *supra* note 14, at 711 (describing contractual enforcement as the "forcible holding of a man . . . to a promise").

damages. It does not secure voluntary compliance; it coerces compliance with
a contract when one party has decided not to comply.

In other words, law comes into play when a voluntary agreement at t_1
does not lead to voluntary compliance at t_2. This difference between t_1 and
t_2 frequently arises because intervening events have made a contract that
appeared to serve both parties' interests cease to serve one party's interests.[18]

If follows that law usually comes into play when performance of a contract
becomes inefficient. Recall that neoclassical economics defines efficiency
during contract formation in terms of a transaction generating a Pareto optimal
exchange, meaning a transaction that benefits *both parties*. Nonperformance
triggering contract law usually indicates that the transaction itself did not
benefit both parties. The transaction, of course, occurs at t_2. Contract law
comes into play when a transaction that appeared Pareto optimal at t_1 reveals
itself to be inefficient, or at least not Pareto optimal, at t_2.

Contract law generally does enforce contracts in some fashion, even when
one party does not want to perform. Classical contract law, summarized by the
dictum *pacta sunt servanda* (agreements must be observed), provided at best
limited exceptions to this duty to perform.[19] Indeed, some early English cases
appear to take the position that even the impossibility of performance does
not excuse a breach of contract.[20] Under that theory, even if our hypothetical
house went up in flames before the painter could complete his paint job, a
court would hold the painter liable for breach of contract. More commonly,
the common law excused performance only for acts of God and other similar
unusual contingencies outside the parties' control.[21]

---

[18] *See* Sykes, *supra* note 11, at 48–49 (characterizing cases involving "sellers whose fixed-price
contracts have become highly unprofitable" as "the most commonly litigated cases"); Charles
Goetz & Robert Scott, "Liquidated Damages, Penalties, and the Just Compensation Principle:
A Theory of Efficient Breach," 77 *Colum. L. Rev.* 554, 564 (1977) (describing "changed
conditions" modifying an agreement's "perceived advantages" as the ordinary "motivation for
breach").

[19] *See Waukesha Foundry v. Industrial Eng'g*, 91 F.3d 1002, 1010 (7th Cir. 1996) (equating *pacta
sunt servanda* with the idea that "a deal's a deal"); *see, e.g., Stees v. Leonard*, 20 Minn. 494,
20 Gil 448 (1874) (awarding damages for failure to comply with a contract for erection of a
building, when the contractor constructed a three-story building twice, only to have it collapse
because of quicksand); *Butterfield v. Byron*, 27 N.E. 667 (Mass. 1891) (holding a contractor
liable when the building he constructed burned to the ground after being struck by lightning).

[20] *See, e.g., Paradine v. Jane*, Aelyn 26, 82 Eng. Rep. 897 (K.B. 1647) (stating that when a party
"by his own contract creates a duty . . . upon himself, he is bound to make it good, if he may,
notwithstanding any accident or inevitable necessity").

[21] *See, e.g., 407 East 61st Garage, Inc. v. Savoy Fifth Ave. Corp.*, 244 N.E.2d 37, 41 (N.Y. Ct.
App. 1968) (describing the impossibility defense as limited to "destruction of the means of
performance by an act of God, *vis major*, or by law") (citations omitted). *Cf.* William Herbert
Page, "The Development of the Doctrine of Impossibility of Performance," 18 *Mich. L. Rev.*

Even under the modern law of contracts, which excuses performance more liberally,[22] a price rise that does nothing more than make a contract a money-loser for one party does not excuse performance.[23] The Uniform Commercial Code (UCC) § 2–615(a) provides an impracticability defense to sellers failing to deliver goods in a timely manner, but the commentary on that section insists that "increased cost alone does not excuse performance," while acknowledging that some unusual contingencies raising prices might furnish a valid excuse, such as war or local crop failure.[24] Furthermore, "a mere showing of unprofitability" – a showing sufficient to show a lack of Pareto optimality – does not (without more) "excuse performance."[25] For example, in *Neal-Cooper Grain Co. v. Texas Gulf Sulphur Co.*,[26] the Seventh Circuit ordered damages paid for breach of a contract to deliver fertilizer.[27] In response to Texas Gulf Sulphur's argument that the Canadian government's closure of the mine it intended to rely on as a supply source made fulfillment of the contract "impracticable," the court held that "the fact that performance has become burdensome or unattractive is not sufficient for performance to be excused."[28] In demanding "unattractive" performance, it implicitly denied the relevance of efficiency to contract law, for Pareto optimal exchange is, by definition, attractive to both parties. The law regularly enforces bargains that the parties expected to be Pareto efficient, but proved not to be.[29]

Notice that models to address the problem of an unforeseen event occurring between t_1 and t_2 cannot be based on perfect information. The problem of an unforeseen event arising occurs because parties cannot have

---

589, 592–94 (1920) (noting that although the courts sometimes cite an act of God in excusing performance, the impossibility defense extends to acts of human agency and does not include all acts of God).

[22] *See* Kevin M. Teevan, "Development of Reform of the Preexisting Duty Rule and its Persistent Survival," 47 *Ala. L. Rev.* 387, 422–23 (1996) (describing the liberalization of the impossibility doctrine).

[23] *See, e.g., Louisiana Power & Light Co. v. Allegheny Ludlum Industries*, 517 F. Supp. 1319, 1324 (1981) (declaring that a contractual loss does not justify a holding of impracticability).

[24] U.C.C. § 2–615(a) cmt. 4 (1977).

[25] *Schafer v. Sunset Packing Co.*, 256 Or. 539, 474 P.2d 529, 530 (1970). *Cf. Florida Power & Light v. Westinghouse*, 826 F.2d 239, 277 (4th Cir. 1987) (finding impracticability when a loss was "four or five times the expected profit"); Sykes, *supra* note 11, at 77–79 (criticizing the reasoning in *Florida Power* and finding it has nothing to do with efficiency).

[26] 508 F.2d 283 (7th Cir. 1974)

[27] Id. at 293–95 (denying a defense of commercial impracticability and giving instructions to the trial court about how to ascertain the amount of damages).

[28] Id. at 293.

[29] *See, e.g., Transatlantic Financing Corp. v. United States*, 363 F.2d 312 (1966) (closure of Suez Canal producing an additional $44,000 in cost from longer shipping route does not excuse payment of the $305,843 contract price).

perfect information about the future, which is, in a fundamental way, always unknowable.[30]

Neoclassical law and economics indirectly addresses the problem of efficient transactions becoming inefficient through the doctrine of *efficient breach*. That doctrine holds that if a contract becomes inefficient, the breaching party should not perform. This approach would make contractual compliance uncertain and therefore interfere with contract law as a stable force fostering macroeconomic growth.

Most contract scholars, however, do not recommend discharge of contracts that have become inefficient; instead, they endorse the common law rule that the breaching party should pay damages representing the expectations of the promisee – the homeowner in my painting example.[31] They typically justify this endorsement of the expectation damages remedy by arguing that it provides sufficient incentives to avoid inefficient breach.[32] To see why expectation damages should provide incentives to avoid inefficient breach, imagine that the painter's costs for the $5,000 paint job have risen to $6,000, but that the contracting homeowner's expected utility from the $5,000 job equaled $7,000. In that case, performance for a $5,000 payment would produce a $2,000 benefit to the homeowner ($7,000 – $5,000) and only a $1,000 loss to the painter ($5,000 – $6,000). Breach would be inefficient, say the proponents of expectation damages, because performance would generate a $1,000 net benefit ($2,000 – $1,000).[33] As long as the painter must pay the $2,000 net benefit that the homeowner expects under the contract in the event of a breach as expectation damages, the painter has an incentive to perform this unprofitable

---

[30] Ian R. Macneil, "The Many Futures of Contract," 47 *S. Cal. L. Rev.* 691, 727 (1974) (describing "much of the future" as inherently unknowable); *see* Eric Posner, "Economic Analysis of Contract Law After Three Decades: Success or Failure?," 112 *Yale L. J.* 829, 865 (2002) (commenting that if parties "could foresee every possible future state of the world" and contract accordingly, "contract law would be simple and uninteresting").

[31] *See* Posner, *supra* note 30, at 834–35 (explaining that law and economics scholars have argued that an expectation measure of damages encourages only efficient performance); *see generally* Atiyah, *supra* note 1, at 210–11 (distinguishing expectation damages from damages predicated on reliance). *Cf.* Daniel Friedman, "The Efficient Breach Fallacy," 18 *J. Legal. Stud.* 1, 3 (1989) (claiming that although the efficient breach theory was "originally... preached" without "qualification," the modern position distinguished between "opportunistic breach" and other inefficient breaches).

[32] *See* Posner, *supra* note 6, at 90 (explaining the reasons for this conclusion); J. A. Sebert, Jr., "Punitive and Nonpecuniary Damages in Actions Based on Contract: Toward Achieving the Objective of Full Compensation," 33 *UCLA L. Rev.* 1565 (1986) (discussing in detail the reasons that damages often are not fully compensatory).

[33] *See* Michelle J. White, "Contract Breach and Contract Discharge Due to Impossibility: A Unified Theory," 17 *J. Legal Stud.* 353, 357 (1988) (explaining the efficient breach theory algebraically).

contract, because not performing will raise his losses from $1,000 to $2,000.[34] Hence, neoclassical law and economic scholars argue that expectation damages make contract law efficient.

Notice, however, that the painter performing his job to avoid paying expectation damages experiences a loss. So this damages remedy, in principle, is not efficient in the sense of Pareto optimality. Rather, it only can achieve less desirable Kaldor-Hicks efficiency.

This justification for preferring expectation damages to discharge of an inefficient contract depends upon a strong perfect information assumption. The painter, in order to receive the proper signal to avoid inefficient breach and commit efficient breach whenever possible, must know the utility function of the homeowner. In this example, the painter must somehow have figured out that notwithstanding the $5,000 contract price, the homeowner, in fact, was willing to pay up to $7,000 for the job. This sort of knowledge may often prove difficult to come by[35] for the following reasons. A contracting party has an incentive not to disclose his or her utility function to the other party, because doing so helps the other party secure more of the gains from trade at the disclosing party's expense.[36] Second, a utility function is an abstract concept used in economic modeling that in many contexts proves difficult to discover.[37] Because the painter probably does not know the homeowner's

---

[34] *Cf.* Llewellyn, *supra* note 14, at 738 (expressing doubt that damages deter breach).

[35] *See* Friedman, *supra* note 31, at 10 (pointing out that it is very difficult to know how much value a homeowner would place on a renovation); Alan Schwartz, "The Case for Specific Performance," 89 *Yale L. J.* 271 (1979) (arguing that valuation difficulties are ever-present so specific performance is a better default rule than the payment of damages).

[36] *Cf.* Posner, *supra* note 30, at 836 (finding expectation damages undesirable when information is asymmetric).

[37] *See* Mark Sagoff, *Price, Principle, and the Environment* 80–83, 94–100 (2004). Sagoff distinguishes between market prices and the maximum willingness to pay, arguing that market prices do not measure consumer benefit, because they are more driven by production costs than willingness to pay. Id. at 81–82. He shows a utility function's abstractness by demonstrating that maximum willingness to pay is not measurable. Id. at 82–83, 94–100. Unfortunately, maximum willingness to pay, not a market price, determines the amount of consumer surplus (or, more precisely, promisee surplus) involved in an unprofitable transaction. And it is this surplus that a promisor must measure to determine whether a breach would be efficient or not.

Goetz and Scott argue for using market prices of performance as the basis for expectation damages, as courts generally do. Goetz & Scott, *supra* note 18, at 569. But this remedy should be seen as a second-best proxy for the party's actual utility function, as a market represents an average of various arrangements reflecting intersections of different utility functions, not the actual benefit from a transaction to an individual promisee. Goetz and Scott go on to acknowledge that promisees may attach "idiosyncratic value" to performance that varies significantly from market valuation. Id. at 570. Sagoff, however, shows that the problem is more systematic than that. Market prices just do not measure consumer (promisee) benefit

utility function, the painter cannot predict whether breach will prove efficient under a rule embracing expectation damages. Accordingly, the expectation damages rule does not necessarily enable a promisor to carry out "efficient" breach while eschewing inefficient breach. Hence, if one relaxes the perfect information assumption at the heart of neoclassical law and economics and acknowledges that breach occurs with uncertain knowledge about its future effects on the nonbreaching party, then a key argument for regarding contract law as efficient (at least in a very limited way) falls apart.

Thus, parties contract in order to realize an efficient exchange. But the law of contracts exists to force the exchange to occur, or an appropriate monetary substitute, when the transaction proves inefficient and therefore induces the losing party to breach the contract.

THE MACROECONOMIC PURPOSES OF ENFORCING
INEFFICIENT BARGAINS

Enforcing inefficient bargains serves the purpose of fostering economic cooperation over extended periods of time.[38] In societies without well-developed formal legal systems to enforce inefficient bargains, some exchange still occurs. But the exchanges may often be limited to instantaneous sales.[39] Long-term cooperation in such societies typically arises between people sharing kinship ties or other long-term affiliations that allow them to trust each other to carry out bargains without invoking a legal system's formal mechanisms of coercion.[40] Long-term cooperation between strangers may be hard to come by in such societies, and this dearth limits opportunities for economic development.[41]

except in cases in which transactions generally confiscate all consumer (promisee) surplus. *Cf.* Sagoff, *supra* at 94–96 (showing that the amount of consumer surplus cannot be measured, because divergence between consumer utility and market prices cannot be observed); Alfred Marshall, *Principles of Economics*, III, vi, 5 (1890). In addition, some goods, such as unique goods, have no markets, so in some cases market prices do not exist as a basis for damages and courts order specific performance. Goetz & Scott, *supra* note 18, at 569–70.

[38] *See* Schwartz & Scott, *supra* note 13, at 558–59 (pointing out that the law of property adequately governs simultaneous exchange, but that the law of contract governs promises about future behavior).

[39] *See* Posner, *supra* note 6, at 66 (claiming that the absence of enforceable contractual rights biases investment toward short-term projects).

[40] *See* Goetz & Scott, *supra* note 10, at 1272 (modeling the tendency of people to keep promises to family members and close friends); Macneil, *supra* note 30, at 718 (suggesting that in "traditional societies" kinship helps "project" exchange "into the future.")

[41] Schwartz & Scott, *supra* note 13, at 548 (describing "good contract law" as "a necessary condition for a modern commercial economy"); Llewellyn, *supra* note 14, at 720–21 (explaining that informal sanctions may suffice when close ties and face-to-face dealings prevail, but that contract law is essential for long-range impersonal bargains and investment).

Enforcement of inefficient transactions increases parties' willingness to contract in the first place.[42] If a party can count on enforcement of a bargain, then it makes sense to contract at t_1 for performance at t_2, rather than just wait for t_2 in order to realize an instantaneous exchange.[43] Parties in a system with regular enforcement of inefficient contracts will make contracts that appear efficient at t_1. They still have no incentive to choose contracts they expect will prove inefficient, because one party usually will not voluntarily agree to assume losses. And, as mentioned previously, many of the contracts that appear efficient at t_1 will prove efficient at t_2. Thus, enforcement of a few inefficient exchanges encourages many more efficient exchanges. In other words, optimizing each transaction that happens to end up in court does not necessarily optimize the far larger universe of contractual exchange, of which litigated cases form a tiny part.[44]

The willingness to enforce inefficient exchange at the heart of contract law serves many macroeconomic purposes apart from encouraging efficient contracting.[45] The ability to count on performance (or a monetary equivalent) of a contract facilitates all sorts of economic planning and cooperation.[46] It creates important economic growth opportunities,[47] and may do so even when the exchange itself is inefficient.

Contracts do not merely allocate existing resources; they sometimes create economic growth opportunities. A contract between an inventor and a manufacturing firm to produce a new kind of product provides an example. Such a contract may bring to life an innovation having positive spillover effects benefiting society, leading to fresh economic opportunities for people other than the contracting parties.[48] In such cases, even a contract that causes losses to

---

[42] See Goetz & Scott, *supra* note 10, at 1264 (decisions to enforce promises influence "future promising").

[43] See Schwartz & Scott, *supra* note 13, at 559–61 (explaining that absent enforcement of an original contract, sellers would refuse to contract to sell a specialized product at a future date). The law of anticipatory breach seeks to deal with this problem. Id. at 561.

[44] Cf. Jay M. Feinman, "Relational Contracting in Context," 94 Nw. U. L. Rev. 737, 740 (2000) (explaining that "relational contracts" sometimes require subordinating "short-term self-interest" in order to produce long-term cooperation).

[45] Cf. Posner, *supra* note 6, at 66 (emphasizing that contract law provides for more efficient allocation of resources, because a seller can look for the best deal with more temporal flexibility).

[46] See Feinman, *supra* note 44, at 742 (identifying allowing implementation of plans as a central norm in relational contract theory). Cf. Schwartz & Scott, *supra* note 13, at 556 (pointing out that enforcement of contract permits "persons to enlist other persons in their projects").

[47] See Schwartz & Scott, *supra* note 13, at 562 (the absence of contractual enforcement helps explain the dearth of foreign investment in former Soviet states and many third world countries).

[48] See generally Brett M. Frischmann & Mark A. Lemley, "Spillovers," 107 Colum. L. Rev. 257 (2007) (explaining that intellectual property often generates positive spillovers, benefits that accrue to nonparties to a transaction).

one or both of the contracting parties can produce economic growth of much greater value than the losses stemming from contractual performance.[49]

Economic growth frequently involves inefficiency, since it often stems from sometimes unsuccessful experimentation and loss.[50] For example, e-commerce – commerce conducted over the Internet – rests on a foundation of inefficient transactions. Amazon.com, which pioneered the e-commerce model, engaged in numerous inefficient money-losing transactions, leading to years of business losses, in order to entice customers to become accustomed to making purchases in cyberspace.[51] Although the law and economics of contract has focused on the microeconomics of individual exchange, the economic dynamics of contract law may have greater importance.[52] That is, contract law may create the security people need to take the risks that produce economic growth in the long run, even if many transactions leading to this growth prove inefficient.[53] In other words, the macroeconomics of contract law – its role in providing a framework for economic growth – may matter far more than the consistent achievement of microeconomic efficiency in each transaction.

Contract law seeks to give economic actors a stable framework in which to plan, in spite of the inevitability of change in a dynamic world. It manages change over time, not by ensuring that every transaction has a happy ending for all involved, but by making economic cooperation between strangers over time a reasonable thing to undertake.[54]

This implies that contract law does not ensure efficiency. Rather, it provides a framework that parties can employ to pursue their own purposes, including

---

[49] Cf. Richard Craswell, "In That Case, What is the Question? Economics and the Demands of Contract Theory," 112 *Yale L. J.* 903, 909 (2003) (suggesting that a supply contract making both parties better off can be bad for society if too much pollution is emitted in producing the supply); Barbara White, "Coase and the Courts: Economics for the Common Man," 72 *Iowa L. Rev.* 577, 593–94 (1987) (pointing out that optimizing a transaction between two parties does not necessarily improve society's efficiency).

[50] See Driesen, *supra* note 1, at 5 (noting that innovation and growth depend upon experimentation, which often involves failure and inefficiency).

[51] See id. at 6 (explaining that Amazon.com incurred substantial losses in its early years and predicting that if the company survived, it would show that "inefficient investment" proved beneficial over the long term).

[52] See id. at 4 (questioning whether static efficiency merits the "obsessive attention" it has received in light of the importance of economic growth stemming from innovation and change).

[53] See generally Atiyah, *supra* note 1, at 197–98 (noting that the primary purpose of contract enforcement is to encourage people to keep their promises).

[54] See id. at 199 (describing contract as encouraging cooperation and planning but accepting that "some would rise and some would sink").

the purpose of mutually beneficial exchange.[55] Markets may tend toward efficient outcomes. But the law's pursuit of inefficiency plays an important role in making that possible and in providing even more important benefits.[56]

UNDERSTANDING IMPRACTICABILITY DOCTRINE AS MANAGEMENT OF CHANGE OVER TIME

An understanding of contract law as an effort to encourage cooperative relationships over time provides a much more satisfying explanation of contract law's main features than the efficiency-based perspective. A good illustration of this comes from the law of excuse mentioned earlier, which provides the major exception to the rule that courts enforce inefficient bargains.

Traditional law and economics scholarship finds it difficult to account for the rationales courts actually offer for rulings when parties raise defenses of impossibility or impracticability. Alan Sykes finds the excuse cases unsatisfying from an efficiency perspective because the judges writing these decisions fail to grapple with the question of how much unexpected cost is too much relative to benefits – the question that should lie at the heart of an effort to make contract law efficient (at least at the time of judicial enforcement, t_3).[57] Sykes draws the logical conclusion from this lack of interest in the scale of potential losses as compared with the possible benefits – the courts simply have no interest in economic efficiency.[58] Richard Posner, by the way, does not exactly disagree with him. Instead, he argues that an *implicit* economic logic accounts for the cases' main results, but admits that the "courts have not explicitly characterized the problem" of when to excuse performance as "one of identifying the superior risk bearer."[59] It would be surprising indeed

---

[55] *Cf.* Paul J. Gudel, "Relational Contract Theory and the Concept of Exchange," 46 *Buff. L. Rev.* 763, 776–77 (1998) (describing contract as involving norms of "solidarity and reciprocity," not just maximization of net utility).

[56] *See generally* Macneil, *supra* note 2, at 893 (stating that there may be good reasons for contract law not to track the norms governing contracting).

[57] *See* Sykes, *supra* note 11, at 75 (lamenting the lack of judicial guidance about how great a cost increase is too much and pointing out that efficiency does not turn solely on the magnitude of cost increases).

[58] *See id.* at 44 (finding legal doctrine "quite insensitive to the economic factors" determining the efficiency of discharge and questioning "the efficiency of the impracticability defense in practice").

[59] *See* Richard A. Posner & Andrew M. Rosenfield, "Impossibility and Related Doctrines in Contract Law: An Economic Analysis," 6 J. *Legal Stud.* 83, 84, 107 (1977) (concluding that the excuse doctrines have an "implicit economic logic" but admitting that courts do not explicitly seek to identify superior risk bearers).

if judges expressing little or no interest in efficient results somehow stumbled upon rules that produced efficient outcomes. Alan Sykes' conclusion that the courts do not pursue efficient results in these cases (and could not achieve them with any regularity if they tried) has the virtue of aligning judges' purposes with what the judges say they are doing.[60]

We can, however, more easily understand the excuse doctrine in terms of the economic dynamics of change over time. If one sees these doctrines as trying to provide a stable environment for contracting in a world that sometimes upsets parties' expectations, then the justifications judges actually offer for their decisions become much easier to understand.

Judges seeking to make contracting for future performance a reasonably stable exercise should not excuse performance based on circumstances likely to reoccur in a large number of cases. Hence, the main thrust of an excuse doctrine should be to excuse performance only when *extraordinary* circumstances make performance impossible or extremely difficult.[61] Accordingly, in the opinion of the drafters of the Second Restatement of Contracts, judges have made extraordinary circumstances a prerequisite for abrogation of contract under the excuse doctrines.[62] Ordinary circumstances cannot justify excused performance, not because they cannot render a contract inefficient (ordinary circumstances can do that just as often as extraordinary circumstances), but because they arise too frequently.[63]

This focus on extraordinary causes also manifests itself in the courts' emphasis on foreseeability. As a general rule, courts will not discharge contracts based on foreseeable contingencies that arise after contracts are signed making performance difficult.[64] Parties tend to foresee the sorts of contingencies that recur frequently, but often fail to anticipate unusual events. Hence, the foreseeability

[60] See Sykes, *supra* note 11, at 93–94 (finding existing doctrine "devoid of any apparent economic foundation," but suggesting that courts will rarely have sufficient information to craft efficient discharge doctrine).

[61] See *Corbin on Contracts* § 1355 (pointing out that "variations in the value of performance . . . are the rule not the exception" and suggesting that, therefore, parties should "swallow their losses" unless caused by unforeseeable events).

[62] Restatement (Second) of Contracts, introduction to Chapter 11 (emphasizing that the excuse doctrines address the question of when "extraordinary circumstances" justify excusing performance).

[63] See, e.g., *Lloyd v. Murphy*, 25 Cal. 2d 48, 57, 153 P.2d 47, 52 (1944) (expressing reluctance to apply impracticability doctrine to a leasehold, because government regulation interfering with particular contemplated land uses is common during wartime).

[64] See *Waldinger Corp. v. CRS Group Engineers, Inc.*, 775 F.2d 781, 786 (7th Cir. 1985) (stating that "the impracticability defense . . . turns largely on foreseeability").

requirement leads to enforcement in the mine run of cases, confining discharge of contractual obligations to unusual cases.[65]

The focus on foreseeability also seeks stability by discouraging resort to litigation. Hence, courts sometimes justify the foreseeability requirement by stating that foreseeable circumstances do not excuse performance because the party seeking discharge "might have protected himself in his contract."[66] This expresses a judicial preference for more complete contracts that would allow parties to cope with foreseeable changes in circumstances without resort to the courts.

This focus on the unusual helps explain a central preoccupation of courts in these cases with the nature of the causes of failures to perform. Hence, the courts excuse compliance with a contract to hold a concert when the hall specified in the contract disappears, having burned to the ground, when the person to perform a personal services contract dies, or when a legal change makes performance impossible.[67]

By contrast, the failure of a supplier to come through does not ordinarily excuse a seller of goods dependent on the supplier from delivering goods to the buyer.[68] Suppliers mess up all the time, and if that excused performance, breach of contract would become routine in a large class of cases involving inefficient performance. This helps explain why Justice Benjamin Cardozo declined to excuse compliance with a supply contract as a general matter, declaring that obligations will persist though "times turn out to be hard and labor charges high," but conceded that if the supplier's facility is destroyed, a defense based on impossibility or impracticability might succeed.[69] Similarly,

---

[65] *See generally* id. at 786 (linking foreseeability to an inquiry into whether the occurrence triggering the defense "was so unusual or unforeseen" as to justify a conclusion that this is not what the parties bargained for).

[66] *See, e.g., Eastern Air Lines, Inc. v. Gulf Oil Corp.*, 415 F. Supp. 429, 441 (1975).

[67] *See Taylor v. Caldwell*, 3 B. & S. 826, 122 Eng. Rep. 309 (King's Bench, 1863) (excusing performance when Surrey Garden and Music Hall burn to the ground before the concert date); Page, *supra* note 21, at 600–02 (describing cases involving destruction of the subject matter of a contract, death of a party to a contract, and legal changes as "three well settled classes" of impossibility cases).

[68] *See* Restatement (Second) of Contracts, § 261 cmt. e (stating that a party contracting to render performance "that depends on some act of a third party" ordinarily cannot escape its obligation if the third party fails to perform). *cf. Selland Pontiac-GMC, Inc. v. King*, 384 N.W.2d 490 (Minn Ct. App. 1986) (honoring an escape clause excusing the seller of school buses if its source of supply for chassis failed).

[69] *See Canadian Industrial Alcohol Co. v. Dunbar Molasses Co.*, 179 N.E. 383, 384–85 (N.Y. 1932) (assuming that destruction of the supplier's facility would excuse performance, but rejecting excuse based on the supplier's underproduction).

a supplier's lack of financial resources does not excuse performance, even though this lack might make performance literally impossible in some cases.[70] Creation of a stable environment for managing change can explain the courts' emphasis on the causes of nonperformance, a feature having no obvious relationship to efficiency.

The courts do, at least occasionally, consider the costliness of performance, but not in a way that suggests any particular concern with economic efficiency. I have explained that the courts have specifically renounced any allegiance to efficiency by declaring that a contract becoming unprofitable, and therefore presumably not Pareto optimal, does not justify discharge of contractual obligations. Mainstream decisions adjudicating impracticability claims under the UCC usually pay no attention to the relationship between the promisor's increased cost and the economic value of the benefit to the promisee – that is, to the issue of efficiency. Typically, they focus on evaluating the question of whether the increased cost produces an unacceptable economic hardship for the promisor.[71] This inquiry more closely resembles the feasibility inquiry in environmental law (which asks whether proposed pollution control requirements might bankrupt a large number of plants) than the CBA associated with economic efficiency's pursuit.[72]

The case usually cited as the font of the commercial impracticability doctrine, *Mineral Park Land Co., v. Howard*,[73] for example, reflects some concern about costs, but refutes the idea that economic inefficiency could justify excusing compliance with a clear contract. The *Mineral Park Land* court released a party from a contract to take all the gravel and earth needed for a bridge construction project from the plaintiff's land.[74] The defendant discovered that half the gravel and earth needed lay below the water table and therefore

---

[70] *See La Motte v. Hilgedick*, 1992 U.S. App. Lex. 4020, *12 (9th Cir.) (unpublished opinion).

[71] *See, e.g., Eastern Airlines*, 415 F. Supp. at 441 (rejecting claims for impracticability when Gulf Oil cannot show that the increased price of crude oil created any hardship for the company in carrying out a supply contract).

[72] *See* David M. Driesen, "Distributing the Costs of Environmental, Health, and Safety Protection: The Feasibility Principle, Cost-Benefit Analysis, and Regulatory Reform," 32 *Bost. Coll. Envtl. Aff. L. Rev.* 1, 12 (2005) (describing feasibility analysis as focused on figuring out whether the costs of environmental regulation will produce plant shutdowns and contrasting it with cost-benefit analysis); *ALCOA v. Essex Group*, Inc., 499 F. Supp. 53, 72 (W.D. Penn. 1980) (stating that impracticability doctrine focuses "distinctly on hardship"). I am grateful to Robin Malloy for suggesting that I make this parallel explicit here. This is not to say that courts do this consistently, but rather that this is the central meaning of suggesting that cost renders a contract impracticable, as opposed to undesirable.

[73] 172 Cal. 289, 156 P. 458 (1916).

[74] *Mineral Park Land*, 172 Cal. at 293 (finding no recovery because it was impracticable to remove all the gravel and earth needed for a bridge).

took only about half the amount contracted for.[75] The trial court rejected the defendant's argument that taking the gravel below the water table was impracticable, even though it found that removal of that gravel would cost "10 to 12 times as much as the usual cost."[76] The California Supreme Court reversed, construing the contract as limited to "available" gravel.[77] It found the gravel unavailable both because the defendants "could not take it by ordinary means" (a rationale sounding in extraordinary circumstances) or without "prohibitive cost."[78] Although relying in part on an unreasonable cost rationale, even this court disclaimed any allegiance to efficiency, explaining that it did not "mean to intimate" that a mere showing of financial loss would suffice to justify discharge.[79] In other words, lack of Pareto optimality could not justify discharge, but a combination of some unusual circumstances and extremely high costs could. And *Mineral Park Land* constitutes something of an outlier in the emphasis it places on the amount of costs.[80]

This inattention to the relationship between costs and benefits suggests that courts not only regularly enforce contracts that no longer exhibit Pareto efficiency, but also that they do so without regard to the question of whether a Pareto inefficient bargain might pass a Kaldor-Hicks efficiency test. By focusing solely on the costs of compliance, and not the benefits, they eschew consideration of the question of whether an unprofitable, and hence Pareto inefficient, contract might nevertheless prove Kaldor-Hicks efficient, because performance's benefits to the promisee might outweigh the negative costs to the promisor. This further cements the case for contract law's inefficiency, showing that it goes beyond enforcement of Pareto inefficient agreements.

Hence, although judges disclaim any intent to excuse inefficient performance under the excuse doctrines, they regularly focus on factors that matter to an effort to promote a reasonably stable environment for contract law. They generally manage contract's economic dynamics by excusing performance only in exceptional circumstances that make performance ludicrous. The main rule remains that contract law enforces inefficient bargains in order to encourage long-term cooperation through contracts.

[75] Id. at 291 (noting trial court's finding that the land contained about 101,000 cubic yards of gravel and earth, but that the plaintiff only took about 50,131 cubic yards, the amount above the water table).

[76] Id.

[77] Id. at 293.

[78] Id.

[79] Id.

[80] See Subha Narasimhan, "Of Expectations, Incomplete Contracting, and the Bargain Principle," 74 *Cal. L. Rev.* 1123, 1177 n. 143 (1986) (characterizing *Mineral Park Land* as a rare exception to the rule that increased costs do not justify discharge).

ECONOMIC DYNAMIC ANALYSIS IN CONTRACT LAW

Although law and economics scholars have not explicitly faced the tension between efficient contracting and inefficient performance, they exhibit acute awareness of the fact that new circumstances can arise that make performance economically inefficient. As a result, the law and economics of contract has, for at least two decades, explicitly included the analysis of transaction costs and imperfect information.[81] The reality that an assumption of perfect information and zero transaction costs assumes away many of the most interesting problems in the field has forced the law and economics of contract to grapple with institutional law and economics.[82]

An economic dynamic approach derived from institutional economics holds great promise for further improving our understanding of contract law. Economic dynamic analysis provides a useful tool for contract lawyers, because contract law usually manages change over time. Laws constitute temporarily extended commitments that shape a society's trajectory.[83] Even in the contract realm, typified by transactions, law manages change over time, not instantaneous exchange.[84]

Therefore, it is not surprising to see that the field is evolving away from a neoclassical economic approach toward an economic dynamic approach. Perhaps the best example of the move toward adopting an economic dynamic approach rooted in the tradition of institutional economics involves Ian Ayres

---

[81] *See* Richard Craswell, "Contract Remedies, Renegotiation, and the Theory of Efficient Breach," 61 S. *Cal. L. Rev.* 630, 638–40 (1988) (discussing articles from the 1970s through the middle 1980s that focus on the transaction costs of renegotiation); *see, e.g.*, Richard Craswell, "Property Rules and Liability Rules in Unconscionability and Related Doctrine," 60 *U. Chi. L. Rev.* 1, 64 (1993) (arguing that the choice between property and liability rule protection in a contract case should depend on the "cost of overcoming the impediment to consent that provides the reason for invalidating [a] . . . contract"). *Cf.* Harold Demsetz, "Toward a Theory of Property Rights II: The Competition Between Private and Collective Ownership," 31 *J. Legal Stud.* S653, S657 (2002) (claiming that "[n]eoclassical economists ignored" contractual puzzles, because "discussion of market-clearing prices sets aside" problems stemming from incomplete information and an uncertain future).

[82] *See* Craswell, "Contract Remedies," *supra* note 81, at 634–35 (showing that the problems of efficiency analysis being hopelessly indeterminate led to efforts to take transaction costs into account). *Cf.* Posner, *supra* note 30, at 865 (pointing out that if "individuals were rational, with no cognitive limits, and if transaction costs were zero" contract law would be "simple and uninteresting.")

[83] Jed Rubenfeld, *Freedom and Time: A Theory of Constitutional Self-Government* 85 (2001) (pointing out that law on exists "over time," because law implies that after a rule is established it is followed).

[84] *Cf.* Eisenberg, *supra* note 3, at 816 (characterizing "discrete contracts" as "almost nonexistent" because contracts generally "create or reflect relationships").

and Robert Gertner's seminal work on default rules in contract law.[85] Ayres and Gertner begin with a legal fiction that serves as a staple of the law and economics of contract, the idea that economic analysis should favor the rules that the parties would have agreed upon if they had only thought of them (notice that if they did not, probably transaction costs were too high).[86] They label rules that apply to fill out incomplete contracts (such as rules about what remedies to employ in the event of nonperformance in the absence of an express contractual term on the subject) as default rules.[87] But they notice that the law does not permit parties to contract around all default rules.[88] They question the fiction that contract rules simply supply terms that the parties would have wanted by examining these "immutable" default rules – rules that parties may not abrogate.[89] Examples of immutable default rules include the duty to act in good faith under the UCC and the requirement of consideration to form a valid contract.[90] In particular, they show that some rules – "penalty" default rules – deliberately seek to provide contractual terms that at least one party does not want in order to encourage the revelation of information leading to more complete contracts than the parties would otherwise agree to.[91]

This idea of a penalty default rule and the theory Ayres and Gertner develop to guide judicial choice of default rules depend heavily on taking imperfect information and transaction costs seriously. They point out that the transaction cost explanation of contractual incompleteness suggests that courts can minimize contracting costs by choosing rules that the parties would have wanted.

But Ayres and Gertner go on to conduct an economic dynamic analysis of how these rule choices might influence both parties to a contract. This yields the conclusion that sometimes choosing a default rule favored by a minority of parties may produce more efficient outcomes than majority default rules.[92] Furthermore, courts face information deficits and transaction costs that may make determination of the rule that parties would have wanted difficult.[93] In that case, courts may want to establish penalty default rules establishing terms of contracts that at least one party does not want, in order to induce the

---

[85] *See* Ayres & Gertner, *supra* note 5.
[86] *See* id. at 89–90 (explaining that law and economics typically insists that default rules "should be set at what the parties would have wanted.").
[87] *See* id. at 87.
[88] *See* id. at 87–88.
[89] *See* id.
[90] Id.
[91] *See* id. at 91.
[92] *See* id. at 93.
[93] Id.

parties to contract explicitly about the issue the default rule addresses.[94] For example, the UCC voids contracts that do not mention the quantity of goods to be supplied.[95] Since a contract indicates that parties did not intend a supply of zero goods, this rule penalizes parties for not including a quantity term, thereby forcing them to negotiate about the amount of goods to be sold.[96] Ayres and Gertner take incomplete information into account when they argue that the need to encourage parties to reveal information to each other or the court can justify penalty default rules.[97] Thus, they analyze the dynamics of negotiation that can either preserve or remedy informational asymmetries.

Their analysis also explicitly considers how the bounds of rationality will lead some actors to disregard incentives the law creates. For example, they argue for a penalty default rule requiring that earnest money paid by a buyer as security against breach of a real estate contract go to the seller, rather than the real estate broker, in the event of buyer default.[98] They rationalize this result by pointing out that the seller "may not even consider the issue of how to split the earnest money in the event of default,"[99] thereby assuming that bounds on the seller's rationality usually lead the seller not to consider information about the splitting issue. Instead of assuming that the legal rules governing splitting of earnest money will provide an incentive that the seller will respond to, they recognize that the seller probably will not know the legal rule governing this issue.[100]

By contrast, they argue, the real estate broker will likely know the default rule for splitting earnest money.[101] This observation relies implicitly on the notion that brokers engage in a routine of facilitating multiple real estate transactions that make the question of how to treat earnest money in a failed transaction salient enough for the legal rule to fall, at least fairly often, within the bounds of the brokers' rationality. Accordingly, the knowledgeable brokers, unlike the ignorant sellers, will likely respond to the legal incentives that the earnest money splitting rules create. Hence, if the governing rule states that the broker keeps the money, a broker will not raise the issue, because the broker will profit from the seller's ignorance.[102] Conversely, if the rule states that the sellers keep the earnest money, the broker may raise the issue, thereby

[94] Id.
[95] U.C.C. § 2–201(1) (1976).
[96] *See* Ayres & Gertner, supra note 5, at 96–97.
[97] *See* id. at 97.
[98] *See* id. at 98–99.
[99] Id. at 99.
[100] *See* id.
[101] *See* id.
[102] Id.

informing the ignorant buyer, in hopes of persuading the buyer to split the proceeds with the seller.[103] This analysis depends heavily on analyzing the nature of bounded rationality for particular classes of parties, as economic dynamic theory recommends.

Similarly, Ayres and Gertner argue for a rule not requiring damages when a buyer breaches a promise to buy a retail good, relying on the observation that "the customer may not know the default rule for breach."[104] Accordingly, a zero damages rule creates a dynamic that may induce the seller, who probably does know the default rules for retail sale promises, to inform the buyer about the rules if the seller wants to put herself in a position to claim damages.[105] Thus, Ayres and Gertner implicitly analyze the limits of bounded rationality of particular classes of parties in order to examine the economic dynamics of contractual rules. More generally, Ayres and Gertner display an admirable awareness of the economic dynamics of contracting in the face of bounded rationality when they admonish judges to "consider the possibility that some parties will fail to contract around penalty defaults out of ignorance or oversight."[106]

They go on to consider a countervailing incentive that may defeat the incentives that a zero damages default rule creates to bargain for a contractual term creating a damage remedy for breach of a promise to buy from the retailer, thereby conforming to the demand of economic dynamic theory that analysis include consideration of relevant nonlegal incentives.[107] They note that to obtain the damage remedy envisioned in the legal literature on this problem – lost profits – the seller would have to reveal the markup to the buyer.[108] They explain that revelation of a markup can increase the power of the buyer to obtain a better price.[109] This may lead sellers to decline to reveal their markups, thereby defeating the zero damages default rule's incentive to create informed negotiation about damages in the event of a breach.[110] Thus, Ayres and Gertner analyze not just the incentives law creates, but also countervailing economic incentives that may defeat the law's objectives.

Although Ayres and Gertner employ an economic dynamic analysis in pursuit of efficient rules, one can employ economic dynamic analysis to model

---

[103] Id.
[104] Id. at 104.
[105] See id. at 104–05
[106] Id. at 128 n. 178.
[107] See id.
[108] See id. at 105.
[109] Id.
[110] Id.

fair results. For this form of analysis enables scholars to predict how rules will influence behavior that can be judged according to either fairness or efficiency norms. The economic dynamic approach provides both a better foundation than the neoclassical model for choosing efficient rules and a superior method for identifying fair rules. It simply offers a better approach than the traditional approach to analyzing legal rules' effects, regardless of the normative values guiding the analysis.

The dynamics of the problem of new circumstances making the apparently efficient contract inefficient have forced legal scholars to abandon neoclassical law and economics in favor of an institutional approach, with some of the best work employing economic dynamic analysis to provide a superior approach to understanding contract law. An economic dynamic approach to this subject shows great promise.

CONCLUSION

Although contracting parties enact bargains they expect to be efficient, courts regularly enforce inefficient bargains after a party has determined that performance no longer serves his or her interests. Doing so produces a sensible economic dynamic that helps parties cooperate and manages change over time. This dynamic serves important macroeconomic ends.

Recognizing contract law as an effort to manage change over time can help explain the exceptions to the rule that courts enforce inefficient contracts, showing that the judicial focus on unusual circumstances allows discharge only when it does not threaten to significantly disrupt future contracting. All of this commends an understanding of contract law in economic dynamic terms, rather than as an exercise in static efficiency. Economic dynamic analysis provides a means of understanding change over time and therefore a fine tool for examining contract law's economic dynamics.

7

Property Law: A Macroeconomic View

Property law, at first glance, seems to have nothing to do with economic dynamics. Traditionally, lawyers have seen property as a profoundly conservative field of law, aiming primarily at establishing order and stability. Economic dynamic theory, however, has a substantial role to play in property law and scholarship, primarily in helping support a move away from a myopic view of property as a mere prerequisite to efficient exchange and helping us see that property manages change over time to facilitate economic growth.

This chapter begins with a review of the law and economics of property, showing that the traditional approach has focused heavily on just one aspect of property – its function as a prerequisite to efficient market exchange – and in so doing, set the stage for deregulation. It shows that scholarship in the field has implicitly employed economic dynamic analysis to call into question law and economics' principal property law project. Furthermore, it shows that some of the most insightful scholarship and important property law focus not on static transactions, but on managing change over time. Therefore, economic dynamic analysis proves useful for analyzing some of the field's most significant and interesting questions. Property performs important macroeconomic functions and, accordingly, can play a key role in providing a framework for economic growth and, at times, in avoiding or creating systemic risks.

Any economic approach, including mine, focuses on the functions law performs or ought to perform. The property law field, perhaps more than many other fields of law, owes much of its current form to history as much as to modern notions of function. But analyzing law's functions proves helpful, as it may explain how the law works today and what we may wish to change. So, the economic dynamic theory does help illuminate the law's functions, even if it does not completely explain its origins.

CONTRACTS, COASE, AND THE CATHEDRAL

As many scholars have noted, traditional law and economics has advanced a thin conception of property, in which it serves merely as a baseline to facilitate transactions.[1] Once property establishes an ownership right, a person other than the owner who wants the thing the owner possesses must pay the owner for it. Hence, property functions as a prerequisite for the operation of markets.

Property law scholars, however, recognize that property implicates social values, such as values of community, autonomy, personhood, environmental protection, freedom, and security.[2] So, a focus on property only as a prelude to contract proves quite narrow. We buy a home to live in it, not just to sell it.

This emphasis on property as a mere adjunct to transactions leads to an emphasis on efficiency as property law's primary goal. This microeconomic focus on efficient transactions stems primarily from Ronald Coase's seminal work analyzing nuisance cases — cases where one owner's activities interfere with a neighbor's use and enjoyment of his or her land. Coase's famous article, "The Problem of Social Costs,"[3] argues that absent transaction costs it does not matter, for purposes of economic efficiency, what a court does in resolving a nuisance case. For no matter how courts allocate the property rights involved, parties, absent transaction costs, will negotiate an efficient outcome. Coase's followers refer to this proposition as the "Coase theorem." So, for example, if a victim of air pollution wins a nuisance case, the polluter can offer the victim some amount of money to put up with the pollution (or move out). Similarly, if the court denies the pollution victim a remedy, the victim may still pay the polluter to abate the pollution. As these examples illustrate, the analysis underlying the Coase theorem views property as a mere prelude to bargaining and market transactions, thereby emphasizing the value of private markets.

---

[1] *See, e.g.,* Abraham Bell & Gideon Parchomovsky, "Pliability Rules," 101 *Mich. L. Rev.* 1, 23 (2002); Thomas W. Merrill & Henry E. Smith, "What Happened to Property in Law and Economics?," 111 *Yale L. J.* 357, 359–60 (2001).

[2] *See* Gregory Alexander, Eduardo Peñalver, Joseph William Singer, and Laura Underkuffler, "A Statement of Progressive Property," 94 *Cornell L. Rev.* 743 (2009); *see, e.g.,* Gregory S. Alexander, "The Social Organization Norm in American Property Law," 94 *Cornell L. Rev.* 745 (2009); Eduardo M. Peñalver, "Land Virtues," 94 *Cornell L. Rev.* 821 (2009); Jedediah Purdy, "A Freedom Promoting Approach to Property: A Renewed Tradition for New Debates," 72 *U. Chi. L. Rev.* (2005). I do not necessarily mean to suggest that scholars working in the law and economics tradition would deny property's social function. But by focusing so much energy on scholarship focused narrowly on facilitating efficient market transactions, the law and economics scholarship surely deemphasizes competing values.

[3] 3 *J. L. & Econ.* 1 (1960).

This point of view also led to broader support for deregulation.[4] Courts have traditionally thought of nuisance law's purpose as harm prevention.[5] When pollution problems became so acute that nuisance law could no longer adequately address them, the U.S. federal government (and other governments around the world) created environmental law, a body of public law that requires pollution abatement. Initially, the first modern environmental law statutes in the 1970s included goals suggesting a continuation of nuisance law's project of preventing harm.

Coase's work, however, reoriented many experts' views about what nuisance law – and by extension, government regulation – was all about. Coase and his followers, using the nuisance metaphor, redefined law as an efficiency-oriented quest for a balance of cost and benefits, abandoning the harm prevention goal.

The title of Coase's article, "The Problem of Social Costs," signals a shift in orientation by suggesting that we should think of pollution, bad smells, noise, or other interference with a neighbor's use and enjoyment of property not as harms, but as "social costs."[6] Coase then develops an analysis suggesting that instead of thinking about nuisance law as an exercise in harm prevention, we should think of it as a reciprocal problem of two property owners harming each other. His examples emphasize that a court order to abate a nuisance would harm the person creating the nuisance, interfering with this person's use of his or her property.[7] This reciprocity approach reconceives nuisance as a problem of efficient resource allocation. It suggests that the proper approach to nuisance law involves balancing the costs and benefits of decisions to abate pollution or some other nuisance to make sure that the harms to a defendant forced to cease harmful activities do not outweigh the harms to the plaintiff from allowing a nuisance to continue.

The Coase theorem helped inspire deregulation, both by undermining the harm prevention ideal and by suggesting, at least to some, that bargaining made regulation useless.[8] Although Coase himself intended his "theorem"

---

[4] *Cf.* A. W. Brian Simpson, "Coase v. Pigou Reexamined," 25 *J. Legal Stud.* 53, 58 (1996).

[5] *See* id. at 91–92 (noting that the common law rejected the idea of permitting an "efficient level" of pollution); *see, e.g., Boomer v. Atlantic Cement Co.*, 257 N.E.2d 870, 872 (N.Y. 1970) (describing the rule in New York prior to this case as requiring issuance of an injunction once a nuisance has been found).

[6] *Cf.* David M. Driesen, "The Societal Cost of Environmental Regulation: Beyond Administrative Cost-Benefit Analysis," 24 *Ecology L. Q.* 545, 560–62 & n. 67 (1997) (noting that the language of cost-benefit analysis converts a harm avoided through regulation into a "benefit" and discussing Coase's role in this reconception); Simpson, *supra* note 4, at 60.

[7] *Cf.* Driesen, *supra* note 6, at 561, n. 67.

[8] *Cf.* Brett M. Frischmann, "Evaluating the Demsetzian Trend In Copyright Law," 3 *Rev. L. & Econ.* 649, 655 (2007) (characterizing Coase's "challenge to" Pigou's view that government

as a reminder of transaction costs' importance, some of those in the policy
world acted as if his theorem showed that private ordering made government
regulation unnecessary. And Coase wrote "The Problem of Social Costs" as an
argument against the widely held assumption of the economist Arthur Pigou
that external costs – costs that are not considered by those engaged in buying
and selling products (like pollution) – generally justify regulation.

Guido Calabresi and A. Douglas Melamed set the stage for an intensive
focus on property as a mere prelude to efficient transactions in a seminal
article, "Property Rules, Liability Rules, and Inalienability: One View of the
Cathedral." They noted that courts can employ either damages or injunctions
forbidding a particular activity to resolve nuisance cases.[9] They characterize a
rule protecting an entitlement through a damages remedy as a *liability rule* and
a rule protecting an entitlement through an injunction remedy as a *property
rights rule*. They argue that when transaction costs are low, property rights rules
lead to an efficient resolution of cases, as parties can cheaply reallocate property
rights if the judge allocates them inefficiently when either granting or denying
an injunction. But when transaction costs are high, a liability rule would work
better, as it could procure an efficient outcome without negotiation. Parties
can adjust their conduct if damages proved too high.

Calabresi and Melamed's introduction of the concepts of property, liability,
and inalienability rules created a framework that focused on nuisance, but
also provided a metaphor for discussing just about any legal problem. As such,
the framework itself understandably proved fascinating to legal scholars, as it
revealed connections between fields usually thought of as wholly distinct.

This framework extended the influence of Coase's emphasis on efficient
bargaining and private markets[10] by stimulating an enormous literature about
how to design remedies to encourage the efficient bargains Coase envisioned,
based on the property/liability rule framework Calabresi and Melamed had
created.[11] Although Calabresi and Melamed saw their framework as useful for

should intervene in the face of externalities as giving "credence to property rights as an
alternative to government... regulation").
[9] Guido Calabresi & A. Douglas Melamed, "Property Rules, Liability Rules, and Inalienability:
One View of the Cathedral," 85 *Harv. L. Rev.* 1089 (1972).
[10] *See* Bell & Parchomovsky, *supra* note 1, at 3 & n. 6 (discussing the Calabresi/Melamed
framework's extraordinary influence).
[11] *See, e.g.*, Ian Ayres & Paul M. Goldbart, "Optimal Delegation and Decoupling in the Design
of Liability Rules," 100 *Mich. L. Rev.* 1 (2001); Richard Craswell, "Property Rules and Liability Rules in Unconscionability and Related Doctrines," 60 *U. Chi. L. Rev.* 1 (1993); Robert
C. Ellickson, "Alternatives to Zoning: Covenants, Nuisance Rules, and Fines as Land Use
Controls," 40 *U. Chi. L. Rev.* 681 (1973); Louis Kaplow & Steven Shavell, "Property Rules
versus Liability Rules: An Economic Analysis," 109 *Harv. L. Rev.* 713 (1996); Robert P. Merges,

thinking about both efficiency and fairness, subsequent scholarship elaborating their framework focuses overwhelmingly on the efficiency objective.[12]

Much of this property/liability rule literature focuses on a stylized problem of post-judgment bargaining after a judicial decision in a nuisance case. Scholars imagine that a judge issued either a damages remedy or an injunction in a nuisance case and that the judge's ruling does not itself produce an efficient outcome. They then analyze the influence of transaction costs upon parties' efforts to bargain around the inefficient judgment to reach a more efficient allocation of property rights. This analysis then leads to conclusions about when property rules and when liability rules would prove efficient.

Calabresi, Melamed, and Coase made nuisance cases and their resolution the preeminent theoretical issue for property law scholars for more than a generation. And much of this scholarship took the form of an analysis of transaction costs' influence on bargaining to an efficient rearrangement of a judicial decree in a nuisance case.[13]

DO PARTIES NEGOTIATE AFTER NUISANCE CASE JUDGMENTS?

Economic dynamic analysis, however, raises the issue of whether this intensive focus on contracting around property and liability rules has become too myopic. Ward Farnsworth published a study in 1999 suggesting that parties to nuisance suits rarely, if ever, negotiate after judgment.[14] He studied twenty then-recent simple nuisance cases and found that no parties in any of these cases negotiated after final judgment. Now Farnsworth himself indicates that his article examines only a small sample of cases and does not claim to have proven that no party *ever* negotiates around a final judgment in a simple nuisance case. Nevertheless, the findings at least suggest that negotiating after judgment might prove a rare occurrence in such cases, although we would

---

"Contracting into Liability Rules: Intellectual Property Rights and Collective Organizations," 84 *Cal. L. Rev.* 1293 (1996); A. Mitchell Polinsky, "Resolving Normal Nuisance Disputes: The Simple Economics of Injunctive and Damage Remedies," 32 *Stan. L. Rev.* 1075 (1980); Symposium, "Property Rules, Liability Rules, and Inalienability: A Twenty-Five Year Retrospective," 106 *Yale L. J.* 2081 (1997).

[12] *Accord* Bell & Parchomovsky, *supra* note 1, at 12 (pointing out that Calabresi and Melamed proposed a focus on justice, distributional preferences, and efficiency).

[13] In recent years, though, some of this scholarship has become more dynamic. Abraham Bell and Gideon Parchomovsky, for example, characterize the scholarship on property and liability rules as static. Bell & Parchomovsky, *supra* note 1, at 5. They focus their work on *"dynamic rules"* that they call "pliability rules." Id. (emphasis in original). These rules combine liability and property protections, sometimes in a sequence to manage change over time.

[14] *See* Ward Farnsworth, "Do Parties to Nuisance Cases Bargain After Judgment? A Glimpse Inside the Cathedral," 66 *U. Chi. L. Rev.* 373 (1999).

need a much larger empirical study to know. Any notion that bargaining around a judgment in a simple nuisance case occurs enjoyed no real-world empirical support when Coase wrote or, for that matter, when Farnsworth wrote decades later; instead, it constituted a theoretical prediction based on the neoclassical rational actor model with empirical support only from artificial laboratory experiments.[15]

Farnsworth's results comport with the economic dynamic model, which suggests that to understand economic incentives properly, one must consider how the actors view the incentives through the lens of bounded rationality. Farnsworth contends that acrimony between the parties partially explains their lack of interest in negotiation. This acrimony, as he describes it, likely derives from a pattern of interaction between the neighbors litigating against each other. Viewed this way, the observed acrimony bears out the economic dynamic theory's contention that actors pay attention to the incentives that their habits and routines make relevant. Another way of viewing this through the lens of economic dynamic theory involves simply noting that countervailing incentives, economic and noneconomic, can sometimes outweigh the economic incentives that law creates. Thus anger creates an incentive not to negotiate or even have contact with the other party, an incentive that, in many cases, cancels out the economic incentives to negotiate.

Farnsworth argues that the unique nature of the rights at issue here – for example, the right to sit on the front porch free from the sound of the neighboring kennel's barking dogs – can help us understand the failure to negotiate and his observations' limits. The parties, he suggests, view such rights as rights, not commodities suitable for trading. And this view impedes negotiation.[16] Thus, bounded rationality may imply a limit to what people consider appropriate subjects for negotiation, even if parties overcome those limits in extreme cases.

Economic dynamic theory's recommendation that researchers hoping to understand economic incentives' influence should study individual and institutional habits and routines reframes some of the additional research topics that arise from Farnsworth's paper. For example, in exploring the potential

---

[15] Elizabeth Hoffman & Matthew Spitzer found that laboratory subjects bargained to abate pollution as Coase predicted. *See* Elizabeth Hoffman & Matthew L. Spitzer, "Experimental Tests of the Coase Theorem with Large Bargaining Groups," 15 *J. Legal Stud.* 149 (1986). But the authors recognize that real-world results might vary because of various impediments to bargaining absent in the laboratory, including the one that Farnsworth subsequently found most salient: hatred between parties. *See id.* at 160–63.

[16] *Cf.* Simpson, *supra* note 4, at 85–88 (explaining how conceptions of rights places some economically efficient solutions beyond the realm of things parties will consider).

limits of the disincentives to negotiate he sees operating in the nuisance cases he studies, Farnsworth suggests that corporate actors might exhibit less rancor than individuals, or at least bargain toward an economically rational result in spite of acrimony. This suggests that some study of the habits and routines of individuals making decisions about litigation within corporations might prove fruitful. Corporations, like individuals, exhibit some behavior that does not appear to conform to the rational actor model. For example, corporations exhibit a strong tendency to litigate cases with relatively small stakes and then settle on the eve of trial. They can easily run up legal bills far exceeding the costs of paying off the plaintiffs in such cases. Do these behaviors reflect workloads that forbid serious consideration of legal cases until a trial looms, or perhaps the bad habits of lawyers who cannot think through a case well, but can carry out litigation routines? Do they reflect convictions by repeat players that paying off plaintiffs promptly will only encourage other plaintiffs? If so, does refusal to promptly pay claims reflect good information about the relationship between the timing of payoffs and future litigation, or the folk beliefs of people feeling under siege from high levels of litigation? Or do corporate employees often feel that matters of principle are at stake, as Farnsworth's individuals did with respect to their property rights? If so, perhaps sociological studies of corporations can pinpoint how perceptions of principles evolve and where they become influential. The economic dynamics of law provides a framework for evaluating a host of questions about individual and institutional response to economic incentives that might seem to favor negotiation.[17] Hence, Farnsworth's study casts doubt on the importance of the choice between property rules and liability rules in encouraging efficient right rearrangements and suggests intriguing possibilities for economic dynamic research.

In a similar vein, Gideon Parchomovsky and Peter Siegelman found "little evidence" that the choice between damages and an injunction remedy played any role in negotiations in which a large polluter, American Electric Power (AEP), bought out the town of Cheshire, Pennsylvania before private litigation had commenced.[18] They, too, study the bounded rationality of relevant homeowners. Their AEP study found that the value people placed on their community figured in complex ways in their decisions about whether to sell their homes, thus raising the question of whether this community value proved

---

[17] *Cf.* Daphna Lewinsohn-Zamir, "The Choice Between Property Rules and Liability Rules Revisited, Critical Observations from Behavioral Studies," 80 *Tex. L. Rev.* 261 (2001) (examining the endowment effect and tendency toward altruism in bargaining revealed by lab experiments informing game theory).

[18] *See* Gideon Parchomovsky & Peter Siegelman, "Selling Mayberry: Communities and Individuals in Law and Economics," 92 *Cal. L. Rev.* 75, 82, 109 (2004).

salient only because Cheshire was a small town. They also found that many children suffered such extreme health problems stemming from the pollution that parents routinely drove their children out of town when pollution reached high levels.[19] For these parents, the inability to sell their homes in order to finance a move prevented them from leaving, and a buyout made possible a solution to their children's health problems. The parents may have viewed a reliable solution to these problems as an imperative, thereby making them amenable to even distasteful negotiations. Furthermore, although AEP claimed not to fear liability, reputational incentives might well have overcome the economic incentives to refuse to pay off the residents, for the company evinced great concerns about damage to its reputation stemming from media coverage of residents' problems in Cheshire.[20] Economic dynamic theory points to the need for more systematic study of the beliefs and incentives that may influence decisions to engage in or refrain from negotiation.

More broadly, the impediments to negotiation based on the property and liability rule distinction identified in the AEP and Farnsworth studies may deprive the scholarly project of designing legal rules to optimize negotiation around property and liability rules of efficacy, thereby suggesting the need to divert some of the enormous scholarly energy devoted to this project to some other purposes, notwithstanding this project's theoretical interest. Although the AEP study suggests that impediments to negotiation can be overcome (at least prior to litigation) when a community feels overwhelmed by serious and widespread pollution, it reinforces Farnsworth's message that distinctions between property and liability rules play no role in fostering or shaping negotiation. Economic dynamic analysis raises questions about myopic microeconomic focus on property as a mere prelude to efficient transactions. In particular, it raises the possibility that some actors' bounded rationality may cause them to pay no attention to the distinction between property and liability rules or that nonlegal incentives may countervail the economic incentives to engage in negotiation at all in many cases.

A FOCUS ON CHANGE OVER TIME

Property law's more clearly practical insights have come from analyzing change over time, rather than the design of rules to stimulate individually efficient static transactions. A good example comes from Garrett Hardin's work identifying the "tragedy of the commons."[21] He observes that a herdsman allowing

---

[19] *See id.* at 111.

[20] Id. at 112–13.

[21] *See* Garrett Hardin, *The Tragedy of the Commons*, 162 *Science* 1243 (1968).

his sheep to graze in an open commons – a land open to all – has an incentive to keep adding sheep to the herd, even though doing so may degrade the land upon which his herd depends. This incentive stems from the fact that he garners all of the economic benefits stemming from owning more sheep, but experiences only a fraction of the detriment associated with additional stress on the common land. This creates an incentive for not just an individual herdsman, but for all herdsmen sharing a commons, to add more and more sheep over time to their herds, even though doing so threatens to destroy, sooner or later, the commons that all the herdsmen rely upon for their livelihood. Hardin labels this economic dynamic tendency to respond to economic incentives in ways that ultimately destroy the commons as "the tragedy of the commons." Hardin's model of tragedy has accurately predicted the fate of a number of commons resources, perhaps most vividly ocean fisheries, many of which have either collapsed or experienced massive declines mainly because of overfishing in the years since Hardin described the basic economic dynamics at work.[22] Notice that his analysis focuses on change over time, describing its general nature and shape, without purporting to quantify, generally or in any individual case, the actual costs and benefits of adding a particular number of sheep to herds.

Hardin created an important economic dynamic insight by simply focusing on how economic incentives influence the shape of change over time. Furthermore, his framework focuses on potential systemic risks.

Although Hardin focused on economic dynamics, he did not conduct an actual economic dynamic analysis: He implicitly employed a rational actor model and did not pay attention to the actual bounds of individual rationality. Subsequent scholars, however, have, at least to a limited extent, improved on his work by studying the bounded rationality of actors using commons resources.[23] Robert Ellickson, for example, studied local grazing practices in Shasta County, California, and discovered that individual landowners usually conformed to community norms that limit overgrazing.[24] These norms stem

---

[22] *See* Christopher D. Stone, "Too Many Fishing Boats, Too Few Fish: Can Trade Laws Trim Subsidies and Restore the Balance in Global Fisheries?," 24 *Ecology L. Q.* 505, 506–10 (1997); *see also* Carl Tobias, "The Tragedy of the Commons: The Case of the Blue Crab," 19 *S. Cal. Interdisc. L. J.* 73, 73–75 (2009) (describing the decline of the Chesapeake Bay's blue crab population as a "tragedy of the commons" and mentioning the destruction of that bay's shad and oyster populations); Michael Heller, *The Gridlock Economy: How Too Much Ownership Wrecks Markets, Stops Innovation, and Costs Lives* 24 (2008) (citing species extinction, ozone depletion, and highway congestion as examples of the tragedy of the commons).

[23] *See, e.g.,* Elinor Ostrom, *Understanding Institutional Diversity* (2009); Elinor Ostrom, *Governing the Commons: The Evolution of Institutions for Collective Action* 35–38 (1990).

[24] *See* Robert Ellickson, *Order Without Law: How Neighbors Settle Disputes* (1991).

from routines that involve fairly frequent interaction between neighbors that generate community expectations about socially acceptable conduct.[25] Ellickson's study therefore argues that relatively cohesive social groups generate norms that help solve the tragedy of the commons.[26] Hence, Hardin's work shows that even without a full economic dynamic analysis, a focus on how economic incentives generally shape trends over time with an eye to avoiding systemic risks can yield powerful insights. But subsequent work examining relevant actors' norms, habits, and routines can qualify and improve the accuracy of analysis that depends too heavily upon a rational actor model.

PROPERTY'S MACROECONOMICS

Hardin's work suggests that property has many more functions than maximizing microeconomic efficiency; it plays a role in larger scale problems and solutions. This macroeconomic view has deep roots in the property literature, highlights important contemporary property problems that receive insufficient attention, and provides a useful lens through which to view key contemporary property insights. Viewing property in this way highlights property's role in providing economic opportunity and, in some circumstances, in avoiding systemic risks.

Traditional Property Law

Property scholars, going back at least to Blackstone, recognize that property performs a macroeconomic function.[27] That is, ownership provides a stable framework facilitating long-term investments, such as those involved in construction, improvement, and the repair of buildings. It does so by managing change over time in a way that ensures that the owner can reap the rewards of his or her investments.[28] Although some may characterize this traditional investment function as a species of microeconomic efficiency, since property owners today will often pay people to make improvements on their land, this macroeconomic function in principle has no dependence at all on efficient transactions. A property owner living on a desert island could likewise invest in improving his land through his own labor, confident that he would reap the

---

[25] Id. at 53–56 (discussing some of these norms and their roots in repeated interactions between neighbors in a host of contexts).

[26] *See* id. at 167 (stating that "members of a cohesive group develop and maintain" welfare-maximizing norms).

[27] *See* 2 William Blackstone, *Commentaries* * 2.

[28] *See* Merrill & Smith, *supra* note 1, at 361.

rewards of his investments in improving the comfort, safety, and utility of his land and whatever structures he erected. Property law exists precisely because people do not live on desert islands;[29] still, property provides incentives for owners to invest through their own labor not just through efficient contracts. This incentive for investment of labor suggests that viewing property as part of a macroeconomic framework more usefully captures its fundamental role than viewing the investment function as yet another example of law spurring efficient transactions.

Furthermore, traditional understandings of the law of estates in land reflect concern about management of change over time, rather than the mere microeconomic efficiency of a single transaction.[30] The basic tradition of permitting bequests suggests a macroeconomic function for property. If property law's creators cared only about allocative efficiency the law might not permit bequests, for a bequest to an inheritor does not ensure that the land goes to the person who values it the most. If the law concerned itself only with efficient transactions, it might require a trustee to auction off land when the owner dies, to make sure that it ended up in the hands of the highest bidder. The custom of permitting bequests, however, makes some economic sense from the perspective of ensuring adequate incentives for investments in property by an owner who will die at some point in the near future.[31] That is, it makes sense from a macroeconomic perspective, even if it is debatable from both an allocative efficiency perspective that focuses on the immediate aftermath of death and from a fairness perspective (witness the debate over the estate tax).

More specific rules that scholars have viewed in microeconomic terms make even more sense from a macroeconomic perspective. Thus, for example, the rule against perpetuities limits land bequests in complicated ways that have the effect of avoiding the creation of very long-lived entitlements benefiting a former owner's descendants. This serves the purposes of limiting the influence of the dead upon the economic activities of the living, thereby providing an incentive for the living to make good decisions about the use and disposition of land.[32] Of course, this limitation on the dead's influence upon the

---

[29] *See* Harold Demsetz, "Toward a Theory of Property Rights," 57 *Am. Econ. Rev Papers and Proc.* 347 (1967) (noting that property rights "play no role" in Robinson Crusoe's world).

[30] *See* Michael A. Heller, "The Boundaries of Private Property," 108 *Yale L. J.* 1163, 1177–78 (1999) (describing the limiting of the fee tail and life estate as thwarting property owners' efforts to "control resources beyond their lifetimes").

[31] In positing an economic function for the custom of permitting bequests, I do not mean to deny that the custom reflects property law's feudal past. History surely matters to property law.

[32] Heller, *supra* note 30, at 1179–80 (describing the rule against perpetuities as limiting owners' ability to control property disposition long after death to avoid too much divergence from the "welfare maximizing use of" land). *Cf.* Gregory S. Alexander, "The Dead Hand and the

living both manages change over time and tends to encourage efficient use of land.

All this suggests that property, insofar as it serves economic functions, serves macroeconomic functions as well as serving as a backdrop to microeconomic transactions. This means that scholars can understand property, in part at least, as an effort to manage the economic dynamics of change over time in a way that encourages long-term investment without too much rigidity.

Key Contemporary Problems

In developing countries, the link between property rights and macroeconomics seems quite obvious. Indeed, one prominent economic development strategy, enjoying strong support from the World Bank, involves conferring clear property rights on poor informal owners of land or businesses in hopes of spurring economic growth and a redistribution of wealth.

Hernando de Soto, a major advocate of this strategy, argues that creation of full legal property rights for the poor provides a key to economic development, because relatively poor people held assets collectively worth about $9.3 trillion (circa 2000) outside of the legal property system in developing countries.[33] These assets function as "dead capital" – capital that its owners cannot fully exploit and can only hold onto at great cost because the owner possess it illegally. He identifies adapting to ongoing mass migration to the cities and the concomitant growth of informal property rights outside the legal system as a key challenge for property rights law in developing countries.

In looking for models of how the law should adapt, de Soto focuses heavily on the dynamics of American property law's effort to manage change over time. Building on the accounts of historians, he views the development of preemption (a form of adverse possession), homesteading acts authorizing settlers to gain title to lands they occupied, and laws recognizing the property rights arrangements gold miners made among themselves as potential models. All these approaches responded to demands of relatively poor people spontaneously occupying and using land. As in developing countries today, the law for a long time marginalized these squatters' property rights claims. But the later laws de Soto views as a model built a "new concept of property" that associated the dynamics of settlement with economic growth and adapted to

Law of Trusts in the Nineteenth Century," 37 *Stan. L. Rev.* 1189, 1258–61 (1985) (questioning economic justifications for legal restrictions on an owner's power of disposition).
[33] Hernando de Soto, *The Mystery of Capital: Why Capitalism Triumphs in the West and Fails Everywhere Else* (2000).

·

settlement in a way that avoided the social catastrophes that sometimes ensue when legal systems instead require ejection of squatters.[34]

Property law theorists face a key problem today of much greater significance for the world than the increasingly arcane debate over the efficiency of liability and property rules in various settings: the problem of how to make property rules adaptively efficient in developing countries (and in formerly communist countries), to effectively cope with change over time in ways that lay a foundation for macroeconomic development and avoid the systemic risks that land conflicts can pose for society. The goal of secure title for squatters sometimes conflicts with goals of fairness and economic development, thereby generating specific questions about how to manage change over time. This conflict arises often when those occupying and making productive use of land are not the formal owners.[35] The common law has always allowed the award of property rights based on use to non-title holders under the doctrine of adverse possession. This doctrine allows those who have occupied a parcel of land long enough in the right way to become the property owners. Rather broader claims for transfer of title to occupiers can arise in countries where gross inequality in land ownership prevails. In such circumstances, demands for property rights transfers can arise in rural areas as part of a movement for agrarian reform and in urban areas from squatters' rights movements.

Laws regularizing shifts of property from formal owners to the poor help manage change over time. They can contribute to a path of economic development and manage social tensions that can destabilize societies.

But designing programs in ways that provide substantial benefits to invaders at the expense of government or private title holders without too much destabilization requires careful economic dynamic analysis of the incentives such programs create for invaders, title holders, and those who have no land but might be tempted to invade if doing so looks potentially fruitful.[36] Economic

---

[34] Id. at 149. Some, however, have contested de Soto's claims about the importance of U.S. acquiescence to squatters in the development of American property law. *See* Alfred L. Brophy, "Hernando De Soto and the Histories of Property Law," in *Hernando de Soto and Property in a Market Economy* (D. Benjamin Barros, ed., 2010) [hereinafter *de Soto and Property*].

[35] *See* Carol Rose, "Invasions, Innovation, and the Environment," in *de Soto and Property, supra* note 34, at 25 (identifying invasion of property held by others as an important aspect of the problem incompletely accounted for in de Soto's work).

[36] *See, e.g.,* Michael Trebilcock & Paul-Erik Veel, "Property Rights and Development: The Contingent Case for Development," 30 *U. Pa. L. Rev.* 397, 449–50 (2008) (discussing expropriation's encouragement of rural land invasions in Brazil); Bernadette Atuahene, "Legal Title to Land as an Intervention Against Urban Poverty in Developing Nations," 36 *Geo. Wash. Int'l L. Rev.* 1109, 1131 (2004) (discussing the Peruvian government's decision to title only those already on the land before the titling program began, to discourage invasion).

dynamic analysis can focus on broad questions about the scope of programs, but also on matters of detail that may prove critical to program success. De Soto assumes that given an opportunity to regularize title, poor landowners will avail themselves of that opportunity and then use their newly regularized title as collateral to obtain capital to expand their businesses and/or improve their dwellings. Economic dynamic analysis would not assume that the poor would necessarily respond to the opportunities regularization of title provides in the rational way that de Soto predicted, but would ask if they would instead sell the property to fund either current consumption or to obtain capital without debt. As it turns out, titling programs have often caused a large increase in land values, but poor squatters have sold their rights to middle- and high-income buyers who reaped most of the rewards of the price rise, sometimes even in advance of titling.[37] Had an economic dynamic analysis studying the bounded rationality of squatters in various regions anticipated this, governments could have considered the desirability of regulation limiting speculation, subjecting such proposed reforms to economic dynamic analysis.[38] A commitment to studying change over time with a view toward explicitly considering uncertainties makes it very likely that one would anticipate problems like this.

Anticommons

Michael Heller points out that property sometimes limits transactional freedom – through limits on certain kinds of bequests, for example.[39] He links this limiting function to what he has called an *anticommons problem*: the problem of ownership in assets becoming so fragmented that projects become impossible, because they require the assent of too many interest holders.[40]

Although scholars may think of an anticommons as inefficient, they might better think of it as a macroeconomic problem. Anticommons problems can arise from multiple transactions selling property, which presumably appear efficient to those undertaking the transactions. From a longer-term perspective, however, these individually efficient transfers might not function very well, because the fragmentation of ownership they cumulatively create prohibits

---

[37] *See* Rashmi Dyal-Chand, "Leaving the Body of Property Law? Meltdowns, Land Rushes, and Failed Economic Development," in *de Soto and Property, supra* note 34, at 91.

[38] *Cf.* David M. Driesen, "Brazil's Transition to Democracy: Agrarian Reform and the New Constitution," 8 *Wis.Int'l L. J.* 51, 78 (1990) (noting that Brazilian law makes title acquired as part of agrarian reform nontransferable for ten years, in order to discourage speculation).

[39] *See* Heller, *supra* note 30, at 1176–81.

[40] *Cf.* Merrill & Smith, *supra* note 1, at 386 (arguing that standardization of property interests does not limit property fragmentation, but instead solves an information problem created by the large number of parties potentially interested in a property).

adaptation needed to solve economic problems. In other words, allocatively efficient transactions can generate adaptively inefficient outcomes. This lack of flexibility can limit economic growth and even create systemic risk.

A good example of an anticommons problem creating systemic risk comes from the problem of workouts of defaulted mortgages in the wake of the financial crisis. Securitization of subprime mortgages meant that ownership of mortgages became highly fragmented. Those involved in securitization viewed each transaction as efficient. But securitization and the fragmentation of ownership it created made the economic system less adaptively efficient in the case of a shock causing borrower defaults by making workouts difficult, as explained in Chapter 2. An economic dynamic approach at least invites the question of whether a particular property rights regime creates an anticommons posing systemic risks to macroeconomic stability.

Furthermore, economic dynamic analysis of the 2008 economic crises has relevance to the debate about how to use property rights to encourage economic development. One can think of subprime mortgage lending as an effort to bestow title on the poor.[41] The crises this led to further demonstrates the need for property law scholars to use economic dynamic analysis to minimize systemic risks that may arise from reforms aimed, at least ostensibly, at using property to better the lot of the poor.[42]

I have emphasized in this section that economic dynamic theory's twin goals of macroeconomic development and the avoidance of systemic risk make it an especially salient theory for property law. Although these goals lie at property law's heart, I do not mean to suggest that all of property's goals are or should be economic. A focus on change over time and use of economic dynamic analysis can prove fruitful even for those pursuing values not featured in economic dynamic theory. Economic dynamic analysis of land titling reforms, for example, can prove useful in securing the social benefits of property for the poor, conferring on them the dignity to participate fully in a community, rather than remaining on the social margins.[43] Thus, economic theory proves important to property law both because of its goals and its methods, even if no coherent general theory can fully account for all possible relevant values.

---

[41] *See* Dyal-Chand, *supra* note 37, at 85 (pointing out that the subprime market made many poor people into new homeowners).

[42] *Cf.* Robin Paul Malloy, "Mortgage Market Reform and the Fallacy of Self-Correcting Markets," 30 *Pace L. Rev.* 79, 108 (2009) (describing government policies addressing subprime lending as combining the goal of helping make housing more affordable with a goal of stimulating speculation).

[43] *See, e.g.*, Driesen, *supra* note at 38, at 57 (quoting a Brazilian advocate of agrarian reform who regards land ownership as essential to citizenship).

CONCLUSION

Some of the most important and interesting problems in property law involve economic dynamics and would benefit from economic dynamic analysis. Now that analysis with some economic dynamic elements has cast doubt on the utility of the academy's myopic focus on optimizing the choices of liability and property rule protection for rights, it is high time to devote more scholarly attention to macroeconomic problems such as the titling reforms discussed earlier. Property does address change over time and provides an infrastructure important to macroeconomic growth and, at times, to creating or avoiding systemic risk.

8

Intellectual Property: Economic Dynamic Scholarship and Neoclassical Legal Change

Many intellectual property scholars view their field in dynamic terms, rather than embrace neoclassical law and economics.[1] Perhaps because this body of law has a major goal of securing innovation's benefits for society, scholars in this field regularly focus on the shape of change over time and innovation's macroeconomic benefits. Intellectual property scholars usually favor combining property rights protections with a free intellectual commons in which those who use intellectual work can gain access to it without payment of license fees, and therefore defend traditional limits on intellectual property and tend to respond to new technologies in ways that preserve or extend the intellectual commons.

Actual intellectual property law, however, has often followed a markedly different course in recent years. Both judges and Congress in recent years have tended to expand intellectual property's domain. They have tended to act consistently with a view of private property associated with Harold Demsetz: more is better. And several neoclassical law and economics scholars have similarly supported expansion of intellectual property rights.

This chapter begins by discussing the Demsetzian view broadly favoring private property, which forms part of neoclassical law and economics. It then contrasts this Demsetzian view with traditional intellectual property law and the view of most intellectual property scholars that preserving common space for sharing ideas is important enough to require some significant limits on intellectual property. This view sees intellectual property as providing important incentives for innovation, but sees a need to limit intellectual property's reach sufficiently to permit diffusion and further development of innovation.

---

[1] *See, e.g.*, Brett M. Frischmann, "Cultural Environmentalism and the Wealth of Networks," 74 *U. Chi. L. Rev.* 1083, 1096 (2007) (book review) (criticizing a focus on measurable outputs and characterizing the cultural environment as dynamic).

This chapter shows, however, that lawmakers have recently moved in the direction of expanded property rights, which comports well with the market glorification that neoclassical law and economics has supported and, more specifically, with Demsetz's view of the world. The chapter closes with a look at economic dynamic analysis' actual and potential uses in the field, including an analysis of the implicit economic dynamic elements found in Lawrence Lessig's work on the Internet, Yochai Benkler's work on open source software (software produced by teams of cooperative programmers scattered around the world and made available for free), and then Harvard law professor, now Supreme Court Justice, Stephen Breyer's work on copyright. In general, an economic dynamic approach already plays a very substantial role in this field's scholarship and law could do even more. An economic dynamic view that does not assume the superiority of privatization makes much more sense than the automatic favoring of privatization that one finds in the work of Demsetz and some others in the Chicago school of law and economics.

THE DEMSETZIAN VIEW: MORE IS BETTER

Hardin's work on the tragedy of the commons mentions two possible remedies for the overuse of commons resources: government regulation and division of a commons resource among private owners. Intellectual property scholars associate Demsetz with a strong preference for the privatization solution.

Demsetz famously argued that private property rights arise where the benefits of establishing a private property right exceed the costs of establishing and enforcing it.[2] This proposition seems like an economist's fantasy – and, indeed, Demsetz avoids claiming that those crafting property rules, Congressmen and common law judges, explicitly weigh costs and benefits.[3] Nor does he claim rich empirical support for this proposition, although others have sought to supply more.[4] Yet he does provide examples where a correlation exists between changes in benefits and changes in property rights regimes.[5] Neither Demsetz nor, to my knowledge, anybody else has actually carried out CBA showing one property regime's superiority to another. But by proposing that private property should prevail when its benefits exceed the costs of enforcing it Demsetz elevates efficiency considerations.

---

[2] *See* Harold Demsetz, "Toward a Theory of Property Rights," 57 *Am. Econ. Rev. Papers and Proc.* 347, 350 (1967).
[3] *See id.*
[4] *See id.* (noting that "a rigorous test" of his assertion "will require extensive . . . empirical work").
[5] *See id.* at 351–53.

The next step in Demsetz's argument has provoked intellectual property scholars. He argues that private property owners stand in a better position to internalize external costs and benefits (such as pollution or clean water flowing from a property) than communal property owners. He gives several reasons for this belief. He argues, for reasons wholly unexplained, that an individual owner will care about costs and benefits accruing after he or she dies (albeit on a discounted basis) but suggests that a communal owner will not care about the community's descendants.[6] He also advances a Coaseian argument that somebody affected by an externality may more easily negotiate an appropriate arrangement with a single owner than with the owner of communal property, since any arrangement respecting use of communal property would require many people's assent.[7] These arguments suggest that one should always favor a private property regime, except when the costs of establishing and enforcing property rights prove prohibitive. Thus, Demsetz generally supports a strong presumption favoring private, rather than communal, property.[8]

A number of intellectual property scholars draw on Demsetz to argue for expanding private intellectual property.[9] For example, Paul Goldstein finds that the "logic of property rights" that Demsetz developed dictates "their extension into every corner" of artistic and literary endeavor,[10] and Trotter Hardy argues for a unified substitute for copyright law with few of its limitations left intact, relying squarely on Demsetz.[11] Edmund Kitch and F. Scott Kief support patents not only on the grounds that they will create an incentive for invention, but also on the Demsetzian ground that patent holders, like other owners of private property, will efficiently manage the inventions covered by their patents in a way that advances social welfare.[12] Other scholars draw on

---

[6] Id. at 355.

[7] Id. at 356–57.

[8] See Richard A. Epstein, "The Allocation of the Commons: Parking on Public Roads," 31 *J. Legal Stud.* S515–16 (2002) (characterizing Demsetz's argument as maintaining that "systems of private property generally outperform systems of common property"); *cf.* Brett M. Frischmann, "Evaluating the Demsetzian Trend In Copyright Law," 3 *Rev. L. & Econ.* 649, 657 (2007) (pointing out that although it is debatable whether Demsetz intended to advance this argument, it "permeates his article" and strongly influenced his successors).

[9] See Mark Lemley & Brett Frischman, "Spillovers," 107 *Colum. L. Rev.* 257, 264–67 (2007) (discussing Demsetz's influence on intellectual property); *see also* Julie Cohen, "Lochner in Cyberspace: The New Economic Orthodoxy of 'Rights Management'," 97 *Mich. L. Rev.* 462, 472–80 (1998) (reviewing the work of fans of freedom of contract in the intellectual property realm).

[10] Paul Goldstein, *Copyright's Highway: From Gutenberg to the Celestial Jukebox* 178–79 (1994).

[11] See I. Trotter Hardy, "Property (and Copyright) in Cyberspace," 1996 *U. Chi. Legal F.* 217.

[12] Edmund W. Kitch, "The Nature and Function of the Patent System," 20 *J. L. & Econ.* 265, 276 (1977); F. Scott Kief, "Property Rights and Property Rules for Commercializing Inventions,"

neoclassical law and economics without invoking Demsetz to characterize the
fair use doctrine – which permits limited copying of copyrighted materials for
teaching, research, or other favored purposes without fee – as inefficient and
to embrace the concept of allowing contract to limit fair use rights.[13]

But in this area, traditional law and economics does not present a monolith.
In intellectual property we have free market fundamentalists like Hardy seeking to sweep away traditional limitations on intellectual property and some
positivists seeking to justify the tradition (or much of it anyway) in law and
economics terms.[14] The leading positivists, William Landes and Richard Posner, recognize a need for balance between private and public intellectual
property.[15] Having no data on the costs and benefits of copyright, they concede that "it may be difficult to determine whether, on balance, copyright is
a good thing."[16] Yet Landes and Posner endorse the existing copyright regime
as efficient, albeit in qualified terms. Overall, their work well illustrates the
tendency in law and economics to use CBA to justify a result as efficient, without actually measuring the costs and benefits.[17] The main point here, though,
is that law and economics divides into two camps in this realm, that of the
market fundamentalists, who follow Demsetz in calling for increased property
rights, and that of the positivists, who call for balance.

The insistence on efficiency as an important goal for intellectual property
unites both of these camps, but suffers from a number of fundamental problems. First, as a technical matter, economists often define an efficient market

85 *Minn. L. Rev.* 697, 717 (2001); *see* Shubha Ghosh, "Patents and the Regulatory State:
Rethinking the Patent Bargain Metaphor after Eldred," 19 *Berkeley Tech. L. J.* 1315, 1353–57
(2004) (noting that the prospect and commercialization theories exemplified in Kief and Kitch
stem from Demsetz's work).

[13] *See* Tom W. Bell, "Fair Use v. Fared Use: The Impact of Automated Rights Management
on Copyright's Fair Use Doctrine," 76 *N.C.L. Rev.* 557 (1998); Maureen O'Rourke, "Drawing
the Boundary Between Copyright and Contract: Copyright Preemption of Software License
Terms," 45 *Duke L. J.* 479 (1995) (supporting use of contract to expand intellectual property
rights beyond those conferred under the copyright law).

[14] There are also some who resist easy classification. *See, e.g.,* O'Rourke, *supra* note 13, at 485
(describing the lack of incentives to produce and a communal space for sharing as a dual
market failure en route to endorsing contractual erosion of common space).

[15] *See* William M. Landes & Richard A. Posner, "An Economic Analysis of Copyright Law,"
18 *J. Legal Stud.* 325, 326 (1989) (describing striking "the correct balance between access and
incentives" as copyright law's "central problem").

[16] Id. at 331. They argue, however, that copyright does avoid certain "distortions" that would
occur absent copyright. *See* id. at 332.

[17] Another law and economics positivist, Edmund W. Kitch, does the same thing for patents.
See Kitch, *supra* note 12. He recognizes that patent terms are appropriate, but deploys a highly
speculative argument to endorse the terms of patent actually in the law, with no actual data on
costs and benefits. *See* id. at 284–85 (suggesting that patents should be short for short jumps,
but that the risk of poor innovation for big jumps justifies treating the two alike).

as one that balances costs and benefits for a given technological state. So it is a bit odd to specify efficiency as a goal for a body of law that specifically aims to change the technological state. Presumably, adherents of law and economics would respond by redefining their goal as dynamic efficiency, but doing so introduces problems of specifying whose benefits we hope to maximize, this generation's or a subsequent one's.

The problem, however, goes beyond mere indeterminacy (which the lack of data ensures anyway). This goal looks like a category mistake. After all, technological innovation plays a major role in determining economic growth rates. It would seem that economic growth serves as the appropriate economic goal here, not efficiency.[18] And since intellectual property seeks to spur creativity and experimentation, some inefficiency might prove essential to realizing the more salient economic goal of long-term growth. Often growth and change follow some unsuccessful experiments. Furthermore, intellectual property has some important noneconomic goals. Copyright, for example, should play a role in helping us create and sustain a viable culture. Landes and Posner arguably subsume this idea within the concept of consumer surplus. But economic models, by assuming that all preferences have equal value (as expressed through dollar expenditures at least), crowd out room for qualitative debate about copyright's influence on culture and creativity. This treatment of all consumer preferences as being of equal value becomes especially problematic when it comes to questions about the fair use doctrine. Fair use often arises in academic and research settings, places that play a role in preference formation. To the extent that education and technological change shape preferences, viewing the question of whether researchers and teachers should enjoy free access to copyrighted materials as a question of maximizing satisfaction of existing preferences simply ignores the change over time that intellectual property, education, and research aim to bring about.

BALANCED LAW

Traditionally, intellectual property law has sought to provide adequate monetary incentives to create new work without eliminating free access to the intellectual resources needed as the basis for advances in the arts and sciences. In broader terms, it has privatized some intellectual property while preserving an intellectual commons for information sharing.

---

[18] *See* Frank H. Easterbrook, "Intellectual Property Is Still Property," 13 *Harv. J. L. & Pub. Pol'y* 108, 110 (1990) (describing intellectual property with its dependence on monopolies as trading off dynamic growth against allocative "losses," i.e., efficiency); Frischmann, *supra* note 1, at 1107 (associating positive spillovers with economic growth).

Thus, for example, copyright law prevents the copying of original works, such as books and records, but includes significant limitations that facilitate sharing of information. Allowing the author a copyright has the effect of requiring those who would like to read the book to pay the publisher for the privilege, since they cannot simply copy it. These payments provide the publishers with the means to compensate authors. Thus, the copyright aims to provide authors with a potential means of support, so that they can create new works. But copyright protection does not apply to the ideas underlying the works. This limitation allows authors to draw on the ideas in one book to create a new one or parody an old book. Furthermore, even the copyright itself traditionally had a limited term. This goal of incentivizing new work implies that copyright need not continue indefinitely. Accordingly, after a limited term traditionally designed to facilitate adequate compensation to a living author, copyrighted works have become part of the public domain, available for copying without fee. Copyright expiration allows for freer use of the work itself as a basis for creating new work and allows new publishers to print the book, thereby introducing competition in the packaging of a book that may, by then, have an established value. Thus, copyright has traditionally created a dynamic with some potential to compensate old authors and to provide information for new ones.

Patent law similarly sought to provide adequate incentives for innovation – in this instance, by providing a monopoly on the use of inventions, while allowing new ideas and methods to spread. As in copyright law, the intellectual property right applies only to actual artifacts, not to the ideas used in creating the artifacts.[19] Hence, one has to actually produce something prior to obtaining a patent. Also, upon receiving a patent, the patent holder must disclose the patent to the public, so that competitors can use the ideas underlying the patented object to create new inventions.[20] Traditionally, patent law has limited that which inventors and corporations could patent in ways that kept the intellectual commons open. For example, one could not patent life or facts, just inventions.[21]

Patent law seeks to allow those who make extraordinary advances to profit from a limited monopoly without cutting off competition to make obvious improvements on the existing art in a field. Accordingly, patent rights apply

---

[19] Kitch, *supra* note 12, at 269 (to obtain a patent, the inventor must have produced a device or process that works).

[20] *Cf.* id. at 287 (noting the disclosure requirement, but commenting that the patent system has failed to secure adequate disclosure in practice).

[21] *See Feist Publications v. Rural Telephone Service*, 499 U.S. 340 (1991) (declining to apply copyright protection to the white pages, since they merely compile facts).

only to novel inventions, those not obvious from prior art.[22] Furthermore, governments traditionally grant patent holders monopoly rights only for a limited term, thereby mirroring a basic feature of copyright law. Since monopolies raise prices and limit access to inventions, patents eventually expire, at which point others can manufacture the formerly patented invention. Thus, for example, a pharmaceutical firm developing a patent medicine can count on extracting monopoly rents from doctors and hospitals for a needed drug, which might justify the expense of developing and testing a new drug. But once that patent expires, new entrants can make generic versions of the same drug, thereby bringing down the price. Thus, granting a patent for a limited term both creates incentives to continually advance the state of the art by coming up with a new patentable drug that provides a superior treatment and makes the new drug more easily available to consumers than it would be if a monopoly persisted indefinitely.

The U.S. Constitution even reflects recognition of the importance of limits on intellectual property to technical and artistic progress. It links promotion of "Progress of Science and useful Arts" to securing rights "for *limited times*" to "authors and inventors."[23]

THE INTELLECTUAL PROPERTY LAW SCHOLARS' VIEW: SEEKING A BALANCE THAT MANAGES CHANGE OVER TIME

Almost all leading intellectual property scholars, unlike the Demsetzians (but like the positivists), call for balance.[24] They recognize that intellectual property rights provide incentives to produce creative work. Yet they point out that granting too strong a property right can make it very hard for creative work to generate more creative work.[25] Innovations frequently create "positive spillovers" – benefits to the larger society.[26] These benefits include learning better manufacturing techniques by building on previous advances, writing more interesting literary works inspired by predecessor works, deriving humor

---

[22] Edmund W. Kitch, "*Graham v. John Deere Co.*: New Standards for Patents," 1966 *Sup. Ct. Rev.* 293; 35 U.S.C. § 103.

[23] U.S. Const. Art. 1, sec. 8, cl. 8 (emphasis added).

[24] *See, e.g.*, Cohen, *supra* note 9, at 514 (stating that the "trick" in copyright is to properly balance "[i]ncentives to create and limits on author/owner control").

[25] Rochelle Cooper Dreyfuss, "Does IP Need IP? Accommodating Intellectual Property Outside the Intellectual Property Paradigm," 31 *Cardozo L. Rev.* 1437, 1441 (2010) (explaining that the cumulative nature of knowledge means that "exclusive rights" can "slow progress in the name of promoting it"); Cohen, *supra* note 9, at 498–99 (arguing that extension of copyright protections can discourage valuable new work).

[26] *See* Lemley & Frischmann, *supra* note 9.

from previous works through satire, and creating fresh musical arrangements of and variations on older tunes. This implies that new creators must have access to previous intellectual artifacts and the ability to use and reformulate them in order for the state of the art to advance.

Recognition of positive spillovers implies that Demsetz has missed the boat, even with respect to efficiency. If an intellectual commons provides spillover benefits beyond what private intellectual property produces, then analysts cannot measure efficiency by simply comparing private property's benefits to the costs of protecting it. Rather one would have to include the incremental benefits a commons resource provides the public, beyond those offered by licensing of intellectual property held in a private monopoly.

Consistent with their belief in the value of an intellectual commons, intellectual property scholars have proposed, in various ways, maintenance of traditional limits on property rights and some expansion of older limits designed to allow access at some time to the works needed to generate positive spillovers and to avoid such broad protections that ideas themselves become off limits to further development.[27] And, in some cases, they have argued that a commons can flourish without intellectual property.[28]

For example, Yochai Benkler has chronicled the development of the open source software movement, which suggests that complex sharing and development can occur in some contexts without formal property protection.[29] A number of scholars have defended fair use doctrine in copyright law.[30] They have also defended the traditionally limited duration of copyright terms. In these and many other cases, intellectual property scholars have sought to maintain or expand space for sharing of ideas and the artifacts that embody them.

In taking into account the need to preserve positive spillovers even while providing sufficient incentives for new creation, intellectual property scholars implicitly focus on change over time. They envision a new work inspiring another work, and that work in turn inspiring another, and so on. They imagine

---

[27] *See, e.g.,* Frischmann, *supra* note 1, at 661 (noting that intellectual property rights scholars have "questioned the wisdom" of making copyright protection too absolute); Maureen A. O'Rourke, "Toward a Doctrine of Fair Use in Patent Law," 100 *Colum. L. Rev.* 1177 (2000); Cohen, *supra* note 9 (questioning extension of copyright through digital rights management).

[28] *See* Dreyfus, *supra* note 25, at 1443–47 (discussing a literature on creative work being completed and shared without intellectual property protection).

[29] *See* Yochai Benkler, "Coase's Penguin, or Linux and the Nature of the Firm," 112 *Yale L. J.* 369 (2002).

[30] *See, e.g.,* James Boyle, *Shamans, Software, and Spleens: Law and the Construction of the Information Society* 139 (1996) (defending fair use on the ground that "creators need some raw material to work *with*") (emphasis in original).

a chain of innovation in the arts and manufacturing transforming knowledge and, therefore, production of artifacts over time.

This vision suggests that intellectual property law embraces the macroeconomic objective of creating economic growth as a major goal. Surely, the patent regime, at least, aims at the achievement of this goal. It seeks to provide proper incentives for creating and bringing to market new inventions, usually with commercial potential, which constitute the heart of economic growth. Indeed, the information economy has likely made intellectual property law more central to economic growth than ever before.[31] As information itself, new media, and medical information stemming from efforts to sequence the human genome play an ever greater role in our economy, proper management of those resources becomes a key element in providing opportunities for economic growth. That said, intellectual property plays a key role in the arts, not just in the economy. Without meaning to deny that the arts have a role to play in the economy (or vice versa), intellectual property's role in the arts must embrace creation of a rich culture, not just the creation of wealth, as a key goal.[32] Hence, in claiming that the creation of economic opportunity constitutes a major goal of intellectual property law, I do not mean to suggest that it constitutes its only goal.

DEMSETZIAN LAWMAKERS

In recent years, legislatures and judges have tended to expand intellectual property's sphere, rather than to protect the commons.[33] In doing so, they have acted consistently with the Demsetzian view,[34] or, as Brett Frischmann describes it, an "unreflective glorified view of property rights and markets."[35]

Congress expanded the term of copyright protection to unprecedented lengths in 1998. In 1790, Congress established a copyright term of twenty-eight years. In 1831, Congress extended it to forty-two years and in 1909 to fifty-six years. All these terms might expire while the author still lived (although, since 1909, only in the case of a young author living a long time) and therefore seem at least sufficient to pay authors for their works.[36] In 1976, however,

---

[31] *See* id. at x (characterizing information as "one of the main sources of wealth" in our society).

[32] *See generally* id. at 60 (linking the idea of the "author" in intellectual property to remaking "individual life and collective existence").

[33] *See, e.g., San Francisco Arts and Athletics, Inc. v. United States Olympic Committee,* 483 U.S. 522 (1987) (enjoining the use of the word "Olympics" in promotions for a Gay Olympics).

[34] *Cf.* Frischmann, *supra* note 8, at 651 (noting that copyright protection has expanded in recent years as the value of copyrightable work, such as software, has grown).

[35] *See* Frischmann, *supra* note 1, at 1103.

[36] *See* Deven R. Desai, "The Life and Death of Copyright," 103 *Wis. L. Rev.* 219 (2011).

Congress extended the copyright term to the author's lifetime plus fifty years, meaning that the term became excessive (assuming it was not already excessive in 1909) if the goal is simply to compensate the author himself. Posner and Landes, however, despite their balanced approach to intellectual property generally, defended this extension on the basis of the potential rewards to the authors' children, which might motivate an author.[37] This position illustrates even relatively moderate law and economics proponents' tendency to favor expansion of private property rights. And Posner and Landes' extension of the model of self-interested utility maximization to include an interest in advancing one's children's welfare suggests a willingness to treat the rational actor model flexibly in order to achieve pro-market results.

In 1998, Congress added yet another twenty years to the copyright term, making it last for the author's lifetime plus seventy years.[38] This means that the term would extend beyond the lifetime of an author's children, unless the author died when the children were quite young and these very young children lived to a quite ripe old age. Furthermore, Congress applied this copyright extension to existing works, where it could not possibly provide an incentive for the creation of new work.[39] Congress also responded to the possibility of new digital media expanding the commons by providing enhanced private rights to digitized products in 2006.[40]

The courts, meanwhile, limited the fair use doctrine.[41] The Second Circuit, for example, held in *American Geophysical Union v. Texaco*[42] that unauthorized copying of scientific articles for research purposes did not constitute fair use, a ruling in tension with a host of previous cases. The Sixth Circuit held that an educational use – the assembly of course packs for university courses consisting of book excerpts – does not constitute fair use.[43] Similarly, the Ninth Circuit prohibited an offshoot of an established church from photocopying that church's annotated Bible under the fair use doctrine.[44] All of these cases reflect the view that the possibility of privatization, of earning market revenue

---

[37] *See* Landes & Posner, *supra* note 15, at 363 (justifying the length of copyright in terms of the interests of descendents).

[38] *See Eric Eldred v. John D. Aschcroft*, 537 U. S. 186, 195 (2003).

[39] *Accord* id. at 254 (Breyer, J., dissenting).

[40] *See* Sonny Bono Copyright Extension Act, Pub. L. No. 105–298 § 102, 112 Stat. 2827, 2827 (1998) (codified at 17 U.S.C. §§ 301–304 (2006)); Digital Millennium Copyright Act, Pub. L. No. 105–304, 112 Stat. 2836 (1998) (codified as amended at 17 U.S.C. §§ 1201–1205 (2006)).

[41] *See Princeton Univ. Press, Inc. v. Michigan Document Serv., Inc.*, 99 3d 1381 (6th Cir. 1996) (*en banc*); *American Geophysical Union v. Texaco, Inc.*, 60 F.3d 913 (2d Cir. 1994).

[42] 60 F.3d 913 (2d Cir. 1994),

[43] *Princeton Univ. Press*, 99 F.3d at 1383.

[44] *Worldwide Church of God v. Philadelphia Church of God*, 227 F. 3d 1110 (9th Cir. 2000).

from a use that might be considered fair, strongly argues against fair use and place little emphasis on the fair use doctrine's original purpose of limiting the domain of markets to protect a limited intellectual commons for copyrighted works.[45] Since advancements in digital technology almost always make it possible to create a market for a use formerly considered fair, this approach severely threatens the viability of fair use doctrine as a preserver of the intellectual commons.

The courts extended patents to all sorts of things not previously covered, such as business methods[46] and genetically modified organisms.[47] And the patent office, long notorious for excessive liberality in granting patents, extended patent protection to a golf putting method and to legal strategies.[48]

These constitute but a few of many examples of lawmakers, in recent years, acting consistently with the pro-market worldview that neoclassical law and economics helped spawn, rolling back traditional limits on intellectual property and creating property rights in new media. This extension of intellectual property rights helps create markets in intellectual property where a commons with free access to information might otherwise prevail.

ECONOMIC DYNAMIC ANALYSIS

Intellectual property scholars, however, have employed economic dynamic analysis to insist on the intellectual commons' value. Lawrence Lessig, in *The Future of Ideas*, implicitly relies on an economic dynamic analysis grounded in the concept of bounded rationality to argue for an open access Internet regime.[49] Lessig implicitly invokes bounded rationality when he notes that the

---

[45] *See* id. at 1119 (emphasizing potential Bible sales even though the church producing the Bible had stopped selling it because of doctrinal changes); *Princeton Univ. Press*, 99 F. 3d at 1385–87 (putting emphasis on the potential market and finding that payment of royalties for course packs is possible); *American Geophysical Union*, 60 F.3d at 931 (putting emphasis on the possibility of new subscriptions or licensing substituting for photocopying).

[46] *State St. Bank & Trust Co. v. Signature Fin. Group, Inc.*, 149 F.3d 1368 (Fed. Cir. 1998). *Cf. Lab. Corp. of Am. Holdings v. Metabolite Labs., Inc.*, 548 U.S. 124, 125–39 (2006) (Breyer, J., dissenting).

[47] *Diamond v. Chakrabarty*, 447 U.S. 303 (1980).

[48] U.S. Patent No. 5,616,089 (May 29, 1996); U.S. Patent No. 6,567,790 (filed Dec. 1, 1999) (grantor retained annuity trust). *See* Michael Risch, "Everything is Patentable," 75 *Tenn. L. Rev.* 591 (2008); *see also* Dreyfuss, *supra* note 25, at 1441 (detailing some international and foreign expansion of intellectual property as well).

[49] *See* Lawrence Lessig, *The Future of Ideas: The Fate of the Commons in a Connected World* 88–89 (2001). This chapter's analysis of Lawrence Lessig's work draws upon David M. Driesen, "An Economic Dynamic Approach to the Infrastructure Commons," 35 *Ecology L. Q.* 215 (2008).

Internet's creators could not know what sort of innovations it might spawn.[50] This bound upon rationality makes optimization of the Internet for particular applications a poor choice. Because the Internet's founders could not intelligently optimize the Internet for innovations they could not identify, they relied on a "dumb" end-to-end design, which makes it easy for end users to use the commons of the Internet as an innovation platform.[51] Lessig then uses the notion of path dependency, another pillar of economic dynamic theory,[52] to further his argument. Building on the work of Clayton Christensen, the author of *The Innovator's Dilemma*,[53] he shows how path dependency limits the innovation capacity of established companies. He shows that companies tend to become expert in refining the technologies they know about and serving the markets they have helped create, but can easily miss opportunities for innovation that would disrupt these markets.[54] He fears that established firms' path-dependent bounded rationality and the economic incentive they have to discourage disruptive technology can lead them to squash innovation.[55] Therefore, he suggests, leaving the infrastructure commons of the Internet open might be a very good idea.[56] When we have little understanding of how a resource might be used we should favor disruption by leaving it in the commons, writes Lessig.[57]

This preference for leaving options open in the face of uncertainty closely tracks another pillar of economic dynamic analysis, Douglas North's idea of adaptive efficiency.[58] When we cannot sum relevant costs and benefits, we should choose the option that maximizes our future flexibility, our ability to grow and experiment.[59] Lessig does exactly what the economic dynamic theory recommends: he analyzes economic incentives based on bounded rationality and path dependence to predict the shape of change over time as a guide to optimal policy, using a concept of adaptive efficiency that works even when we cannot quantify salient benefits.[60]

[50] Lessig, *supra* note 49.
[51] Id. at 88–89.
[52] *See* David M. Driesen, *The Economic Dynamics of Environmental Law* 7 (2003).
[53] Clayton Christensen, *The Innovator's Dilemma: When New Technologies Cause Great Firms to Fail* (1997). *See* Driesen, *supra* note 52 at 109–10 (citing Christensen to support the idea that firms can fail if they "forgo innovation in favor of the status quo").
[54] *See* Lessig, *supra* note 49, at 89–91.
[55] Id. at 91–92.
[56] Id. at 92.
[57] Id. at 88–92.
[58] *See* Driesen, *supra* note 52, at 7.
[59] Id.
[60] *See* id.

Yochai Benkler also employs economic dynamic analysis in analyzing open source software (along with other examples of "peer production") and its implications for intellectual property law. He relies on bounded rationality for a key analytical move in developing the case for open source software as a viable approach to its production. Traditionally, economists studying institutional organization have followed Coase in thinking in terms of two main alternatives. Firms can organize resources through hierarchical command structures to carry out tasks.[61] Conversely, markets can coordinate actions among diverse actors through price signals and contracts.[62] Benkler, however, finds that open source software and similar collaborative efforts do not primarily rely on either the hierarchy of a firm or the market's price signals to coordinate efforts of individuals, and sets out to explain the basis for open source collaboration and what it has to teach us about the potential value of maintaining an intellectual commons.[63] A key analytical move involves attention to the bounds of the rationality of the creative individuals involved in producing open source software. He argues that under some conditions people will participate in common projects, such as creating open source software, because of "social-psychological," rather than monetary, reward.[64] For example, relying on a study by two economists, he finds that people's desire for creative work and recognition motivate their participation in open source software projects.[65] He develops a model that incorporates these motivations as well as monetary ones to inform analysis of when and how such collaboration will work, based on observations of the bounded rationality of academics, artists, and others who often seem to engage in activities for nonmonetary rewards.[66] Recognizing that a full understanding of these rewards and the circumstances under which they suffice to motivate successful collaboration requires more intensive study of bounded rationality, Benkler calls for anthropological and social-psychological study of those involved in such projects.[67] He observes that certain groups, such as young people with few financial obligations and a hunger for recognition, may find nonmonetary rewards more important than monetary ones.[68] His analysis shows that fairly well known aspects of human psychology can produce a pretty good model of bounded rationality to inform

---

[61] *See* Benkler, *supra* note 29, at 372.
[62] *See* id.
[63] *See* id. at 375–81.
[64] *See* id. at 378.
[65] *See* id. at 424; *see also* Josh Lerner & Jean Tirole, *Some Simple Economics of Open Source*, 50 J. Indus. Econ. 197 (2002).
[66] *See* Benkler, *supra* note 29, at 426–33.
[67] *See* id. at 424.
[68] Id. at 434.

understanding of the intellectual commons, even if a full description would require substantial empirical study.

Having shown that bounded rationality indicates that open source software production (or more generally, peer production) offers a viable approach, Benkler implicitly employs economic dynamic analysis to reach conclusions about his insights' implications for intellectual property law. He begins with a simple observation: strong intellectual property rights raise the costs of access to existing information that could contribute to the creation of open source software.[69] Conversely, according to Benkler, intellectual property law provides no benefits to peer production. It follows that the current trend of strengthening of intellectual property law proves ill-advised if peer production can prove important.[70]

My point is not necessarily that Benkler's analysis definitively answers all pertinent questions about intellectual property in software and other important questions that his argument raises.[71] But he gets much further than others have in figuring out important questions and likely answers to intellectual property puzzles by focusing on economic dynamics, instead of pretending he can determine an efficient outcome through summation of costs and benefits under a rational-actor model. Furthermore, subsequent work suggests that Benkler does not consider efficiency the main objective; he claims that peer production can enhance participation in political, intellectual, and cultural activities in ways that enrich society.[72]

Stephen Breyer's work on copyright from the 1970s tries to analyze copyright in terms of efficiency, but makes headway only when he switches to an economic dynamic approach.[73] His work illustrates the point made in Chapter 4 that economic dynamic analysis proves essential to CBA as well as the point that it provides a way to analyze legal problems even though calculation of costs and benefits usually proves impossible for significant legal policy questions.

Breyer begins by arguing for efficiency as the analytically appropriate criterion for analyzing the desirability of copyright protection.[74] He purports to

[69] Id. at 445.
[70] Id..
[71] Cf. Frischmann, *supra* note 1, at 1117, 1132–36 (suggesting the need for further economic dynamic analysis to fully assess the potential and limits of peer production and its implications for policy); Steven A. Hetcher, "Hume's Penguin, or, Yochai Benkler and the Nature of Peer Production," 11 *Vand. J. Ent. & Tech. L.* 963, 1000 (2009) (arguing that copyright may have an important role to play in sustaining exchange of user-generated content by supporting privacy).
[72] See Yochai Benkler, *The Wealth of Networks: How Social Production Transforms Markets and Freedom* 2 (2006).
[73] Stephen Breyer, "The Uneasy Case for Copyright: A Study of Copyrights in Books, Photocopies, and Computer Programs," 84 *Harv. L. Rev.* 281 (1970).
[74] Id. at 289.

carry out a CBA, but concedes, in a gross understatement, that he cannot make
"exact quantitative estimates" of costs and benefits.[75] He does not carry out a
"cost–benefit analysis" by making imprecise estimates of aggregate costs and
benefits, but rather identifies the "sources" of costs and benefits.[76] What follows, however, basically involves an economic dynamic analysis. He focuses on
questions about whether copyright would "seriously injure book production"
and what might be gained by eliminating copyright.[77] He employs scenario
analysis to answer some of these questions, such as, for example, considering
the possibilities of buyers combining to pay for the production of books made
noneconomic by the abolition of copyright and the ability of a publisher to
amortize fixed costs through the advantage of being the first to publish a book
unprotected by copyright.[78] He also considers countervailing economic incentives, as economic dynamic theory recommends. Thus, for example, he doubts
that abolishing copyrights will kill textbooks, because universities can support
textbook writing through professional recognition and increased salaries for
authors.[79] Subsequently, other scholars have made the related point from the
perspective of bounded rationality, the desire for recognition or influence may
motivate professors, so a decline in monetary rewards through a copyright system may not matter much.[80] In the end, Breyer, unable to quantify costs and
benefits, finds the case for copyright weak.[81] His analysis reaches this rather
tentative conclusion primarily through economic dynamic analysis, since in
the end he has no estimates, precise or otherwise, of copyright benefits. But
he does develop an economic dynamic analysis to try to approximate a CBA.
One should draw a fairly broad lesson from this. Since, as Brett Frischmann
has pointed out, one can measure the benefits of intellectual property in terms
of numbers of patents and copyrights granted, but not the opportunity costs
forgone,[82] CBA just does not work in this area, but economic dynamic analysis
does.

Breyer's analysis becomes much more definitive when he deploys economic
dynamic analysis to focus on the question of efficacy. He argues that Congress
should not extend the fifty-six-year copyright period in effect when he wrote
to "life plus fifty years."[83] He reaches this conclusion primarily through an
analysis of the bounded rationality of authors and publishers to figure out how

---

[75] Id. at 291–92.
[76] Id. at 292.
[77] Id. at 293, 313.
[78] Id. at 299–308.
[79] Id. at 309.
[80] *See, e.g.,* Cohen, *supra* note 9, at 505.
[81] Breyer, *supra* note 73, at 321.
[82] Frischmann, *supra* note 1, at 1136–37.
[83] Breyer, *supra* note 73, at 323–29.

the incremental economic incentive created by the extra years of copyright protection would influence them. Since only one in a hundred books remains in print after fifty-six years, few, if any, authors will take the extra length of the term into account in deciding whether to write.[84] Even for a wildly confident author who does expect his work to remain in print that long, the added sales, Breyer writes, provide negligible additional income unlikely to influence writing decisions.[85] His analysis of publishers' incentives includes some data about how the publishers actually think about books, which show that publishers base their decisions about expected returns over the first twenty years of publication or less (usually much less).[86] Thus, he employs specific information about the bounded rationality of institutions to show that an extension of a copyright term does not succeed in stimulating additional publications. So Breyer employs economic dynamic analysis both to approximate an unobtainable CBA and to analyze basic questions of efficacy leading to fairly clear conclusions about the value – or, more precisely, lack of value – of proposed legal reforms. Many leading scholars in the field have made important contributions through implicit deployment of economic dynamic analysis.

Some Possible Extensions Using Economic Dynamic Analysis

The preceding materials show that intellectual property has the creation of economic opportunity as a central focus and that its leading scholars tend to focus on change over time in seeking to understand and strengthen intellectual property regimes. We see that much of the field's leading work implicitly employs economic dynamic analysis to evaluate how bounded rationality may influence change over time.

In spite of an implicit consensus among many prominent intellectual property scholars that the field is an economic dynamic enterprise, intellectual property scholars' works appear ad hoc and eclectic. This oddly puts them at a disadvantage in the competition with practitioners of neoclassical law and economics for control of the field, even though these practitioners do not have a consistent approach to intellectual property.

Part of the problem involves the failure, until now, of anybody to identify what analytical elements permeate the work of many of our best legal scholars. Lawrence Lessig sounds almost apologetic when he characterizes his

---

[84] Id. at 324.

[85] Id.

[86] Id. at 325. Indeed, Breyer explains that publishers consider only ten to twenty years of revenue for reference works. For trade books and textbooks, the figures are two years and five years, respectively. Id.

economic dynamic analysis as merely identifying some factors to consider in making decisions about whether to preserve the Internet as a commons, rather than comprehensively analyzing its costs and benefits.[87] Yet a comprehensive evaluation of costs and benefits proves impossible, as Lessig recognizes, because we cannot know the future. And Lessig has done much more than just identify some random relevant factors. He has analyzed key factors that shape change over time. We cannot know the future, but we can have some sense of where we are going and what needs to change. Lessig's deployment of economic dynamic analysis allows his work to succeed in a way that many authors would envy.

We can, however, go further in analyzing the desirability of an open access Internet regime and other intellectual property questions, if we explicitly and carefully apply economic dynamic analysis. As Brett Frischmann points out, many resources, including the Internet, function as infrastructure. He defines infrastructure as that which provides inputs into a great variety of public and private goods.[88] This implies, of course, that leaving infrastructure in a commons provides a path toward a lot of future economic and social benefits, an observation about change over time. Privatization, by contrast, limits infrastructure's uses to those things the owner finds desirable. This may help justify our practice of keeping the Internet open, as well as the public trust doctrine's protection of navigable waters from privatization, and the custom of making highways publicly available.

In describing the nature of the infrastructure commons, Frischmann characterizes infrastructure commons as, at least partly, nonrivalrous. A resource is nonrivalrous when its uses do not interfere with one another. Ideas constitute nonrivalrous resources because two people can use the same idea without interfering with each other. Thus, if this book's readers decide to use the idea of economic dynamic analysis in their own work, they have not interfered with my future use of the idea. Indeed, they may enhance it. By contrast, the cup of coffee I sip as I write is a rivalrous resource. If you come and drink it, I have no coffee to drink (assuming away the backup stash in the kitchen). This suggests that commons infrastructure should remain in the commons because it lends itself to myriad uses without conflict, so privatization would simply limit the scale of potential use. Hence, an analysis of the extent to which a resource proves rivalrous or nonrivalrous can help us predict whether leaving the resource in the commons will lead over time to a tragedy of the commons,

---

[87] Lessig, *supra* note 49, at 1039 & n. 15.
[88] *See* Brett Frischman, "An Economic Theory of Infrastructure and Commons Management," 89 *Minn. L. Rev.* 917, 974 (2005).

suggesting the need to consider privatization, or to a plethora of unpredictable and potentially useful uses, thereby suggesting advantages to leaving it in the commons.

We can use this analysis of the nature of uses of infrastructure to evaluate the benefits of open access or access limits when combined with an economic dynamic analysis showing how different commons uses influence incentives. For example, some uses of the Internet, spam and viruses, are rivalrous in the sense that they impede other uses of the Internet. We can ask whether, over time, an open commons would lead these uses to seriously diminish the positive values of the resource. If so, we would need to at least evaluate whether an end-to-end architecture is compatible with effectively limiting these rivalrous uses that have the capacity to destroy, or at least seriously limit, the common's capacity to deliver benefits.

Consideration of whom particular architecture empowers can also aid analysis of the value of an open Internet.[89] The Internet that Professor Lessig so admires once served a relatively small, albeit rapidly growing, community. Enabling the larger community to use the Internet requires capacity increases over time. An economic dynamic analysis must address the question of whether funding this capacity increase remains consistent with open access. One must evaluate whether the bounded rationality of those in a position to add bandwidth will cause them to desist unless they gain some measure of control over the architecture.[90] If they would desist absent some control, then economic dynamic analysis can support open access only by making a case for some alternative way of building capacity or for the idea that society does not need additional capacity. On the other hand, if we can add capacity without handing over some control over architecture to large firms, then this would strengthen the case for open access.

Economic dynamic analysis could help frame and inform new questions about the production of various kinds of literature. Many prominent analysts recognize that academics usually write because they enjoy the intellectual engagement, hope to influence the world, or seek recognition, with the prospect of royalties playing, at most, a minor role in their thinking. This might imply that copyright should be less robust in this area than in some other areas. That is, if monetary incentives play only a marginal role in securing production of new work, then one might want to maximize cheap access to academic work to spread its influence. Currently, we seem to be moving in

---

[89] *See* Driesen, *supra* note 52, at 8.
[90] *See* Lessig, *supra* note 49, at 156–58 (listing examples of cable companies' efforts to limit access and use through control of Internet "architecture").

the opposite direction. The cost of academic journals has risen so high that many university library directors find themselves discontinuing subscriptions to print journals. Even this, however, provides only a little relief, as costs of online subscriptions have become very high relative to the costs of publication. For institutions that can afford the subscription prices, students and scholars have easier access than ever before, because of the new technologies, but it would be worth studying whether access has declined in some academic institutions. If access has declined, one could employ retrospective economic dynamic analysis to figure out what caused this loss. Such an analysis could look at trends in the academic publishing industry, including mergers and consolidations, and the dynamics that have created these changes and evaluate potential reforms, whether in copyright, antitrust, or some other area, that could reverse this trend.

CONCLUSION

Intellectual property is about change over time, not about maximizing the satisfaction of existing preferences. It has a major goal of providing opportunities for economic growth. Economic dynamic analysis has already played a role in some of the leading work in the field and scholars could use it to make work in the field more rigorous and fruitful.

9

Size Matters: Antitrust, Empowerment, and Systemic Risk

Congress passed the antitrust statutes, as the term *antitrust* suggests, to limit the power of large economic entities.[1] Conversely, the antitrust statutes sought to empower consumers, farmers, and small business owners, all of whom felt threatened by the trusts. Thus, Congress considered whom the law should empower and whom it should disempower. Empowerment analysis constitutes one aspect of economic dynamic theory – its "public choice dimension." And antitrust law, as mentioned in the introduction, provides an example of Congress making a conscious decision about whom to empower.

This chapter explores the role of empowerment analysis in meeting economic dynamic theory's goal of avoiding systemic risks while keeping economic opportunities open. It begins by discussing the role of power in the thinking of the Congresses that created antitrust law and in early judicial decisions, showing, among other things, that the preservation of economic opportunities for small actors figured prominently among its goals. It then critically discusses the role of neoclassical law and economics in justifying empowerment of big business through very limited antitrust enforcement from an economic dynamic perspective. In particular, it criticizes the Chicago School emphasis on static efficiency at the expense of innovation, even in the face of a consensus among economists that dynamic efficiency is more important than static efficiency. It also shows that the Chicago School has tended to use justifications for empowering big business that enjoy limited support in the economics literature, but instead rest on faith in free markets (surpassing that of many economists), a faith undermined by attention to bounded rationality.

Finally, this chapter discusses the economic dynamics of deregulation's empowerment of large businesses as an aid to plotting the future of antitrust

---

[1] *See, e.g.*, Gerald Berk, *Louis D. Brandeis and the Making of Regulated Competition 1900–1932* 104–05 (2009).

and other business regulation. It shows that the concerns about the political, social, and economic power that animated early antitrust law have become more important because of the dynamics created by the end of government limits on corporate campaign contributions, the gross misdistribution of wealth in our economy, and the rise of too-big-to-fail institutions. It argues that efforts to limit the size and influence of large enterprises, especially in the financial sector, can help create economic opportunity and avoid systemic risk in the future. This chapter closes with some specific reform suggestions to illustrate how taking the dynamics of empowerment seriously could transform antitrust enforcement to help move us in a more positive direction than the direction we seem headed toward now.

ANTITRUST'S PURPOSES

Concerns about large entities' acquisition and use of economic, social, and political power permeate the antitrust statutes' legislative histories. Many, but not all, of these concerns involve the use of economic power to obtain advantages in the marketplace. Congress repeatedly expressed concern that the trusts would "oppress" individual consumers. Some of these consumers were also businesspeople. Thus, the high rates railroads charged farmers and other small businesspeople to ship their goods offer a paradigmatic example of the type of oppression Congress had in mind. Hence, one finds embedded within the concern for consumer welfare a concern for the viability of farms and other small businesses. Congress viewed the propensity of trusts to extract exorbitant rents from consumers, both product purchasers and businesspeople dependent on services offered by trusts, as "unfair," not just inefficient.

At the same time, Congress expressed concerns about large entities driving small competing firms out of business. It sought, in a variety of ways, to make competition fairer and avoid "predation."

Congressional suspicion of bigness, however, went beyond concerns about large entities wielding vast economic power in the marketplace. Congress expressed concern about the social and political ramifications of burgeoning corporations.[2]

A major social concern that emerges from the early judicial pronouncements and legislative history involves economic freedom.[3] The Supreme Court

[2] *See* Robert Pitofsky, "The Political Content of Antitrust," 127 *U. Pa. L. Rev.* 1051 (1979).
[3] *See* Jesse W. Markham, "Lessons for Competition Law from the Economic Crisis," 16 *Fordham J. Corp. & Fin. L.* 261, 266 n. 12 (mentioning that early antitrust cases frequently reflected the Sherman Act Congress's concern with providing "personal freedom to pursue economic opportunity").

in the *Standard Oil* case cited the danger of "slavery" stemming from capital aggregations.[4] While Congress did not spell out exactly what its members meant by their various statements about economic freedom, some reflection reveals that too much economic concentration can curtail the freedom of smaller economic actors in a variety of ways. First, market power can enable dominant firms to impose prices on suppliers that they have little choice but to accept. Second, proliferation of large enterprises can make it very hard, or impossible, for an entrepreneur to establish a new business.[5] Third, in an economy dominated by monopolies and oligopolies, most people cannot enjoy anything approximating the freedom and independence that business owners enjoy.[6] Instead, nearly everybody becomes an employee of large entities and must live with the loss of freedom and control associated with life in large bureaucracies.[7] And finally, consumers can lose the freedom to choose among multiple providers of goods and services when a monopoly or small oligopoly dominates markets.

The Supreme Court characterizes the Sherman Act as seeking "preservation of our democratic political... institutions," thereby reflecting the congressional concern with economic concentration's political ramifications.[8] While the legislative history does not spell out the precise nature of the threat the trusts (or other large economic entities) pose to democratic institutions, the economic dynamics of this do not appear difficult to explain. Large entities collect great sums of money from consumers. These entities can use some of this money to influence elections and lobby (or even bribe) government officials to protect their interests at the expense of everybody else. Thus, large entities acquire political power. In effect, consumers end up subsidizing well-funded efforts to create policies that may negatively influence their interests. Furthermore, very big companies employ large numbers of people, so

---

[4] *Standard Oil Company of New Jersey v. U.S.*, 221 U.S., 1, 83 (1911).

[5] *See* David W. Barnes, "Revolutionary Antitrust: Efficiency, Ideology, and Democracy," 58 *U. Cin. L. Rev.* 59, 61, 64 (1989) (discussing the willingness to accept "a reduction in the supply of goods and services" in exchange for an opportunity to "pursue ... the 'American Dream'" and suggesting that antitrust policy might protect self-employment and rights to enter a new line of business).

[6] *See U.S. v. Columbia Steel*, 334 U.S. 495, 536 (1948) (Douglas, J. dissenting) (stating that the antitrust law evinces hostility to the idea of concentration of power in a few people's hands and favors scattering economic power "into many hands").

[7] See *U.S. v. Falstaff Brewing Corp.*, 410 U.S. 526, 543 (1973) (Douglas J., concurring) (finding antitrust hostile to the notion of "a nation of clerks"). *Cf.* Lawrence Anthony Sullivan, "Economics and More Humanistic Disciplines: What are the Sources of Wisdom for Antitrust?," 125 *U. Pa. L. Rev.* 1214, 1223 (1977) (pointing out that people like decentralization of decision-making power).

[8] *Northern Pacific Railway v. U.S.*, 356 U.S. 1, 4 (1958).

harming almost any giant firm's economic interests will prove politically difficult. Hence, economic concentration creates an economic dynamic that favors increased corruption over time, making the political system increasingly unresponsive to most people's needs as it seeks to satisfy the demands of large entities with the capacity to make big donations to political campaigns and to lobby vigorously to protect their interests.[9]

Accordingly, trustbusters, such as Teddy Roosevelt, saw the trusts as a threat to the power of government and sought to constrain them for that reason. Modern public choice theory supports this fear, as it predicts that well-organized and powerful special interests will tend to dominate political decision making. Limiting the size and activities of large entities would therefore limit this threat to democracy. Hence, the Congresses that created antitrust law implicitly relied on an empowerment analysis in constructing antitrust law.

Congress believed that a laissez-faire policy empowers large entities at the expense of smaller economic actors and governments. Congress chose to enact antitrust laws to empower consumers and small business people at the expense of large firms.

In addition, Congress examined the shape of change over time and decided to change direction from one of ever-increasing concentration of economic power to one of preserving space for farmers and small business owners while protecting consumers. Thus, for example, the Congress that passed the Clayton Act feared a "rising tide" of economic concentration.[10] The view that the process of economic concentration, if not checked early on, would, like a tidal wave, simply sweep away all impediments to wholly unacceptable economic domination led the Clayton Act Congress to favor curtailing mergers in their "incipiency" – that is, long before they produced monopoly-like effects.[11] One might ask why it was necessary to curtail mergers that did not themselves produce undesirable effects just because they might lead to more mergers that would produce bad effects. One can justify this in two ways. First, it may reflect some modesty about regulators' ability to predict mergers' bad effects, a kind of procompetitive precautionary principle. Second, the incipiency doctrine reasonably addresses the problem of economic concentration's political impact. Large entities may acquire sufficient political power to

---

[9] *See* Barnes, *supra* note 5, at 70 (discussing about antitrust as a means of "for ensuring that views of private citizens will not be lost"); Berk, *supra* note 1, at 108–09 (quoting Woodrow Wilson as saying that monopolies are "more apt to control government than be controlled by it"); *Louis K. Ligget Co. v. Lee*, 288 U.S. 517, 565 (1933) (Brandeis J., dissenting) (stating that large corporations sometimes "dominate the state").

[10] *Brown Shoe Company v. U.S.*, 370 U.S. 294, 315 (1962).

[11] *Id.* at 317–18.

prevent attempts to limit their efforts to grow still larger through anticompetitive mergers or predation.[12] The incipiency doctrine drowns monsters before they become too powerful to control. The antitrust laws, then, seek a change of direction in response to an undesirable trend toward economic concentration.

The antitrust laws reflect a commitment to a particular economic dynamic: the dynamic of competition. Congress believed that competition would force producers to offer goods and services at low prices and foster innovation and progress. This makes sense because in a highly competitive market, producers live in fear of losing market share to competitors and therefore feel compelled to improve their offerings to avoid losing out. Greed also motivates progress in a competitive market, as the path to great riches usually requires innovation and certainly involves improvement. Hence, an economic dynamic that Congress implicitly understood undergirds its preference for competitive markets.

Congress wrote antitrust law to counter an economic dynamic it considered politically, socially, and economically dangerous in favor of one that would maximize economic opportunity and avoid wildly inequitable distribution of wealth and power.[13] It considered the preference for empowering small actors consistent with consumer protection.

THE CHICAGO SCHOOL AND THE ABANDONMENT OF ANTITRUST'S TRADITIONAL GOALS

The founders of the Chicago School of antitrust famously argued that antitrust should abandon practically all of the goals mentioned previously, instead adopting the single goal of maximizing efficiency.[14] Robert Bork, a leading law and economics scholar in this area, equates the goal of maximizing efficiency with antitrust law's traditional goal of protecting consumer welfare.[15] But scholars have shown that the two goals differ.[16]

Bork focuses on two types of efficiency, allocative efficiency and productive efficiency. Allocative efficiency involves the relationship of production

---

[12] *See* Darren Bush, "Too Big to Bail: The Role of Antitrust in Distressed Industries," 77 *Antitrust L. J.* 277, 280 (2010).

[13] *See* Barnes, *supra* note 5, at 69 and n. 24 (citing legislative history suggesting an intent to leave opportunities open to the "little fellow" who wants to go into business).

[14] *Cf.* Richard A. Posner, *Antitrust Law: An Economic Perspective* 4 (1976) (arguing that efficiency should be antitrust law's sole goal, because the only other competing goal advanced consistently, protection of small business, has no merit).

[15] Robert H. Bork, *The Antitrust Paradox: A Policy at War With Itself* 90–106 (1978).

[16] Barnes, *supra* note 5, at 73; *see* John B. Kirkwood & Robert H. Lande, "The Chicago School Foundation is Flawed: Antitrust Protects Consumers, not Efficiency," in *How the Chicago School Overshot the Mark: The Effect of Conservative Economic Analysis on U.S. Antitrust* 89–97 (Robert Pitofsky, ed., 2008).

costs to the benefits delivered to consumers. The term *allocative* captures this efficiency goal's aim of allocating resources optimally among competing uses. Productive efficiency corresponds more to a lay understanding of what efficiency means. It refers to producing a given quantity of goods at the least possible cost.[17]

Neither allocative nor productive efficiency necessarily corresponds with protection of consumer welfare, an important goal of the antitrust statutes. One can see this most readily in the case of productive efficiency. A monopolist may produce goods at a very low price, but sell them at a high price to consumers. If a competitive market would result in higher production costs but lower costs to consumers, a competitive market would prove better for consumers, but not for efficient production. So productive efficiency does not necessarily improve consumer welfare. Consumer welfare does not coincide with allocative efficiency either. The concept of allocative efficiency focuses not on consumer welfare alone, but on a relationship between production costs and consumer benefits.[18] Economists typically define an allocatively efficient transaction as one that equates costs and benefits at the margin. Economists identify competitive markets with consumer welfare, because such markets tend to produce "consumer surplus," a value to consumers greater than the price paid for the good or service producing the value. Transactions generating benefits exceeding, rather than equaling, marginal costs maximizes consumer surplus.

Robert Bork quite clearly advocates an antitrust law that abandons the goal of maintaining consumer surplus, which measures consumer welfare.

---

[17] *See* Wikipedia, http://en.wikipedia.org/wiki/Productive_efficiency (2010); Timothy J. Coelli, D.S. Prasada Rao, Christopher J. O'Donnell, & George E. Battese, *An Introduction to Efficiency and Productivity Analysis* 3 (2005) (defining technical efficiency, which is sometimes treated as synonymous with productive efficiency); Bork, *supra* note 15, at 91* (defining productive efficiency in terms of "effective use of resources by particular firms"). Although I have offered a very simple definition, which corresponds to what most people mean when they use this term, economists do not agree about what the term means. *See* Bork, *supra* note 15, at 104 (claiming that many economists do not understand the term). Bork, except in the footnote cited here, defines the term in a confusing way. He defines it as any activity that produces wealth. Id. But wealth-producing activities can be either productively efficient or inefficient. He then quotes from definitions, not of productive efficiency, but of economic efficiency generally. Id at 105. In the end, he claims that a firm's success in the market provides a measure of productive efficiency, but then seeks to distinguish success from profitability, leaving it unclear what measure of success he has in mind. Id. at 105–06. In any case, a measurement method is not a definition. Defining productive efficiency in terms of market success makes it hard to distinguish market power from efficient production. His definition seems like more of an ideological attempt to justify firm "success" than a technically sound definition of a concept.

[18] *See* Richard Schmalensee, "Thoughts on the Chicago Legacy in U.S. Antitrust," in *How The Chicago School Overshot the Mark*, *supra* note 16, at 12–13.

He considers the question of whether producers or consumers capture the difference between production costs and the value consumers place on goods and service a distributional question that should play no role in antitrust policy.[19] In doing this, he largely abandons a major goal of antitrust law, which involves protecting consumers from high prices, substituting a goal of maximizing overall wealth for society defined in efficiency terms. In Bork's world, it does not matter if some producers become fat and rich off monopoly profits while farmers lose the family business because railroads charge shipping rates well above marginal costs, as long as output does not decline.

His argument for ignoring consumer surplus as merely distributional makes clear that he, and by extension, the Chicago School of law and economics, has abandoned another major concern of Congress, fairness.[20] Bork argues that the legislative history shows that efficiency constitutes antitrust law's sole goal. But other scholars have not found this argument at all convincing.[21] Congress regularly spoke of fairness in passing antitrust legislation, thus evincing a concern about distribution (the concentration of wealth).

The Chicago School's relentless focus on efficiency as the sole goal of antitrust provided a conceptual underpinning for recommendations to abandon almost all antitrust enforcement. And this recommendation has influenced courts and antitrust enforcers, even though they have adopted only part of the Chicago School's agenda.[22]

According to the Chicago School, antitrust law generally should prohibit only price fixing agreements and some extremely large horizontal mergers. This leaves out many anticompetitive practices that have traditionally fallen within antitrust's domain. For example, antitrust law has traditionally regarded tie-in arrangements, in which a seller demands that a buyer of one product purchase a second product as well, as anticompetitive. The Chicago School generally treats tie-in arrangements as efficient price discrimination.[23] Antitrust law has generally treated resale price maintenance, in which sellers and buyers agree to floors on resale prices, division of sales territories, or deals establishing exclusive outlets for products, as anticompetitive. The Chicago School replies that such actions might benefit potential purchasers by facilitating information

[19] Bork, *supra* note 15, at 110–11.
[20] *Cf.* Robert H. Lande, "Wealth Transfers as the Original and Primary Concern of Antitrust: The Efficiency Interpretation Challenged," 34 *Hastings L. Rev.* 65, 70, 115 (1983).
[21] *See, e.g.,* Kirkwood & Lande, *supra* note 16, at 89–97; Pitofsky, *supra* note 2; Lawrence Anthony Sullivan, "Economics and More Humanistic Disciplines: What are the Sources of Wisdom," 125 *U. Pa. L. Rev.* 1214 (1977).
[22] *How The Chicago School Overshot the Mark, supra* note 16.
[23] *See* Richard A. Posner, "The Chicago School of Antitrust," 127 *U. Pa. L. Rev.* 925, 926 (1979).

flow to consumers.[24] Antitrust law has traditionally prohibited predatory pricing – below-cost pricing designed to drive competitors out of business. The Chicago School teaches that predatory pricing will prove both rare (because unprofitable) and ineffective (because targets can fight back and new entrants can substitute for bankrupt competitors), and suggests that it therefore merits little antitrust scrutiny.[25]

The Chicago School has largely rejected the idea that size matters, suggesting that most mergers merit approval under antitrust law. Specifically, it largely rejects prohibition of "vertical" mergers – those that integrate manufacturing with distribution.[26] It also evinces much more acceptance of horizontal mergers – mergers among businesses carrying out the same type of activity – than antitrust law traditionally exhibited.

While a minute analysis of all of these positions will contribute little to our understanding of neoclassical law and economics generally, examination of the rationales undergirding some of these positions will help us understand neoclassical law and economics more deeply. The Chicago School's "results" depend heavily upon the ideological assumptions of the law professors leading the Chicago School. If one has faith in free markets, it makes sense to assume that firms behave more or less as a rational actor with perfect information would. One not possessing much faith in markets would regard such assumptions as too unrealistic to form the basis for sound policy, even if they can lead to some useful insights on occasion. Economists themselves, although usually favorably disposed toward markets as well,[27] tend to adjust their assumptions to take reality into account, at least occasionally. So incongruities have always existed between the Chicago School's views and the teachings of many economists not ensconced in law schools.[28]

For example, the Chicago School view of mergers depends heavily on rational actor assumptions at the firm level. The Chicago School builds on an unobjectionable insight from economic theory, that sometimes economies of

---

[24] Id. at 926–27.

[25] Id. at 927.

[26] Id.

[27] F.M. Scherer, "Conservative Economics and Antitrust: A Variety of Influences," in *How the Chicago School Overshot the Mark, supra* note 16, at 31 (describing "virtually all" U.S. economists as "conservatives," in the sense that they "believe in free markets and capitalism as instruments of discovery and engines of progress").

[28] *See* Posner, *supra* note 14, at 4 (expressing his awareness that some of "the economic views presented" in his book are "highly controversial" among economists); Bork, *supra* note 15, at 117 (noting disagreement with "some economists"); Schmalansee, *supra* note 18, in *How the Chicago School Overshot the Mark, supra* note 16, at 22 (stating that many of the Chicago School's 1970s proposals are "inconsistent with current economic thinking").

scale can make bigness economical. They therefore infer that many mergers
might enhance efficiency. Given that inference, one might expect the Chicago
School's leaders in this area, Richard Posner and Robert Bork, to call for an
analysis of whether a particular proposed merger would enhance or diminish
efficiency. Both of them, however, argue against this solution on the grounds
that courts and enforcers cannot obtain the information needed to analyze a
particular proposed merger's effect on efficiency.[29] This reliance upon CBA
as a heuristic to signal the objectivity and rigor of the law and economics
enterprise, combined with a refusal to perform any actual CBA, characterizes
law and economics as a whole, even if economists outside the legal academy
do sometimes carry out CBA. This refusal reflects not obstinacy or disingenu-
ousness on the part of law and economics scholars, but simply the fact that the
project of calculating costs and benefits usually proves deeply problematic,
because law looks forward to an uncertain future.[30] So, faced with this problem, Bork and the rest of the Chicago School assume that firms behave more
or less like rational actors to derive legal policies from neoclassical economic
theory.[31]

Based on this firm-level rational actor assumption, Bork imagines that firms
choosing mergers over internal growth must have figured out that a merger will
prove more efficient than internal growth.[32] The likelihood that market actors'
chosen methods will likely prove efficient provides a basis for the Chicago
School's position favoring no restrictions on mergers, except in cases of very
large horizontal mergers.

Economists studying actual data about mergers do not find this particular
manifestation of faith in the prescience and wisdom of markets (or, more precisely, market actors) terribly convincing.[33] They just see too many cases where

---

[29] See Bork, *supra* note 15, at 124, 219 (stating that the "trade-off" between output restriction
and enhanced efficiency cannot be measured); Posner, *supra* note 14, at 112 (characterizing
efficiency measurement as an "intractable subject for litigation").

[30] See Bork, *supra* note 15, at 125–27 (explaining why direct measurement of merger efficiency
poses enormous challenges).

[31] See id. at 120 (relying on the assumption that firms behave as if rationally maximizing profits
with perfect information).

[32] Id. at 206–07.

[33] See, e.g., F.M. Scherer, *Industrial Market Structure and Economic Performance* 103 (1970);
Spencer Waller, "Corporate Governance and Competition Policy," Loyola University of
Chicago School of Law Research Paper No. 204–006, available at http://wwww.ssrn.com/
abstract=1681673, 43 (2011) (discussing "mounting evidence" in the corporate finance litera-
ture that mergers destroy shareholder value); James Fanto, "Braking the Merger Momentum:
Reforming Corporate Law Governing Mega-Mergers," 49 *Buff. L. Rev.* 249 (2001); James A.
Fanto, "Quasi-Rationality in Action: A Study of Psychological Factors in Merger Decision
Making," 62 *Ohio St. L.J.* 1333 (2001).

mergers destroy long-term value. Accordingly, many students of mergers abandon the model of rational profit-maximizing firms. For example, many analysts note that although firms might have an incentive to choose only efficient mergers, a countervailing incentive exists. Managers can sometimes make a great deal of money from mergers, even if the merger harms shareholders.[34] This illustrates another ambiguity of the rational actor model, that the choice of which actor to make the subject of analysis has a large impact on "results."

Moreover, some economists implicitly recognize the value of an economic dynamic analysis of merger questions. Close observers of mergers doubt that merger proponents regularly act rationally in the economic sense. They describe a form of bounded, and rather feeble, rationality that appears all too familiar to those of us who have dealt with businesses that have more in common with Dilbert than with neoclassical economic models.[35] Corporate leaders may choose mergers because their egos demand the satisfaction of building empires and their hubris makes them imagine (incorrectly) that they can successfully integrate complex operations that defy efficient management.[36] For example, even *Forbes* magazine, a publication not noted for an especially critical stance toward big business, published an article characterizing Citicorp, the product of multiple mergers, as "a dysfunctional unmanageable behemoth."[37] All this echoes the views of Louis Brandeis, who championed economic efficiency but saw the formation of giant trusts as destroying economic value.[38] Brandeis, too, assumed bounded rationality, explaining in

---

[34] *See generally* Scherer, *supra* note 33, at 35–36, 114–15; *U.S. v. Falstaff Brewing*, 410 U.S. 526, 540–45 (1973) (Douglas J., concurring) (pointing out that the increase in business volume can enrich managers of a large enterprise when creation of a large enterprise does not enhance efficiency).

[35] *See* Amanda P. Reeves & Maurice E. Stucke, "Behavioral Antitrust," 86 *Ind. L.J.* 1527, 1540 (2011) (discussing the bounded rationality model in antitrust).

[36] *See* Scherer, supra note 33, at 112; 120–22; Jonathan B. Baker & Carl Shapiro, Reinvigorating Horizontal Merger Enforcement, in *How the Chicago School Overshot the Mark*, *supra* note 16, 235, 256; Waller, *supra* note 33, at 46–47; Maurice E. Stucke, "Behavioral Economists at the Gate: Antitrust in the Twenty-First Century," 38 *Loy. U. Chi. L.J.* 514 (2007); Troy A. Paredes, "Too Much Pay, Too Much Deference: Behavioral Corporate Finance, CEOs, and Corporate Governance," 32 *Fla. St. U.L. Rev.* 673 (2005); Ellen R. Auster & Mark K. Sirower, "The Dynamics of Merger and Acquisition Waves: A Three-Stage Conceptual Framework With Implications for Practice," 2 *J. Applied Behav. Sci.* 216 (2002); Matthew Hayward & Donald Hambrick, "Explaining Premiums Paid for Large Acquisitions: Evidence of CEO Hubris," 42 *Admin. Sci. Q.* 103 (1997).

[37] Peter C. Beller, "Escape from Citicorp: Can the U.S. Collect its Paper Gain on Citicorp Shares" (December 10, 2009), available at http://www.forbes.com/2009/12/10/citigroup-government-bailout-tarp-capital.html.

[38] *See* Berk, *supra* note 1; Louis Brandeis, *Other People's Money and How the Bankers Use It* (1914).

congressional hearings leading to passage of the Federal Trade Commission Act that few businesses knew enough about their own costs of operations to make efficient choices.[39] He saw antitrust as a means of steering businesses away from "predation" and toward efficient practices.

Thus, economic theory cannot tell us what merger policy to adopt, even assuming that efficiency should rule. If we choose one economic theory, one based on the egotistical manager seeking to maximize his or her own psychic and pecuniary gains, we should assume that mergers generally prove efficiency destroying. If we choose a rational actor economic model, focusing on the firm rather than on individual decision makers within the firm, we might presume that mergers are a great idea. The data, though showing some evidence of successful mergers, do suggest that an awful lot of them reflect executive folly. This would suggest a strong anti-merger policy.

Antitrust scholars generally admire the Chicago School contribution to the debate on mergers, even if they do not agree with many of its positions. They tend to view the Warren Court's disapproval of even fairly small mergers as going overboard and thank the Chicago School for correcting that excess. A good case exists to impose some limits on the law's opposition to mergers. If there were none, then absorption of a small bankrupt firm with useful assets by a company able to make use of them, or even the formation of a small partnership among formerly competing businesspeople, would violate the law. These examples are not realistic, because limitations on enforcement resources would make that kind of overreach virtually impossible, even if legal doctrine allowed it. But the Chicago School point that these enforcers must somehow limit the law's merger prohibitions seems undeniable, and its longing for a principled precise way of defining such limits understandable. Yet, the Chicago School looks in vain for economics to supply definitive rules to resolve these questions. As even Posner and Bork admit and economists readily and regularly confess, once we move from questions about monopoly's effects to the question of how much of a tendency toward oligopoly we should tolerate, economics provides no clear answers.[40] In other words, the results law and economics generate depend upon the assumptions its leaders choose to make.

Chicago School law and economics also famously rejects vigorous policing of predatory pricing, on the grounds that rational actors will rarely eschew profits and that if they try, new entrants will likely enter the market, making it impossible for them to recoup their losses after they drive their targets from the market. The Supreme Court embraced this view in *Matsushita Electric Industrial Co., Ltd. v. Zenith Radio Corp* and in *Brooke v. Group Ltd. v. Brown and Williamson Tobacco Corp.*, describing such schemes as "rarely tried, and even more rarely successful."[41] Modern economics, however, partly because of employment of economic dynamic models employing strategic thinking and imperfect information, now rejects the Chicago School view on this.[42] The relevant work eschews static analysis based on perfect information in favor of a dynamic analysis based on imperfect and asymmetic information.[43] The analysis concludes that predation can signal small firms – and, perhaps more important, their creditors – that market conditions are not favorable for investment, even if they are.[44] By employing more realistic assumptions, this more dynamic work has helped explain why recent studies have observed predation empirically.[45]

It seems very clear that a set of assumptions (such as the rational actor and perfect information assumptions) reflecting the view that market actors' decisions generally serve the public undermines a body of law designed to change the direction of markets over time, so that they function differently – that is, in a more decentralized competitive way. To the extent that a set of assumptions should guide legal analysis, they should, according to economic dynamic theory, reflect characterizations of rationality and information based on actual studies of norms and behavior at firms. Although the economics shows some sign of moving in that economic dynamic direction, the simplistic neoclassical law and economics emanating from Chicago continues to have an enormous influence on policy.

INNOVATION AND STATIC EFFICIENCY

More fundamentally, the emphasis on static allocative efficiency that the Chicago School has insisted on focuses on the relatively trivial at the expense of the more important. Economists agree that innovation, a product of dynamic

---

[41] *Matsushita Electric Industrial Corp. v. Zenith Radio Corp.*, 475 U.S. 574, 590 (1986).
[42] *See* Patrick Bolton, Joseph F. Brodley, & Michael H. Riordan, "Predatory Pricing: Strategic Theory and Legal Policy," 88 *Geo. L. J.* 2239, 2241 (2000) (describing the view that predatory pricing "can be a successful and fully rational business strategy" as "the consensus view in modern economics").
[43] Id. at 2247.
[44] Id. at 2248.
[45] Id. at 2244–47 (discussing empirical evidence); *cf.* Shubha Ghosh & Darren Bush, "Predatory Conduct and Predatory Legislation: Exclusionary Tactics in the Airline Markets," 45 *Hous. L. Rev.* 343, 347–48 (2008) (noting that predatory pricing was recognized in articles contemporaneous with the *Matsushita* decision).

change, is likely much more important than static allocative efficiency (and short-term productive efficiency) from the standpoint of wealth creation.[46]

I do not mean to resolve here the debate between the view associated with Joseph Schumpeter that large businesses innovate better because of their ability to fund research and development and those who think that atomistic markets do best.[47] It suffices for present purposes to point out that this debate about innovation is more important than the debate about static efficiency and that the evidence so far does not provide a solid case for abandoning the preferences of the Congresses passing antitrust laws for small business over monopoly and oligopoly.

Frederic Scherer, one of the leading industrial economists, concludes that competition increases innovation within limits.[48] Fragmented markets are especially good for fast-paced innovation and radical innovations. Furthermore, monopolies can suppress significant innovations.[49] A frequently cited example involves the old AT&T monopoly, which for a long time prevented such simple advances as the introduction of push-button and other new styles of phones. Only after the government broke up AT&T did we see cell phones and other major advances in telephony.[50] Although some evidence suggests that monopolies and oligopolies can make slow advances in knowledge pretty well, they can also discourage rivals.[51] Established businesses often have significant investments in infrastructure and skills revolving around some already established technology. This can make them blind, inept, or hostile toward radical innovations that can greatly hasten advances within society at the expense of their core technologies.[52] A famous example of established business's blindness toward radical innovations involves IBM's early failure to appreciate the importance of the personal computer, which largely destroyed the value of its mainframe computing business. Louis Brandeis, one of antitrust law's originators, shared modern economists' skepticism of size helping with innovation, characterizing "modern trade combination[s']" opposition to new processes and products as a "well-known fact."[53]

---

[46] *See* F.M. Scherer, "Antitrust, Efficiency, and Progress," 62 *N.Y.U. L. Rev.* 998–99, 1002 (1987) (stating that deadweight losses are very small, so we should mainly be concerned about dynamic efficiency and "x-efficiency" [a synonym for productive efficiency], but reflecting doubt that antitrust has a big effect on x-efficiency).

[47] *Cf.* id., at 1012 (noting that most R&D has relatively modest cost).

[48] Id. at 1011.

[49] Id.

[50] Id.

[51] Id.

[52] *See* Clayton M. Christensen, *The Innovator's Dilemma: When New Technologies Cause Great Firms to Fail* (1997).

[53] Brandeis, *supra* note 36.

The standard objection to focusing heavily on innovation involves the difficulty in analyzing any particular merger's influence on innovation rates. Yet we have already seen that we cannot reliably analyze merger efficiencies either. So this difficulty cannot justify focusing on the unimportant (static efficiency) instead of the important (innovation over time).

DISTRIBUTIONAL CONSIDERATIONS AND ECONOMIC OPPORTUNITY

The foregoing critique, in a bit of a bow to the Chicago School, focused on wealth maximization, suggesting that an economic dynamic approach would better serve that goal. Yet there is little evidence that wealth maximization matters much to human happiness.[54] Past a certain minimum point, increased riches do not significantly increase happiness.

Economic opportunity, however, matters a lot. It creates the adaptive efficiency needed to enable society to rise to new challenges. It nurtures the spirit of entrepreneurism. It gives people hope. And it makes freedom an economic reality.

This is reason enough to validate, within reasonable limits, the late nineteenth and early twentieth century congressional preference for an antitrust regime that protects small businesses and approaches questions of how much size and potentially predatory practices matter with healthy suspicion of the value of economic concentration.[55] We should care more about the creation of economic opportunity for new businesses than we care about maximizing the production or efficiency of the old. The economic culture's openness is extremely important.[56]

---

[54] *See* Mark Sagoff, *Price, Principle, and the Environment* 102 (2004) (pointing out that "virtually all . . . empirical evidence" shows "no correlation" between preference satisfaction and well-being "after basic needs are met"); E. Diener & R. Biswas-Diener, "Will Money Increase Subjective Well Being: A Literature Review and Guide to Needed Research," 57 *Soc. Indicators Res.* 119 (2002); R. Easterlin, "Will Raising the Incomes of All Increase the Happiness of All?," 27 *J. Econ. Behav. Org.* 35 (1995); Robert H. Frank, *Luxury Fever: Why Money Fails to Satisfy in an Era of Success* 6 (1999) (arguing that after a certain threshold has been reached increases in material wealth do not correlate with increases in subjective well-being); *see also* L. van Boven & T. Gilovich, "To Do or to Have? That is the Question," 85 *J. Personality & Soc. Psychol.* 1193 (2003) (finding that experiences rather than possessions bring happiness); John Kenneth Galbraith, *The Affluent Society* 131, 145 (1960) (questioning the link between increased production and consumption and increased welfare).

[55] *See, e.g.*, Brandeis, *supra* note 38, at 62 (stating that even a showing that interlocking directorships were "efficient" would not remove his objections to them, since the "Money Trust" must be abolished).

[56] *Accord* Irwin Seltzer, "Some Practical Thoughts About Entry," in *How the Chicago School Overshot the Mark, supra* note 16, at 24–25.

The preference for maximizing economic opportunity over maximizing efficiency found in the antitrust statutes' legislative histories makes at least as much sense today as it did at the time of these laws' enactment, because of the importance of distributional issues in today's American economy. The period of maximum antitrust enforcement coincided with an economic expansion coupled with a reasonable degree of equality. Although this does not even suggest that antitrust enforcement caused post–World War II economic growth, it does show that vigorous antitrust enforcement does not prevent economic growth. This period saw the growth of a middle class consisting of a large number of people enjoying a level of material welfare that no large mass of people has ever experienced before in human history. Whereas most societies throughout human history involve misery and impoverishment for the masses with great wealth for a very select few, our society during the post–World War II era tempered wealth with high tax rates and ushered millions into membership in a relatively prosperous middle class.

This middle-class lifestyle and our tradition of rough equality has come under assault. Foreign competition has put pressure on firms to reduce wages and benefits; unions that played an important role in creating a broad middle class have become decrepit; and the government has slashed tax rates, especially for the rich, thereby depriving government of the means to maintain basic infrastructure and educational services. The 2008 financial crises wrecked the finances of many formerly middle-class households, producing widespread unemployment and a wave of foreclosures throwing people out of their homes.

Inequality in America, as measured by gini coefficients, has grown so that our pattern of income distribution no longer resembles that of a developed country.[57] In 2005, U.S. inequality rivaled that of Brazil, Mexico, and Russia.[58] By 2008, the U.S. gini coefficient ranked among the highest in the world.[59]

The middle class has lost ground since 1973, when the average income of 90 percent of Americans (excluding the richest 10 percent) reached a peak of $33,000.[60] And the poor, in recent decades, have seen an even greater decline in income than the middle class.[61] The rich, however, became much richer

---

[57] David Kay Johnston, *Free Lunch: How the Wealthiest Americans Enrich Themselves at Government Expense (and Stick You with the Bill)* 11 (2007).

[58] Id. at 11.

[59] *See* Max Fisher, "U.S. Ranks Near Bottom of Income Inequality," September 19, 2011, http://www.theatlantic.com/international/archive/2011/09/map-us-ranks.

[60] Johnston, *supra* note 57, at 10.

[61] *See* id. at 274 (showing that the bottom 50 percent of average income saw a decline in earnings exceeding that of the bottom 90 percent, both in absolute dollar value and in percentage terms between 1980 and 2004).

during this period.[62] Over a thirty-year period ending in 2005, the bottom 90 percent of Americans saw their incomes decline by 3 percent, while the top 1 percent of Americans, people with average incomes of $1.1 million a year in 2005, saw their incomes more than double.[63] The superrich, a group of just 30,000 people with average incomes of more than $25 million a year in 2005, saw their incomes increase more than sixfold during this period.[64]

During the period between 1980 and 2005, the economy more than doubled in size in real terms.[65] Perhaps some of this gain reflects increased economic efficiency. But this increase in wealth did little or nothing for 90 percent of Americans. There is a simple reason for this failure: the gains went to the rich. By 2005, the rich owned the largest share of national income since the end of the Roaring Twenties – the decade immediately preceding the last Depression prior to 2008.[66] During the period of vigorous antitrust enforcement from 1950 to 1975, each person on average in the top 1 percent of earners got four dollars of additional income for every extra one dollar earned by the bottom 90 percent. Between 1960 and 1985 (a period including vigorous enforcement and some of the swing away from vigorous enforcement), this ratio shifted from 4:1 to 17:1. Between 1981 and 2005, the period when the Chicago School triumphed, the top 1 percent got $5,000 of additional income for every new dollar going to the bottom 90 percent. Hence, the key question for our time is not how to make production more efficient; it is how to have a fair open economic system that provides real economic opportunities for the 90 percent of Americans who have not benefited from the national wealth increases of the decades preceding the 2008 crash and how to avoid more debacles.

In this context, the preservation of economic opportunity for individuals of ordinary means is more important than ever. Indeed, for most people (meaning 90 percent of Americans), national wealth increases have virtually no value. Although they theoretically benefit from new products and price declines even if they earn less, the fact that their *real wages* have declined suggests that these benefits have not offset their lost incomes. Often mergers have maximized profits for shareholders by bringing in new management prepared to cut jobs and/or wages and benefits. Such cuts often can enhance efficiency and, in some cases, prove essential to firm survival in the face of international competition. The presence of so many mergers that have produced lower valuations for the merged firms, however, casts some doubt on whether all

---

[62] Id. at 276 (the rich are getting fabulously richer, while the vast majority are being "savaged").
[63] Id.
[64] Id.
[65] Id. at 8.
[66] Id. at 275.

of these sorts of cuts are efficiency enhancing. One problem with a market for corporate control involves the ability of people to seize control of businesses that they have no experience with and then choose the most obvious efficiency-enhancement methods, such as wage reductions or layoffs, because they simply do not have the skills to improve actual operations. Whether efficiency enhancing or not, mergers have contributed to the inequality that has emerged as a major economic problem in the United States.[67] As inequality grows, so does the importance of keeping economic opportunities open to people, including the opportunities to start new businesses. This argues for making openness and freedom, not just enhanced efficiency, a major goal of antitrust. If efficiency means enriching a tiny elite in society while chucking the masses from the middle class, it might be a bad thing. We could sacrifice some efficiency at the margins to create a society with greater economic opportunity.

Economic dynamic theory's recognition of law as a framework, rather than as determinant of efficiency, implies that antitrust law usually has only a marginal role in business efforts to enhance efficiency. If antitrust authorities deny a merger application in a case where the merged entity would permit the management to realize certain efficiencies, managers may realize these efficiencies, or others of equal or greater value, through other kinds of agreements or other changes in operation. Accordingly, section 10 of the 2010 Merger Guidelines issued by the Federal Trade Commission and the Department of Justice already declines to recognize an efficiency if firms can realize the *same efficiency* without a merger. And prohibiting an efficiency-enhancing merger does not necessarily imply a loss of overall efficiency, even if firms must forgo the particular efficiency the merger achieves. For firms can often find new efficiencies to make up for the one forgone. Hence, recognition of law as a framework should lead enforcers to place little weight on potential efficiency gains from mergers.

The suggestion that we should care about economic opportunity because of antitrust law's traditional distributional concerns will invite the usual objection that we should address distributional concerns through taxing and spending. This objection rings especially hollow in an environment in which the rich enjoy so much political influence that many politicians consider significant (and often insignificant) tax hikes anathema, even in the face of a fiscal crisis.

---

[67] *See* Bush, *supra* note 12, at 287 (pointing out that the structure–conduct–performance school of antitrust maintains that "concentrated market structures lead to a redistribution – or perhaps a 'maldistribution' – of income").

POLITICAL POWER

The concern about economic concentration's potential influence on democracy that animated the creators of the antitrust statutes has become extraordinarily salient in recent decades. Congressional efforts to staunch the flow of corporate money into political campaigns in the 1970s and since have largely failed, thanks to a First Amendment jurisprudence that treats money as if it were speech, rather than just a means of amplifying speech's impact.[68] Campaign spending has risen grossly – and with it, the time elected officials spend raising money.

This period has given rise to a vast increase in government spending benefiting the wealthy at the expense of everybody else.[69] Much of this spending takes the form of subsidies and tax breaks to benefit big business, often at the expense of smaller competitors.[70] The states, desperate to attract jobs, have engaged in a vast bidding war to attract investments, producing expenditures probably exceeding $70 billion a year that produce few, if any, net economic benefits.[71] Although this subsidy war began with manufacturing plants, billions of dollars of subsidies now go to big-box retail stores, which offer only low-wage jobs and generally obtain revenue by taking business away from smaller retailers, rather than by expanding the pie.[72] These incentives do not generally affect overall national investment or employment levels. They do, however, substantially influence state revenues, shifting tax burdens from businesses to individuals and weakening state and local capacity to provide education, infrastructure, and public safety, the foundations of economic growth.

While a rational actor model does not explain this, as the expenditures often outweigh any conceivable benefit to the state, the economic dynamics explain this phenomenon well. States face a prisoner's dilemma. While they would benefit from cooperating to get rid of tax credits and subsidies for big business, officials in each individual state fear that their state will lose out if they do not offer expensive inducements while competing states are doing so. Elected officials may risk losing elections if they do not appear to be doing all they can

---

[68] *See Buckley v. Valeo*, 424 U.S. 1 (1976).

[69] *See* Johnston, *supra* note 57.

[70] *See* id. at 95–109 (discussing an example of subsidies for big outdoor supply chain stores that compete with small shops).

[71] See Kenneth P. Thomas, *Investment Incentives and the Global Competition for Capital* 106 (2010); David Cay Johnston, "On the Dole Corporate Style," January 4, 2011, available at http://tax.com/taxcom/taxblog.nsf/Permalink/UBEN-8CSNLH?OpenDocument.

[72] *See* Johnston, *supra* note 57, at 100 (discussing the $1 billion of known subsidies to Walmart, and statements by Walmart spokesmen suggesting that received subsidies might be 14 times larger).

to attract business to their state. On the other hand, passing out state money can lead to lucrative campaign contributions. Hence, one can predict that this sort of subtle corruption will increase over time, as the economic dynamics favor this trend.

As corporations experience the benefits of corporate welfare, their willingness to make campaign contributions in hopes of gaining yet more influence will increase. For many years, Congress and the states limited – and, at times, even prohibited – corporate campaign contributions as part of an effort to limit large corporations' power in political life.[73] But in 2010, the Supreme Court, in *Citizens United v. Federal Election Commission*,[74] overruled two prior precedents, *McConnell v. Federal Election Comm'n*[75] and *Austin v. Michigan Chamber of Commerce*,[76] to find limits on corporate campaign contributions unconstitutional.

In doing so, the Court rejected the idea it espoused in *Austin* that the "corrosive and distorting effects of immense aggregations of wealth" on the political process justified some restrictions on corporate campaign contributions.[77] In short, it rejected any place for empowerment analysis in the First Amendment.

In the wake of this decision, corporate campaign contributions have increased to unprecedented levels. Whether because of these contributions' importance to reelection of politicians or other reasons, Congress and state legislatures have, in the wake of the financial crisis, done precious little that might tread on corporate interests. Congress extended tax breaks for high-income individuals, many of whom work for large corporations, in spite of the massive budget deficit the crisis had created. Many states, likewise, ruled out tax increases as a means of contributing to deficit reduction, focusing instead on slashing spending on schools, Medicare, and other programs generating benefits for ordinary citizens. The government, as we saw, responded to the crisis by bailing out the banks. It did not, however, vigorously implement law designed to encourage workouts of mortgages, which banks did not favor.[78] In the aftermath of the crisis, many economists called for the breakup of banks that had become too big to fail, a standard International Monetary Fund

---

[73] *Citizens United v. Federal Election Comm'n*, 130 S. Ct. 876, 900 (2010) (discussing state bans on corporate spending dating back to at least the latter half of the 19th century and subsequent restrictions on corporate spending).
[74] 130 S. Ct. 876 (2010).
[75] 540 U.S. 93, 203–09 (2003).
[76] 494 U.S. 652 (1990).
[77] *Citizens United*, 130 S. Ct. at 903–13 (citing *Austin*, 494 U.S. at 660).
[78] *See* Peter S. Goodman, "U.S. Loan Effort Is Seen as Adding to Housing Woes", *New York Times*, A1 (January 2, 2010).

prescription for a bank crisis. This suggestion did not get much support from politicians of either party.

Of course, this does not prove that corporations have completely captured legislatures. After the economic crisis, Congress passed the Dodd-Frank bill, a financial reform bill that the financial industry generally opposed, and one probably can find instances of other laws passed since *Citizens United* that large corporations did not favor.

But corporate influence will likely grow in an environment in which the Supreme Court prohibits limits on corporate campaign contributions. One potential check on this influence involves the diversity of interests among corporations, at least on some questions. Economic concentration, however, limits this diversity. Very large entities can afford to make generous (actually, greedy) campaign contributions and still have plenty of spare change for lobbying activities. They can use this influence to help perpetuate barriers to entry and limit opportunities for smaller competitors. In short, *Citizens United* makes the concerns about economic concentration leading to political influence undermining democracy perhaps more salient than ever.

This suggests that empowerment analysis focusing on the economic dynamics that *Citizens United* has unleashed probably supports vigorous antitrust enforcement. *Citizens United* creates an incentive for corporations to increase their campaign contributions, as they have. Once these contributions increase (or have the potential to increase), politicians acquire an incentive to please corporate contributors (or potential contributors). A fuller economic dynamic analysis might look at what sorts of laws corporate interests might support, identifying those that will not pit large entities capable of great influence against one another. Possibilities include getting subsidies and tax breaks that will undermine efforts to cure deficits and fund basic services that society needs. They might also include further extensions of intellectual property rights favoring large holders of such rights, at least in areas where large corporate interests agree on the value of strong intellectual property protection. And they may include the utter destruction of environmental regulation, which tends to benefit nascent corporations (such as providers of renewable energy) and ordinary citizens at the expense of established entities with sufficient resources to make big campaign contributions. Thus, large entitites may already have enough influence to get laws passed enriching them, which will empower them to make still larger donations and obtain still larger economic benefits. This sort of economic dynamic may have led Congress to embrace, and certainly helps justify, antitrust laws.

Ironically, the same aggregation of political power that makes vigorous antitrust enforcement more desirable will tend to make it less likely. It will

take courage in a political environment favoring corporate interests to rein-
vigorate antitrust law. It may become possible only in limited instances when
individual enforcers defy political pressures, but more widely if a populist
backlash changes the political climate in spite of corporate influence.

SYSTEMIC RISK

The economic crisis shows that, at least in the financial sector, powerful
conglomerates create huge systemic risks. Hence, creation of huge businesses
not only may limit rivals' economic opportunities, but it also can, in some
contexts, create unacceptable systemic risks.

While several commentators have suggested the employment of antitrust
law to address this,[79] that suggestion will strike many antitrust scholars as a
little odd. Avoidance of systemic risk just does not figure among the rationales
for antitrust law.[80] Indeed, the concern here seems the opposite of the problems that Congress created antitrust law to deal with. Normally, antitrust law
concerns itself with economic concentration tending to increase profits at the
expense of the public and competitors.[81] Here, society worries that economic
concentration may hasten the demise of an economically concentrated entity,
which may take down the whole economy with it.

In spite of this, the antitrust law's literal language would permit prohibition
of new mergers in the financial sector that posed a systemic risk. Section 7
of the Clayton Act prohibits any merger creating a significant reduction in
competition. Since any merger produces some reduction in competition, this
section makes the legality of mergers hinge upon whether the competition
reduction is substantial. While not an inevitable interpretation of the law,
section 7 can be, and at times has been, construed to reach almost any sizable
merger. Construed in this way, it would surely prohibit any merger of financial
institutions large enough to present a systemic risk.[82]

Also, creation of a too-big-to-fail entity does produce an anticompetitive
effect. The likelihood of a government bailout in the event of the collapse
of a very large institution induces suppliers of capital to regard these large

---

[79] *See* Markham, *supra* note 3; Jonathan R. Macey & James F. Holdcroft, Jr., "Failure is an
    Option: An Ersatz-Antitrust Approach," 120 *Yale L. J.* 1368, 1393 (2011) (suggesting that antitrust
    regulators adopt their breakup proposal, but disclaiming an intent to revise "current antitrust
    laws or regulations").

[80] *See* Markham, *supra* note 3, at 267.

[81] *See* David A. Westbrook, *Out of Crisis: Rethinking Our Financial Markets* 112 (2010).

[82] *Cf.* Markham, *supra* note 3, at 268 and n. 20 (noting that a Federal Trade Commissioner has
    argued for taking systemic risk into account under both the Clayton Act and the FTC Act
    because an economic collapse would reduce competition).

institutions as very safe. As a result, these institutions pay less for capital than an institution small enough to collapse without damaging the economy.[83] Hence, obtaining the capacity to destroy the economy through merger confers a competitive advantage that can make it hard for smaller institutions that pose too little risk to survive.[84] At least one FTC commissioner believes, for that reason, that section 5 of the Federal Trade Commission Act, which prohibits "unfair methods of competition," may prohibit mergers creating or exacerbating too-big-to fail status.[85]

Whether or not current antitrust law prohibits the creation, growth, or existence of too-big-to-fail firms, their existence shows that the problem of economic concentration implicates systemic risk. Accordingly, if existing antitrust law does not authorize actions avoiding further concentration creating or exacerbating systemic risks and provide for the breakup of dangerous institutions, Congress should consider creating new law to do so.[86]

Taking the goal of systemic risk avoidance seriously would usefully change the laws that address, or could address, economic concentration. We shall see that taking the economic opportunity goal seriously also leads to significant reform proposals.

THE IMPLICATIONS OF TAKING EMPOWERMENT SERIOUSLY

The foregoing material has argued for an understanding of antitrust, not as an efficiency-enhancing mechanism, but as the product of an empowerment analysis aimed at managing change over time to maintain economic opportunity, in keeping with economic dynamic theory. It turns out that embracing empowerment of small actors at the expense of larger ones not only would preserve economic opportunity, but would also, at least in the financial sector, avoid systemic risks. Finally, this chapter has suggested that distribution of wealth has become so much more important to economic well-being and democracy than overall efficiency that the revival of antitrust's traditional embrace of decentralization of power and wealth may prove important (although not likely sufficient by itself) in reversing decades of economic failure.

A question remains, however, about what sort of specific reforms an economic dynamic approach in general – and, in particular, an embrace of

---

[83] *See* Macey & Holdcroft, *supra* note 79, at 1374–75.

[84] *See* Bush, *supra* note 12, at 309.

[85] *See* Markham, *supra* note 3, at 283–84.

[86] *Cf.* Adam J. Levitin, "In Defense of Bailouts," 99 *Geo. L. J.* 435, 463 (2011) (pointing out that antitrust regulation can address the too-big-to-fail problem when risk is a function of, or at least correlates with, firm size, but not otherwise).

disempowerment of large entities as a legitimate choice – should lead to. Skepticism toward bigness and a concern about growing concentration of economic power could lead to very specific additions to merger guidelines and recognition of new anticompetitive practices.

I will offer here a few suggestions, but space does not permit a complete analysis of these ideas. My only point is that acceptance of empowerment of consumers and small business as a core goal of antitrust, along with a concern for fostering innovation through competition, can yield, with a little imagination, a fairly specific set of reform proposals that policymakers can mull over. These proposals illustrate what a reorientation of antitrust policy to create and preserve economic opportunity might look like.

Most simply, antitrust enforcers could adopt a presumption against approving mergers among large firms. If we take the preservation of economic opportunity and the dynamics suggesting that increasing wealth concentration undermines its preservation seriously, large mergers just seem like a bad idea, at least in most cases (I discuss some exceptions later). Certainly the possibility that mergers might prove efficient should count for little in deciding such questions. For firms in competitive markets can grow internally only through greater innovation and efficiency. Mergers provide a path to growth that does not require either. Furthermore, as shown earlier, efficiency is much less important than providing economic opportunity for ordinary people and reducing political corruption.

Antitrust authorities should routinely demand comprehensive information about whether managers individually would profit from mergers. Unless managers expect to realize all potential gains solely from improved long-term economic performance, any sign that individual managers will profit from a merger should lead either to automatic disapproval of that merger or further strengthen the presumption that it serves no overwhelmingly important social purpose and should be disapproved.

Since mergers generally can create risks of blocked innovation through economic power or simple bureaucratic ineptitude, antitrust authorities could refuse to approve medium- or large-sized mergers without firm enforceable commitments to significant increases in research and development (R&D) spending. The economics teach that static efficiency gains prove difficult to predict, companies predict such gains much more often than they materialize, and efficiency improvements do not matter as much as innovation gains. Antitrust enforcers, however, can make commitments to R&D legally enforceable to test whether a compelling reason, not just a plausible reason, justifies approving a merger that will tend to increase generally undesirable economic concentration. Recently, the Department of Justice required continued R&D

as a condition of approving a decree consenting to the merger of Google and the travel data company ITA Software. Absent a compelling reason, society may appropriately expect firms to grow, if at all, by pleasing customers instead of by purchasing rivals.[87]

Antitrust authorities could treat receipt of subsidies and tax credits as an anticompetitive practice in many cases. One can fairly easily state the rationale for this. Often large businesses have the political muscle to obtain special concessions that smaller businesses cannot get. This can create an unfair advantage in the marketplace. But antitrust authorities might not judge the receipt of tax credits and subsidies generally available to all without application or lobbying as anticompetitive, at least not on a *per se* basis.

A more fine-grained approach to subsidies and tax credits could help solve a big problem in the antitrust literature. This literature generally recognizes that antitrust law has political and social dimensions, like those elaborated on in this chapter. But the literature only rarely links these concerns to specific proposals to reform antitrust law.[88] The law could treat cases in which a corporation receives a tax credit or subsidy from officials who received its campaign contributions or were potentially subject to influence by higher officials who received its campaign contributions especially harshly. Many ways of manifesting this harshness exist. This could influence penalties. It might trigger an investigation aimed at assessing whether a company needs to be broken up. It might eliminate defenses (such as that the tax credit was generally available).

Treating corruption through campaign contributions as an enforcement trigger would require some First Amendment analysis, as corporate campaign contributions now enjoy the status of protected speech. My own view, which I will not defend here, is that attaching special consequences to acceptance of largesse that may reflect the gratitude of recipients of campaign contributions does not impose an impermissible burden on speech, since corporations would remain free to make unlimited campaign contributions if they simply turn down all largesse. Furthermore, antitrust enforcers could demand a full accounting of subsidies and tax breaks as part of any merger proposal. Receipt

---

[87] *See U.S. v. Grinnell*, 384 U.S. 563, 570–71 (1966) (holding that the Sherman Act prohibits monopolies created by "willful acquisition . . . of [monopoly] power" rather than power flowing from production of a superior product, execution, or accident); Brandeis, *supra* note 38, at 164 (contrasting "natural growth" with "combination"); 21 Cong. Rec. 3151 (April 8, 1890) (opining that the Sherman act did not intend to thwart those who obtained control of a business "by virtues of . . . superior skill").

[88] *Cf.* Ghosh & Bush, *supra* note 45, at 366 (noting that antitrust law's concern with wealth concentration's harmful effects could justify striking down uses of administrative and legislative process that harm competition).

of special tax breaks or subsidies (those not generally available without application to all) could trigger automatic denial of a merger application, lest a concentrated entity acquire too much political capital that it will likely use to engage in more anticompetitive manipulation of government.

These proposals show that taking empowerment of small actors seriously as a strategy to create economic opportunity and avoid systemic risk could significantly change antitrust law, which has generally treated lobbying and legislative activity as off limits to courts and antitrust enforcers.[89] No doubt thoughtful students of antitrust law can think of other proposals that might likewise operationalize a serious commitment to a shape of change over time that favors decentralization over concentration. The need for some such reform has become much greater in recent years than it has been in decades.

CONCLUSION

Congress enacted antitrust laws to create a significant change over time, empowering consumers and small business in order to maximize economic opportunity for small actors. In pursuit of the relatively insignificant efficiency goal, the Chicago School has aided and abetted a trend toward economic concentration that poses a threat to democracy and the economy, and may have contributed to a diminution in economic freedom, opportunity, and wealth for most Americans. An economic dynamic approach to antitrust that takes empowerment seriously would support a set of reforms that grapple with the key problems of our times.

---

[89] *See* id. at 364–389 (discussing antitrust doctrines protecting lobbying and legislation and arguing that they should be limited).

10

On the Dangers of Ignoring the Economic Dynamics
of National Security

It may seem odd to claim that economic theory, either neoclassical or economic dynamic, has anything to say about national security. It turns out, however, that neoclassical law and economics has lent intellectual support to privatizing military functions. On the other hand, CBA of military decisions has not caught on, for a very good reason – the relevant variables defy quantification. National security experts, however, regularly employ elements of an economic dynamic approach, and an economic dynamic approach can provide powerful help in making wise decisions.

This failure of CBA to catch on in the national security context may appear troublesome, however, because the United States has recently taken some rash (some would say disastrous) actions, such as engaging in torture and invading Iraq, that seem to reflect a conspicuous failure to consider tradeoffs. This chapter shows, however, that analysts can better understand the main questions in the national security context that appear to involve tradeoffs as questions of efficacy. Furthermore, economic dynamic analysis, not CBA, provides the proper method for deciding these efficacy questions and any questions that might arise about collateral negative consequences. Use of economic dynamic analysis allows officials to make sensible decisions about how to minimize very serious systemic risks.

While the characterization of national security risks as systemic appears intuitively obvious, it will aid our understanding of systemic risk to pause and defend this characterization before outlining this chapter's goals. National security policy protects our political and social systems. Terrorist attacks and war constitute threats not just because they kill people. Indeed, the 9/11 attacks killed fewer people than die from automobile accidents or from air pollution on an annual basis in the United States. Rather, attacks can potentially topple a government, or so alter its character as it copes with attacks that it ceases to function as an organ of freedom-loving democracy. Similarly, terrorism or war has the potential to engender so much fear that it interferes with people's basic social lives, making such simple actions as going shopping, attending a sporting event, or going to work problematic. Serious national security threats qualify as systemic risks because they put social and political systems at risk.

As the introduction mentioned, exploration of economic dynamic analysis' superiority in the national security context provides an opportunity to develop several significant points. First, economic dynamic analysis provides a method for analyzing causation, a prerequisite for any analysis of actions' consequences. In doing so, it puts the question of efficacy front and center, precisely where it belongs when we analyze actions addressing systemic risks. CBA puts that question in the background and can therefore prove extremely misleading. Second, thoughtful military planners routinely use scenario analysis, a component of economic dynamic analysis, to cope with uncertainty. Third, economic dynamic analysis' focus on change over time provides an antidote to the tendency to fail to think through military commitments' long-term implications.

This chapter first presents an account of how neoclassical law and economics provides important intellectual underpinnings to the privatization of national security functions, with a brief mention of some of the policy questions privatization raises. It will then explain why CBA has not caught on in military circles, and ought not catch on, using decisions about whether to invade Iraq and whether to engage in torture as examples.

The remainder of the chapter uses examples of military and foreign policy leaders' thinking, especially about Iraq and treatment of "enemy combatants," to demonstrate that careful rational thought about tough national security issues often requires economic dynamic analysis. This material will demonstrate the value of emphasizing efficacy, employing scenario analysis to cope with uncertainty, and focusing on long-term change over time. Unfortunately, even when some officials developed dynamic analysis, as they did to some extent in the case of Iraq, top-level officials tended to ignore it. If they had paid attention to a well-developed economic dynamic analysis, they would have either changed their decision to invade Iraq or executed that decision in a much more effective way.

Before proceeding, a caveat is in order. No economic theory can capture all values relevant to national security decisions. But economic dynamic theory does provide a more useful guide to improving national security decision making than the neoclassical law and economics framework.

PRIVATIZING SECURITY FUNCTIONS

The belief in the superiority of markets that neoclassical law and economics spawned led to privatization of all manner of functions that were formerly carried out by government employees, including functions traditionally carried out by military personnel.[1] If private markets are efficient and governments woefully inefficient, then it appears to make sense to contract with the private sector to provide as many government services as possible. Thus, an efficiency framework combined with an assumption that market actors are rational and well-informed leads to privatization.[2]

Privatization of security functions has taken off in recent years. Private contractors guard military facilities, protect diplomats, escort convoys, conduct interrogations, train soldiers, provide logistical support, and perform intelligence functions.[3] At the high point of the U.S. engagement in Afghanistan, the number of contract employees in Iraq and Afghanistan approximately equaled the total number of regular troops.[4] Some of the functions this virtual army of contractor employees performs, such as guarding facilities and escorting convoys, can place contractor employees into what amounts to a combat situation, where they must decide about what to do when facing an actual or potential attack.

The assumption that markets can perform almost any function better than government employees (such as soldiers) may have contributed to a failure to adequately analyze the question of whether private contractors have the necessary incentives or training to perform their functions properly. Soldiers, of course, receive intensive training on how to defend themselves while minimizing civilian casualties. They perform their duties under a command structure and a strict military code, which commanders can enforce, if necessary, through courts-martial. Thus, failure to conform to international norms

---

[1] See John S. Kemp, "Private Military Firms and Responses to their Accountability Gap," 32 Wash. U. J.L. & Pol'y 489, 496 (2010); Allan Stanger, One Nation Under Contract: The Outsourcing of American Power and the Future of Foreign Policy 13 (2009); P. W. Singer, Corporate Warriors 66 (2003). I do not mean to claim that the belief in market actors' superiority constitutes the sole cause of the move to privatize military functions. See Singer at 49–70.

[2] See Clifford J. Rosky, "Force, Inc.: The Privatization of Punishment, Policing, and Military Force in Liberal States," 36 Conn. L. Rev. 879, 929 (2004). Cf. Ann R. Markusen, "The Case Against Privatizing National Security," 16 Governance: Int'l Poly, Admin. Insts. 471 (2003).

[3] See Laura A. Dickinson, "Military Lawyers, Private Contractors, and the Problem of International Law Compliance," 42 N.Y.U J. Int'l L. & Pol. 355, 355–56 (2010).

[4] See Stephanie M. Hurst, "Note: 'Trade in Force': The Need for Effective Regulation of Private Military and Security Companies," 84 S. Cal. L. Rev. 447, 449 (2011).

protecting human rights, for example, can lead to (and has occasionally led to) dishonorable discharge and even imprisonment.

Contractors do not face quite the same incentives. And they have committed some notorious human rights abuses. Most famously, in September 2007 employees of the Blackwater security firm fired into a crowded square in Baghdad, killing 17 Iraqi civilians.[5] Reportedly, Blackwater employees had been involved in 196 firefights in Iraq, "an average of about 1.4 shootings per week."[6] The firm became so infamous that it changed its name. While Blackwater's performance in Iraq provides the most notorious example of a private contractor atrocity, security firm personnel have faced accusations of human rights abuses before. In the late 1990s, for example, employees of DynCorp International "allegedly bought women and girls as sex slaves while deployed in Bosnia."[7] And an Army report found contractor employees, along with military officers, directly or indirectly responsible for the abuse of Iraqi prisoners at Abu Ghraib, a scandal that provided a propaganda coup for Al Qaeda.[8] These abuses have led to some legal reforms and to numerous proposals to make private contractors accountable for human rights violations.[9]

We have already seen that the market glorification at the heart of neoclassical law and economics supported widespread privatization. But the problem of applying neoclassical law and economics to military contracting (or other government contracting) has more fundamental problems than just the tendency to assume that private contractors must perform more efficiently than government employees. Focusing analysis on the question of which type of actor performs most efficiently misses the most important questions – the questions of accountability and the long-run capacity for governance over time.[10] An economic dynamic approach, because it focuses on change over time, at least invites consideration of these questions.

With respect to accountability, the major question becomes : What incentives do government employees and contractors face that tend to encourage

---

[5] See id. at 448.

[6] Id.

[7] Id.

[8] See Martha Minow, "Outsourcing Power: How Privatizing Military Efforts Challenges Accountability, Professionalism, and Democracy," 46 *B.C. L. Rev.* 989, 993–94 (2005).

[9] See, e.g., id.; Katherine J. Chapman, "The Untouchables: Private Military Contractors' Criminal Accountability under the UCMJ," 63 *Vand. L. Rev.* 1047 (2010); Kemp, *supra* note 1; Dickinson, *supra* note 3.

[10] See Paul Verkuil, *Outsourcing Sovereignty: Why Privatization of Government Functions Threatens Democracy and What We Can Do About It* (2007); Devorah D. Avant, *The Market for Force: The Consequences of Privatizing Security* (2005).

them to perform their duties?[11] What incentives do they face that might coun-tervail their incentives to perform their duties?[12] A particularly important exam-ple of the latter question includes the question of whether the incentive to make a profit might interfere in some contexts with performance of a govern-ment duty.[13] In short, an economic dynamic analysis can help separate wise from unwise contracting and facilitate appropriate contracts when contracting is chosen.

An economic dynamic approach focuses on change over time. Contracting raises issues about the erosion of democracy and government capacity over time. While costs matter in making contracting decisions, too great a focus on efficiency tends to draw attention away from these important questions.[14]

Under our Constitution, we commit government decision making to offi-cials ultimately responsible to "the People." Yet when contractors perform some military functions, they may end up making discretionary judgments that a democratic society must commit to government officials. These judgments include how to respond to various real or potential dangers. Do our people patrolling in a hostile environment slaughter entire civilian populations to destroy the danger? Withdraw from dangerous areas? Arrest dangerous people, shoot them, or torture them? All of these questions involve policy judgments that we subject to democratic controls. If these decisions become privatized, we end up ceding that control and weakening democratic accountability over time.

A related problem, which a theory focusing on change over time empha-sizes, involves the erosion of government capacity. Military contractors such as Haliburton and Blackwater recruit former military personnel and offer much higher wages than government can.[15] For government to perform compli-cated functions like making sensible decisions in war zones, running military procurement programs, and rescuing people from disasters, it must have

---

[11] *See* David M. Driesen, "Toward a Duty-Based Theory of Executive Power," 78 *Fordham L. Rev.* 71 (2009).

[12] *See* Kathleen Clark, *Ethics for an Outsourced Government* (Administrative Conference of the United States 2011).

[13] *See* Singer, *supra* note 1, at 151 (claiming that "clear tensions always exist between state "security goals" and contractors' "desire for profit maximization"); Michael J. Trebilock & Edward M. Iacobucci, "Privatization and Accountability," 116 *Harv. L. Rev.* 1422, 1435–36 (2003) (pointing out that government officials may be insufficiently motivated to achieve public objectives and may engage in "political rent seeking.").

[14] *See* Markusen, *supra* note 2, at 493 (pointing out that nobody has been able to calculate the long-term costs and benefits of extensively privatizing national defense).

[15] *See* Singer, *supra* note 1, at 74–76 (private military firms pay 2 to 10 times as much as government and hires ex-soldiers almost exclusively).

employees who have experience with these sorts of functions. If government contracts out essential functions, it may lose the capacity to perform them adequately.[16] This can have a number of consequences. It may make democratic accountability impossible. It can make adequate supervision of contractors extremely difficult. It can leave government a hostage to private monopolies or oligopolies when one or a handful of firms employ all of the people capable of performing some highly specialized government function.[17] While good analysts routinely focus on change over time and appreciate these problems, many policymakers enamored of efficiency mythology pay little attention to these questions.

Not only does an economic dynamic approach draw attention to questions important to sensible decisions about when privatization might make sense and when it might not, it also can aid efforts to structure privatization properly. Once government privatizes a function, it must write contracts that provide incentives to perform properly in the face of countervailing incentives to increase profits at the expense of the mission government needs performed.[18] Effective contracting requires the government to structure contracts to create incentives that encourage contractors to faithfully perform tasks government employees may have performed in the past. This requires at least a rough form of scenario analysis, imagining what situations and countervailing incentives might cause departures from applicable norms that should govern performance of the relevant tasks. Taking into account the bounded rationality of contractors, the contracts must anticipate possible problems and, insofar as possible, establish mechanisms that foster proper performance.

WHY COST-BENEFIT ANALYSIS HAS NOT CAUGHT ON

Many people consider the Bush administration decisions to invade Iraq and to detain and torture "enemy combatants" found in Afghanistan and many other places irrational. (Many people, including me, consider the decision to embrace torture immoral as well, but I do not plan to justify that point here.)[19] How does one make a rational decision about such matters? Neoclassical law and economics would assume that performance of CBA provides the proper antidote to irrationality. Its proponents might characterize Bush's failure as one of not considering the costs and benefits of invasion or torture.

---

[16] *Cf.* Benedict Sheehy & Jackson N. Maogoto, "The Private Military Company-Unraveling the Theoretical, Legal, and Regulatory Mosaic," 15 *ILSA J. Int'l & Com. L.* 147, 173 (2008)

[17] *See* Rosky, *supra* note 2, at 956–57; *see also* Singer, *supra* note 1, at 155 (discussing claims to unique expertise leading to sole-source contracts).

[18] *See* Laura A. Dickinson, *Outsourcing War and Peace* 69–101 (2011).

[19] *See* Thomas E. Ricks, *Fiasco: The American Military Adventure in Iraq* (2006).

Serious commentators who consider these decisions irrational, however, identify a more fundamental problem than a failure to perform CBA: a failure to take into account relevant information that would help us analyze key causal claims. President Bush and his key advisers did not take into account information indicating that these actions might be unnecessary and counterproductive. In the case of Iraq, this information indicated that Saddam Hussein had no weapons of mass destruction and that, as a secular leader, he would probably not share such weapons with Muslim fundamentalists like Al Qaeda if he had them.[20] In the case of torture, this information indicated that torture did not elicit reliable information.[21] As a result, it might well prove useless as an interrogation technique. Hence, the Bush administration gave short shrift to key information relevant to rationally resolving the causal questions of whether torture would prove effective and whether leaving Saddam Hussein in power would lead to a devastating attack on the United States.

CBA does not provide the means of answering these questions. Indeed, it can distract one from understanding their importance and resolving them properly.

These causal questions go to the efficacy of the actions involved. If torture does not elicit useful information, torturing detainees serves no purpose even – indeed, especially – in a so-called ticking bomb scenario, in which an interrogator knows that an imminent attack will kill large numbers of people but hopes to prevent the attack by eliciting key information quickly. If torture produces inaccurate information, then torturing somebody to try to obtain information about when and where a bomb will go off will produce a wild goose chase, reducing the chances of stopping the attack.[22] An interrogator should, in that case, use some other technique more likely to produce accurate information. The key question to ask about torture, putting aside moral questions in order to keep a tight focus on forms of consequentialist analysis, is the efficacy question about whether it elicits accurate information.

Similarly, if Saddam Hussein has no weapons of mass destruction or will not share them with our enemies, then no national security interest favors invasion. Invasion serves no purpose other than to deter human rights violations. And

---

[20] *See* id. at 376–78.
[21] With respect to torture and other interrogation techniques, we have precious little data about effectiveness. *See* Intelligence Science Board, *Educing Information, Interrogation: Science and Art, Foundations for the Future* xv, xxi (2006). The little information we have, however, suggests that torture frequently elicits incorrect information. Id. at xi; xxii–xxiii.
[22] Robert Coulam, "Approaches to Interrogation in the Struggle Against Terrorism: Consideration of Cost and Benefit," in id. at 9 (pointing out that even when seeking information to prevent an "imminent assault" it makes no sense to torture if better methods for getting information are available).

that consideration might not suffice on its own to justify unilateral invasion, since so many countries engage in human rights violations. Conversely, if we knew that absent an attack on Saddam Hussein he would give Al Qaeda nuclear or biological weapons to use against us, then national security would demand an invasion, assuming that an invasion is likely to prevent this. Hence, the key question about whether we should invade Iraq involves the efficacy question: Is an invasion necessary to stop a devastating attack?

Even if one is committed to CBA, one cannot perform one without resolving efficacy questions first. And efficacy questions often require economic dynamic analysis. In other words, CBA depends upon economic dynamic analysis and by itself cannot resolve efficacy questions.

The Iraq case demonstrates CBA's dependency on efficacy questions. Suppose we believe that Saddam Hussein has weapons of mass destruction and will give them to Al Qaeda. It follows that the benefits of invading Iraq might be very great, as we could presumably prevent the use of weapons of mass destruction against us. Suppose, on the other hand, that he has none or that he will not share them with Al Qaeda to be used against us. In this case, the benefit of invading Iraq consists only of the prevention of Saddam Hussein's human rights abuses. This constitutes a much lesser benefit to the world and no direct benefit to us. So, the results of CBA depend on resolving the question of efficacy flagged earlier.

The torture case demonstrates efficacy's primacy as well. Suppose that torture produces no useful information. It follows that it provides no benefit to us and a severe harm to the torture victims. Suppose we believe that torture produces accurate information. It follows that torture generates some benefit to us, and the question of whether that benefit justifies torture's costs looks very different.

Economic dynamic analysis, not CBA, provides the tools to resolve these key *a priori* questions. CBA monetizes and compares known costs and benefits; it provides no method for discovering in a fundamental way what the costs and benefits are. That discovery must come, somehow, from other approaches or disciplines.

In the case of Iraq, the question of whether Saddam Hussein had methods of mass destruction presented a factual issue. But determining the facts requires assessment of intelligence. Sensible intelligence gathering relies on the assumptions undergirding economic dynamic analysis in order to assess the reliability of statements indicating Iraq's possession of weapons of mass destruction. Treating intelligence sources as rational economic actors making statements based on full information – that is, using neoclassical economic assumptions – endangers us. Experienced analysts instead consider the

bounded rationality of intelligence sources and the fact that they have limited information available to them. They consider the incentives they face to
speak the truth and the incentives they face to lie. In the case of Iraq, those
who believed that Saddam Hussein might have weapons of mass destruction
relied heavily (although not exclusively) upon statements by Iraqi exile Ahmad
Chalabi, and the brother of one of Chalabi's aides, known to the government
intelligence community by the code name "Curveball."[23] Chalabi served as a
leader of the opposition to Saddam Hussein in exile and therefore had a motive
to lie (as might his associates of similar mind set).[24] Those who believed that
Saddam Hussein shared weapons of mass destruction with Al Qaeda relied
heavily upon the statements of Ibyn al-Shykh al-Libi, the chief of an Al Qaeda
training camp, made after undergoing torture at the hands of the Egyptians.[25]
Intelligence analysts also consider whether the person making the assertion
actually has access to the relevant information. And these analysts doubted al-
Libi's statements, as Pakastani officials seized him in *Afghanistan* and he had
no reason to know about such events in Iraq.[26] In short, determining the facts
requires analysis of multiple incentives facing individuals making statements,
the bounds upon their rationality, and the problem of limited information.

The link to economic dynamics is even clearer with respect to the question
of whether Saddam Hussein would share weapons of mass destruction with
Al Qaeda. This question involves a prediction about the future, a prediction
dependent upon an assessment of the incentives facing Saddam Hussein and
the limits of his rationality. In this regard, it is important to note that Saddam Hussein was a secular leader with a long history of repressing Muslim
fundamentalists. This would suggest that he would not have an incentive to
empower Al Qaeda by giving its members weapons of mass destruction. Any
rational assessment of whether Saddam Hussein would share these dreaded
weapons would have to consider the incentives he faced, as well as other
information.

Similarly, the question of torture's efficacy must rest on an assessment of
captives' bounded, and sometimes impaired, rationality. Many of those high
up in the Bush administration just assumed, with no look at any information at
all, that aggressive interrogation techniques that many would characterize as
torture would yield good results. This perspective makes sense if one assumes

[23] *See* Ricks, *supra* note 19, at 56–57, 91.
[24] For an account of doubts about Curveball both before and after the Iraq invasion, *see* id. at 91.
  Apparently, he, like al-Libi, was not in Iraq during the time of the events he supposedly spoke
  of. Id.
[25] *See* Jane Mayer, *The Dark Side* 104, 135–36 (2009).
[26] *See* id. at 136–38.

that captives are rational actors with perfect information. Torture is intensely painful. Captives may well assume that giving correct information will stop the pain. So, surely the benefits of coughing up accurate information outweigh the costs to the captive. Yet many experts in the field argue that torture has a long history of producing inaccurate information, and the arguments they make about this implicitly assume bounded rationality and limited information.[27] Those undergoing torture may say anything to make the pain stop. People undergoing torture may hate their interrogators and may want to deceive them for that reason.[28] Torture victims with limited information may make up information when they know nothing of interest to their captors in order to gain some surcease. Furthermore, psychological evidence suggests that torture victims may suffer memory impairment and communication disorders, impairments bounding their rationality in an unconventional sense, which make the reporting of accurate information to interrogators unlikely.[29]

Hence, we see that questions of efficacy necessarily require resolution prior to questions about costs and benefits and that we need to employ economic dynamic analysis to answer many of these questions. But there is more. Even if we perform an economic dynamic analysis and resolve questions of efficacy appropriately, CBA does not facilitate wise choices, because it is indeterminate and obtuse with respect to the relevant issues.

Suppose, for example, that we determined that Saddam Hussein has methods of mass destruction and will likely share them with Al Qaeda. Will CBA enable us to decide whether an invasion is wise?

If Hussein has weapons of mass destruction that he will share with Al Qaeda, we face potential annihilation. In that case, we do not need CBA to see that we need to invade. Serious systemic risks generally require an efficacious response.

Moreover, we could not perform CBA even if we wanted to. All the most important variables thoroughly resist quantification. An invasion would cause deaths on both sides. But we cannot calculate how many deaths we will cause if we invade. We might have an idea of how many of our own troops would die in an invasion, but estimating enemy casualties would prove more difficult. And figuring out how many people might die in a potentially chaotic situation in post-invasion Iraq would prove even more difficult. If a stable government

---

[27] *See, e.g., Educing Information, supra* note 21, at xi, xxii–xxiii (discussing examples from the Inquisition and the Korean War).

[28] *See* id. at xxiii (explaining that psychological theory suggests that torture may increase the subject's determination not to comply).

[29] *See* Steven M. Kleinman, "KUBARK Counterintelligence Interrogation Review: Observations of an Interrogator," in id. at 132–33.

comes into being quickly (which did not happen) then casualties might be few. Conversely, if a long civil war ensued, the casualties might dwarf those of the initial invasion. But knowing the scenario and the numbers in advance would be impossible.

And this is only the beginning of the difficulties this death calculus faces as we peer into the abyss. We must decide whether enemy casualties constitute a cost to us or not.[30] And we would have to assign a dollar value to the deaths we choose to include in our calculus in order to compare them to benefits (not all of which would involve saved lives).

Nor could we calculate the benefits from potentially avoiding an attack with a nuclear or biological weapon. Even if Hussein gives such a weapon to Al Qaeda, there is some chance of our avoiding the attack through counterterrorism actions, but we have no means of making reasonably reliable estimates about the probabilities of preventing an attack. So we cannot proceed by discounting the "value" of the attack by the probability of its occurrence, the procedure economists use to evaluate well-understood risks. Nor could we reliably predict where the attack would take place and how much damage it would cause.

To spell all of this out simply underscores how obtuse this form of analysis is. If we have good reason to believe that an adversary is about to unleash a nuclear or biological weapon upon us and we can prevent it by attacking first, we do not need an elaborate calculation to tell us that we need to attack.

Nor could we resolve questions about torture through CBA.[31] Suppose that we obtained solid information showing that torture can yield useful information. Will CBA help us resolve the question of whether to use torture? Let us start with the relative easy stuff, the benefit to the United States of using torture – the acquisition of information useful in combating terrorism. Interrogation takes place precisely because those asking the questions do not know what information the subject of the interrogation possesses. Accordingly, any CBA of torture in general or in a particular case would be made without knowing what information the torture would reveal. So the potential benefit of the torture represents an unknown. Even if we knew what information torture would bring to light, assessing the monetary value of that information would prove difficult.[32] Suppose, for example, that torture revealed the identity of

---

[30] *See generally* Douglas A. Kysar, *Regulating from Nowhere: Environmental Law and the Search for Objectivity* 126 (2010).

[31] *See* Coulam, *supra* note 22, at 10 (stating that we do not know enough to be able to "calibrate" the costs and benefits of various interrogation methods).

[32] *See id.* at 8 (pointing out that the benefits of successful interrogation can be "enormous" or "quite small").

an important Al Qaeda operative previously unknown to us. Analysts could not determine in advance whether knowing this would allow us to prevent a terrorist attack. Even if we could reliably predict that knowing this would lead to some chain of events preventing an attack, it would be impossible to know how much damage foiling the plot would prevent. So, we have no sound basis for quantifying torture's benefits.

The cost side raises even more fundamental questions about CBA's value. The most obvious cost of torture involves the victim's pain. If the victim is a foreigner, we must decide whether we care, for purposes of CBA, only about members of our own community. In other words, are we concerned only about the costs and benefits to ourselves, or do foreigners' interests count in the cost–benefit calculus?[33] If we treat the pain we inflict as a relevant cost, either because we torture our own citizens or because we decide that a foreigner's pain matters, then we must face the problem of assigning a monetary value to the pain and humiliation we inflict. Doing so would seem utterly immoral and obtuse. We could estimate the costs of medical and psychiatric treatment, but this does not get at the real "costs" (actually, harms) that torture causes – the pain and suffering.

As we think further about torture's "costs," things get even worse for CBA. The questions torture raises go to the heart of the very idea of national security. For national security embodies at its core not just the cost of losing lives, but the idea of protecting the collective entity we call a nation. The protection of our nation has value because the nation itself has value. Democracy and human rights lie at the core of our value as a nation. But when we torture, we change our character from that of a special country that does not engage in the kind of nefarious conduct all too common among nondemocratic governments into that of just another rather evil regime.[34] Unfortunately, this loss of identity is literally priceless, to borrow Frank Ackerman and Lisa Heinzerling's phrase, something of great value that has no particular monetary measure.[35] We also suffer reputational harms from torture. These harms can make it more difficult to get cooperation from governments committed to human rights in the struggle against terrorism.[36] Yet we cannot predict how this loss of prestige will influence us in the future, let alone monetize reputational consequences. Other possible costs of torture resisting quantification include the creation of more enemies, destruction of morale among those involved in

[33] *See* Kysar, *supra* note 30.
[34] *Cf.* Coulam, *supra* note 22, at 12 (discussing loss of legitimacy as a cost of torture).
[35] *See* Frank Ackerman & Lisa Heinzerling, *Priceless: Knowing the Price of Everything and the Value of Nothing* (2004).
[36] *See* Coulam, *supra* note 22, at 13.

interrogations, and a potential increase in the torturing of captured American soldiers.[37] In short, quantification of torture's "costs" proves a fruitless and rather disgusting endeavor.

Now, if one believes that torture is morally wrong, even if the consequences of not torturing might be devastating, then no economic analysis will prove helpful. Hence, application of this book's economic dynamic theory to torture will not prove necessary to those who consider torture immoral. But if one wants to consider the consequences of torture in deciding whether to authorize it, then economic dynamic theory provides a way forward, while CBA leads nowhere. The next section considers economic dynamic analysis in the context of the decision about whether to invade Iraq and decisions about how to treat detainees, assuming that moral considerations do not resolve the latter issue on their own.

ECONOMIC DYNAMIC ANALYSIS OF NATIONAL SECURITY ISSUES AND THE VALUE OF SCENARIO AND WORST-CASE ANALYSIS

Rationality requires an economic dynamic analysis of efficacy, focusing on whether an invasion of Iraq and our treatment of detainees would prevent systemic risk. In fact, our most thoughtful officials use something resembling economic dynamic analysis routinely. Many of the mistakes we have made in the national security realm in recent years stem from a failure of top-level officials to take economic dynamic analysis seriously. Good thinking requires an emphasis on change over time, scenario analysis, and worst-case analysis as we examine the dynamics of uncertain and difficult national security situations.

Indefinite Detention: Focusing on the Big Picture

An amicus brief that former national security officials filed in the case of *Ali Saleh Kahlah Al-Marri v. Daniel Spagone* provides a good example of the implicit use of economic dynamic analysis. The *Al-Marri* case presented the question of whether the president has the authority to subject a U.S. resident suspected of plotting terrorist actions to indefinite military detention as an "enemy combatant."[38] Al-Marri also claimed that the United States had not provided him with a sufficient opportunity to contest his enemy combatant status to meet due process standards. While the case was pending in the Supreme

[37] *See* id. at 13–15.
[38] *See Ali Saleh Kahlah Al-Marri v. Pucciarelli*, 534 F.3d 213 (4th Cir. 2008) (*en banc*).

Court, the government released him from military custody, and the Court dismissed the case as moot.[39] The amicus brief filed in the Supreme Court case, however, contains economic dynamic arguments about why the challenged indefinite detention policy might prove counterproductive in addressing terrorism.

One might describe the Bush Administration's approach to dealing with terrorists, those linked with terrorists in some way, and those who might have information about terrorists as transaction oriented. It created a policy designed to maximize the chances of extracting information from various Muslims whom government officials suspected of having some sort of link to terrorism and to prevent terrorists from carrying out attacks by labeling detainees as enemy combatants and imprisoning them indefinitely, mostly in Guantanamo. Thus, the Bush administration implicitly viewed each person seized as a potential individual threat and an individual opportunity to unravel a plot.

This transactional approach became controversial, leading to several adverse Supreme Court rulings, because it conflicted with the rule of law. We define our national character in part through the idea that we are free people who are innocent until proven guilty. Accordingly, our norms generally demand that we try those who have committed crimes and let those who committed no crime go free. Exceptions to these norms exist, but only limited ones. One can hold suspects for a limited time before deciding whether to charge them, detain persons briefly for interrogation under some circumstances, and keep enemy troops in military custody so that they cannot return to battle. Yet our fundamental norms generally allow governments to deprive individuals of liberty only after they receive due legal process determining that they did something to merit such a serious deprivation. This approach distinguishes a great free nation from a lawless dictatorship.

For purposes of economic dynamic analysis, the question of which of the various aspects of the Bush administration's approach to "enemy combatants" violated due process or other fundamental constitutional and human rights values does not matter a whole lot. A whole literature exists on this subject, along with a body of case law.[40] The policy's *appearance* of inconsistency

---

[39] *See Ali Saleh Kahlah Al-Marri v. Spagone*, 129 S.Ct. 1545 (2009).

[40] *See, e.g., Hamdan v. Rumsfeld*, 548 U.S. 557 (2006); *Hamdi v. Rumsfeld*, 542 U.S. 507 (2004); David Luban, "Lawfare and Legal Ethics in Guantanamo," 60 *Stan. L. Rev.* 1981 (2008); Neal Kumar Katyal, "Equality in the War on Terror," 59 *Stan. L. Rev.* 1365 (2007); Neal Kumar Katyal, "*Hamdan v. Rumseld:* The Legal Academy Goes to Practice," 120 *Harv. L. Rev.* 65 (2006); Neal Kumar Katyal, "Internal Separation of Powers: Checking Today's Most Dangerous Branch from Within," 115 *Yale L.J.* 2314–2349 (2006).

with basic American values, however, does matter for purposes of economic dynamic analysis.

Economic analysis concerns itself with decisions' consequences, not necessarily their legality under established law (constitutional or otherwise). The former national security officials filing an amicus brief on behalf of Al-Marri did not view his case in transactional terms. Rather, they focused on change over time, analyzing the question of what dynamics a practice of indefinite detention of various Muslims created. (As the brief pointed out, the indefinite detention policy in fact swept up only Muslims, although the Bush administration framed it in general terms.)

These experts' analysis indicated that a practice of indefinite detention of Muslims suspected of some connection with terrorism aided the recruitment of new terrorists.[41] Thus, they concluded that indefinite military detention without criminal charges "threatens to undermine our national security." This attention to recruitment of new terrorists involves a shift from a transactional focus to a macro-level focus, in keeping with the spirit of the economic dynamic approach's emphasis on macroeconomics.

These experts reached the conclusion that indefinite detention aids terrorist recruiting by analyzing terrorism's economic dynamics. They began by noting a consensus among practically all terrorism experts that military action alone cannot defeat terrorism. This consensus reflects terrorism's basic dynamics. Killing every terrorist on the planet, if that were possible, cannot prevent terrorism, because people who have never committed terrorist acts in the past can become terrorists. Indeed, terrorist organizations like Al Qaeda recruit new terrorists constantly. For that reason, national security experts describe the battle against terrorism as ultimately a battle for hearts and minds.

In order to analyze the incentives people face to become terrorists, these national security experts examined, at least in a limited way, the bounded rationality of those who might become terrorists. They pointed out that Al Qaeda has constructed a narrative of holy war and martyrdom against Western powers said to be waging a war on Islam. Referring to those we capture as "enemy combatants" supports the terrorists' narrative nicely by characterizing detainees as soldiers in a war rather than just common criminals. And the indefinite detention of Muslims, many of them apparently innocent of any crime, helps Al Qaeda by supporting the myth of a war against Islam. Several U.S. flag officers maintain that the symbols of Abu Ghraib (where we

---

[41] *See* Brief of *Amici Curiae* Former National Security Officials and Counterterrorism Experts in Support of Petitioner, *Ali Saleh Kahlah Al-Marri v. Daniel Spagone*, No. 08–368 (S. Ct. 2009).

tortured Iraqis) and Guantanamo constitute the leading identifiable causes of the death of U.S. fighters, presumably because they incited acts of terrorism. And Al Jazeera and other Arab news outlets have regularly reported on the imprisonment of specific innocents at Guantanamo, thus exposing more than a billion people to information supporting the story Al Qaeda likes to tell. From this perspective, commitment to the rule of law can become a counterterrorism strategy.

Of course, this attention to the way our actions can support narratives that terrorists use to recruit new disciples does not by itself constitute a complete economic dynamic analysis. One would have to study the bounds of rationality Muslim culture creates to evaluate receptivity to such a narrative. And one would want to look at other factors that might countervail the incentive these narratives create to join the jihad. But this narrative does take change over time and incentives seriously and focuses on the macro-level picture.

Nor does recognition of indefinite detention's value in helping terrorist recruitment by itself establish the stupidity of the policy of indefinite detention. But it does show that any good evaluation of this policy's wisdom (as opposed to legality) must not only focus on the immediate advantages and disadvantages of holding prisoners in military detention without charges against them, but must also take a look at change over time and economic dynamics to understand the long-term impacts. To do this, one must consider the incentives facing potential recruits and appreciate the potential receptivity of parts of large Muslim audiences to a jihadist narrative and how U.S. policy might influence that receptivity.

Invading Iraq: Scenarios, Worst-Case Analysis, and Contingency Planning

We have already seen that analysts must employ at least some elements of economic dynamic analysis in order to rationally decide whether to invade Iraq. Scenario analysis, another element of economic dynamic analysis, regularly plays a role in military planning. And it should have played a role in planning for post-invasion Iraq.

The Bush administration invaded Iraq with no operational plan in place for the invasion's aftermath.[42] This bit of irrationality has little to do with either cost–benefit or economic dynamic analysis. Top officials in the Bush administration, especially Vice President Dick Cheney, not only failed to take advantage of the planning efforts of experts within the State and Defense

---

[42] *See* John M. Cushman, *Planning and Early Execution of the War in Iraq: An Assessment of Military Participation* 16 (January 15, 2007).

departments, but also actually fired leading experts in the State Department who had put together coherent plans for winning the peace after the invasion.[43] They apparently saw themselves as spearheading radical reforms and vigorous actions, and treated offering of information indicating a need for careful planning and deployment of appropriate resources as bureaucratic resistance to needed reform.

Their attitudes reflect an arrogance and disdain for the expertise of government officials consistent with a view of government as a deeply dysfunctional bureaucracy. While law and economics acolytes' deep admiration for markets and concomitant skepticism of government is consistent with this view, these officials' attitudes went well beyond what any law and economics scholar would endorse. This is an example of how a particular intellectual climate can lead to excesses that academics helping create the climate would probably resist.

Much of the planning that went on had little to do with economic analysis of any kind, although some of it deals with reconstructing the economy. The State Department Future of Iraq Project, for example, brought together huge amounts of detailed information about Iraqi society, including such things as the salaries of civil servants, the location and condition of specific infrastructure, and the key laws making the legal system corrupt and undemocratic.[44] It then imagined a vast set of actions that might set Iraq on a path to democracy and prosperity, such as revitalizing infrastructure, reforming the civil service, and instituting an independent judiciary.

In planning invasions, however, the military usually employs scenario analysis, because it must prepare for the reactions of an unpredictable enemy. Indeed, by statute, the Joint Chiefs of Staff must carry out "contingency planning," which strongly suggests scenario analysis.[45] In spite of the utter failure of the Bush administration to coordinate the various planning efforts underway within the bureaucracies, let alone to insist on coherent scenario analysis to address uncertainties, elements of scenario analysis did creep into the writing of national security experts seeking to think through what might occur in post-invasion Iraq. They wrote about the potential for looting and therefore the need to protect treasures that might make attractive targets for thieves. Another scenario they envisioned involved sectarian violence, a predictable outcome given Iraq's history of ethnic strife.[46] Some of them also foresaw the

---

[43] See Ricks, *supra* note 19, at 102–104.
[44] See The Future of Iraq Project, National Security Archive Electronic Briefing Book No. 198, http://www.gwu.edu/~nsarchiv/NSAEBB/NSAEBB198/index.htm.
[45] See 10 U.S.C. § 153(a)(3).
[46] See Daniel L. Byman, "Building the New Iraq: The Role of Intervening Forces," 45 *Int'l Inst. for Strategic Studies* 57, 58 (2003); Donald C. Crane & W. Andrew Terrill, *Deconstructing*

possibility of terrorism, since Al Qaeda had announced it would resist an invasion of Iraq.[47] Planning a military invasion requires envisioning the response
to an invasion. The most systematic way to do this is to employ scenario analysis to envision various things that *might* occur and to engage in contingency
planning.

In carrying out such planning, military analysts must pay attention to the
dynamics in play and the bounded rationality of the populace. So, for example, shortly before the invasion, several experts noted that many Iraqis would
assume that the United States "intervened for its own purposes and not primarily to help them."[48] They did not assume that Iraqis would respond as rational
economic actors employing full information, but based on heuristics (note
the word "assume") reflecting their worldview, a view informed by religious
differences and Arab nationalism.[49] This understanding of how the particular
bounds on Iraqis' rationality would likely influence how the dynamics would
play out led them to the conclusion that occupying American forces must
quickly take actions that improve Iraqis' daily lives; otherwise, they might
resist the American occupation with horrible results. The understanding of
the dynamics of the situation also led State Department planners to identify
buildings that looters and resistors might target.[50] Had top officials made use of
these plans, we might have avoided the plundering of Iraq's National Museum
and other sites shortly after the invasion.[51]

When at war, it makes sense to prepare for the most severe problems an
enemy can create, so that one can avoid defeat – in other words, to engage
in some form of worst-case analysis as part of a scenario analysis. Those writing about sectarian strife, terrorism, and looting acted consistently with this
approach and with the basic idea of examining several scenarios seriously. By
contrast, General Tommy Franks, and apparently much of the administration, implicitly rejected worst-case analysis and scenario analysis in favor of
"best-case planning."[52] They thought it likely that Iraqis would welcome us
with open arms and that former Iraqi soldiers would work for the Americans,
making deployment of enough American troops to carry out the needed work
unnecessary. Sensible planning, though, requires scenario analysis to include
some form of worst-case analysis.

    Iraq: Challenges and Missions for Military Forces in a Post-Conflict Scenario, Strategic Stud.
    Inst., U.S. Army War College 2 (January 29, 2003).
[47] *See, e.g.* Byman, *supra* note 46, at 57.
[48] Crane & Terrill, *supra* note 46, at 2.
[49] Id.
[50] *See* Cushman, *supra* note 42, at 18, n. 34.
[51] Id. at 18.
[52] *See* Ricks, *supra* note 19, at 73–74.

For purposes of evaluating the economic dynamic approach's potential contribution to national security, a detailed evaluation of the invasion's aftermath is not necessary. Eventually, top officials concluded that we did not have enough troops on the ground to both provide for security against looting, sectarian violence, and terrorism while delivering sufficient benefits to the Iraq population to win the peace, and they made adjustments and augmented troop levels. But we suffered major casualties and found it difficult to deliver benefits to Iraqis for many years after the invasion because the Bush administration did not adopt a coherent plan based on scenario analysis prior to the invasion.

The larger point, however, is that once we have determined that a particular type of action is needed to address a systemic risk, such as that the Bush administration imagined that Iraq posed, we can use scenario analysis and appreciation of dynamics to prepare and calibrate our actions. This is an important observation for economic dynamic theory, as proponents of CBA often imagine that CBA provides the only way to calibrate actions. On the contrary, CBA of all of the myriad options involved in planning to win the peace is utterly unimaginable. Instead, sensible planners will use scenario analysis and look at the dynamics involved to make choices helping us achieve our objectives.

CBA, moreover, does not substantially aid priority setting, as its proponents sometimes claim.[53] Instead, in this setting, economic dynamic analysis aids priority setting. The dynamics in this situation indicated that top priorities would have to include seizing control of key buildings and providing security to head off looting and then swift actions, such as repair and upgrading of electricity generation, that could bring immediate benefits to Iraqis. While those employing even rudimentary elements of economic dynamic analysis could sequentially order priorities, top officials ignored the analysis and simply failed to provide the resources or planning that would make execution of most of these essentials possible.[54] While one cannot attribute this failure to any form of CBA, the economic dynamics of the situation, not CBA, would inform sensible priority setting.

COLLATERAL NEGATIVE CONSEQUENCES

Efficacy, as some analysts have recognized, goes to the heart of what we need to know in analyzing questions of national security. National security law

---

[53] I make the point here only in terms of national security. But I have defended this point more generally in David Driesen, "Getting Our Priorities Straight: One Strand of the Regulatory Reform Debate," 31 *Envt'l L. Rep.* (Envt'l L. Inst.) 10003 (2001).

[54] *See* Crane & Terrell, *supra* note 46, at 2–3.

generally aims to minimize systemic risk. Accordingly, while officials may need
to understand collateral negatives in choosing among efficacious strategies, the
matter of primary importance involves analyzing proposed actions' efficacy.
Furthermore, we have seen that economic analysis can help us calibrate
responses and prioritize various needed measures.

That said, we must – at least in making major decisions that do not seem
absolutely essential to preventing a catastrophic attack – sometimes consider collateral negative consequences. We considered these consequences
in reducing our involvement in Iraq and we must consider them in deciding
how long to remain deeply involved in Afghanistan. This implies that we must
consider the advantages and disadvantages of our military commitments. Considering advantages and disadvantages differs in a subtle and important way
from considering costs and benefits. The language of costs and benefits implies
an emphasis on dollar values and the ability of quantification to adequately
inform decisions. Considering advantages and disadvantages suggests deemphasizing quantification in favor of qualitative analysis informed by economic
dynamics and value choices.

No sane policymaker would make quantification of costs and benefits central to decisions about whether to remain deeply engaged militarily in Iraq
and Afghanistan. An understanding of the advantages of remaining in those
countries, in particular, requires careful assessment of the situation's dynamics.
Such an understanding relies upon cogent analysis of the relationship between
our presence and prevention of the systemic risks that supposedly justified our
presence in the first place as well as other factors, focusing on efficacy. We
must figure out whether a continued presence foments or reduces terrorism
threats. National security expert Richard Clarke argued that invading Iraq
would foment terrorism by helping Al Qaeda convince potential terrorists that
the West was waging a war on Islam. And our presence did indeed help foment
an increase in terrorism.[55] Once we increased terrorism in Iraq, though, the
equation changed. We had to evaluate the question of whether our continuing
occupation reduces the threat we helped create or instead multiplies terrorist
opportunities. This question, in turn, depends in part on an assessment of the
potential efficacy of a native Iraqi government. Evaluation of these sorts of
questions will necessarily lead to equivocal answers, and trying to represent
the results in dollar terms will only obscure the difficult judgment that our
leaders must make.

Some of the disadvantages of remaining do not resist quantification at
all. We know the monetary costs of remaining (at least roughly). But the key

---

[55] *See* Richard Clarke, Against All Enemies: Inside America's War on Terror (2004).

disadvantages involve lost American lives, a reduced ability to deploy elsewhere if necessary, and potential negative impacts on national security and our reputation. These disadvantages defy quantification. Sensible decision making focuses primarily on qualitative evaluation of advantages and disadvantages by looking at likely future changes over time based on situational dynamics. Quantification of costs plays at best a subsidiary role and quantification of benefits would only obscure the key variables in sound decision making.

While I am not aware of any effort to actually quantify the costs and benefits of our adventure in Iraq (or Afghanistan), some economists did attempt to estimate the economic impacts of an invasion of Iraq on oil prices and the global economy before the invasion.[56] They did not, however, create a point estimate, the typical procedure for CBA in the regulatory context. Instead, they employed scenario analysis to provide a range of outcomes, a range that varied from no adverse effects to a global recession and from lower to significantly higher oil prices. Of course, an analysis that tells you that an action may have no economic impact at all or a very severe impact does not provide much guidance for policy making. Moreover, if policymakers placed significant emphasis on the results of an analysis of costs to the economy, they would miss the boat. The key questions involve the efficacy of various options in eliminating systemic risks, not the temporary effects of invasion on markets. Scenario analysis proves extremely useful when it focuses on key issues of efficacy and less effective when it becomes a component of CBA focusing only on the quantifiable. Although scenario analysis certainly improves CBA, it provides even more help when we abandon CBA and use scenario analysis to illuminate choices without a focus on dollar values.

CONCLUSION

Cogent analysis of national security issues focuses primarily on questions efficacy. It requires analysis of a situation's dynamics, taking into account bounded rationality and the responses of people with limited information about our intentions and other relevant matters. In the case of major decisions, military planners must (and usually do) deploy scenario analysis, including analysis of a worst case, in order to make wise choices in the face of uncertainty. Economic dynamic analysis can inform not only basic choices, such as whether to invade a particular country, but also calibration of responses and consideration of collateral negative consequences when that is appropriate.

[56] *See* Laurence Meyer, *After an Attack on Iraq: The Economic Consequences Conference Summary* (Center for Strategic and International Studies, 2006).

This illustrates a more fundamental point – that we are concerned with efficacy, not efficiency, when we confront systemic risks. For this reason, neoclassical law and economics has enjoyed less influence in the national security field than in many other areas of law (such as property, antitrust, or contract). Still, it has played a role in creating the ideological climate that has led to privatization of many military functions. Cogent analysis of privatization questions, however, requires attention to the shape of change over time, not just short-term efficiency questions. When we privatize a function, economic dynamic analysis can help us design contracts that create accountability and minimize the potential for bad outcomes.

11

Climate Disruption: An Economic Dynamic Approach

This chapter shows that an economic dynamic approach provides appropriate guidance regarding climate disruption policy, has influenced other countries' adoption of sound policies, and has begun to affect officials in the United States. By contrast, neoclassical law and economics contributed to the United States' failure to adequately address global climate disruption.[1]

This chapter's first part shows how a description of climate disruption's dynamic provides a firm basis for understanding the problem well for policy purposes. The second part shows how CBA has failed to provide clear guidance about how to respond to climate disruption. The third part explains that neoclassical law and economics contributed to the United States' failure to adequately address climate disruption. The fourth part shows in some detail how an economic dynamic approach has provided concrete policy guidance. A final section shows that an economic dynamic approach can improve the design of environmental policy instruments and helps us envision new policy instruments focused on maximizing innovation to solve tough long-term problems.

CLIMATE DISRUPTION'S DYNAMICS

Almost all scientists studying climate disruption have considered it a very serious problem for almost two decades, with those offering any opinion at all about what to do about it supporting vigorous regulation. (This excludes a tiny minority of scientists that industry has funded to debunk mainstream climate science or lack credentials in relevant fields.) An elementary understanding of climate dynamics and impacts makes the reasons for characterizing climate disruption as a significant systemic risk apparent.

[1] *See generally Economic Thought and U.S. Climate Change Policy* (David M. Driesen, ed., 2010) [hereinafter *Economic Thought*].

First of all, carbon dioxide and other "greenhouse gases" trap heat. During the industrial era, we have increased our emissions of greenhouse gases and global average mean surface temperatures have risen. Science can find only one plausible cause for this temperature increase: increased human emissions of greenhouse gases.

Rising temperature produces a variety of effects, most of them quite serious and negative. Scientists now predict that climate disruption will raise sea levels, increase flooding, intensify extreme weather events (such as hurricanes), vastly alter ecosystems, eliminate many endangered species, spread insect-borne disease vectors, and produce severe droughts, especially in already dry regions of the world, where more severe water shortages will produce more widespread famine.[2] These problems amount to a very serious systemic risk, because they represent a serious disturbance in fundamental physical systems. They arise from imbalances in the global circulation of carbon, a vast temperature-regulating system that includes the atmosphere, oceans, and land. Scientists consider climate disruption and many of its predicted consequences quite likely, so this amounts to a significant systemic risk, not a minimal risk that one can safely ignore.

Many of the predictions discussed above (and others) flow from rather elementary dynamics. For example, heat melts ice, which implies rising seas. Generally, however, scientists use dynamic models of earth systems to model climate's impacts, as oceans, clouds, terrestrial ecosystems, and other factors can ameliorate or exacerbate the greenhouse gases' tendency to increase heat.

Another basic qualitative fact about climate disruption's dynamics should make any serious analyst extremely concerned about leaving climate disruption unaddressed. Greenhouse gases remain in the atmosphere for decades, if not centuries. This means that once climate disruption begins to occur, even ceasing all greenhouse gas emissions would not reverse its impacts reasonably quickly. It also means that the climate disruption problem is cumulative. Every year that we continue to emit greenhouse gases, we add to a cumulative store consisting of many years' prior emissions, thereby exacerbating the problem.

The most important consequences of climate disruption, however, may be those that involve a dynamic that would make climate disruption a runaway catastrophe beyond the control of human beings simply reducing their emissions. For example, the permafrost covering much of Siberia traps methane, a potent greenhouse gas. If the climate warms sufficiently, it could melt the permafrost, releasing methane trapped underneath. The released methane

---

[2] *See Climate Change 2007: Impacts, Adaptation, and Vulnerability* (Martin Perry et al., eds., 2007).

would, in turn, increase the warming, thereby accelerating the melting of permafrost and the release of yet more methane. Hence, the dynamics show the potential for runaway climate disruption. This would make warming a self-perpetuating phenomenon, in which previous warming, apart from current emissions, causes future warming.

Yet scientists do not pretend to know what amount of temperature increase and emissions would trigger this sort of dynamic, how likely it is, or how severe the runaway warming would be.[3] The dynamic shows that this constitutes a substantial systemic risk with huge potential for danger that we (or our descendants) would have great difficulty coping with. Hence, fundamental dynamics show that taking action would be extremely prudent even in the absence of precise knowledge about climate disruption's effects.[4]

In seeking to provide policymakers with some sense of the problem's magnitude, the Intergovernmental Panel on Climate Change (IPCC) – the expert scientific body charged by the international community with assessing climate disruption's dangers – employs scenario analysis based on climate disruption's economic dynamics to generate a range of estimates of likely temperature increases. Some scientific work seeks to correlate temperature with types, and sometimes magnitudes, of effects.

The amount of atmospheric warming depends on the amount of greenhouse gases in the atmosphere, which, in turn, depends on emissions. Carbon dioxide, which accounts for about 80 percent of global greenhouse gas emissions, comes from burning fossil fuels. In general, because growing economies use more energy, economic growth directly influences future emissions. Hence, scenario analysis of climate disruption features varying assumptions about the amount of economic growth we can expect and therefore of future temperature increases.

This scenario analysis gives one some sense of climate disruption's magnitude, while representing some of the uncertainty in choices of varying scenarios. Even with this approach, however, policymakers cannot rely on the quantitative estimates without taking into account limitations stemming from climate disruption's fundamental dynamics. These analyses leave out important feedback loops (like the methane problem described previously), which remain too poorly understood for modelers to incorporate into a quantitative model. The IPCC, aware of these and other uncertainties, regularly admonishes readers of its reports to "expect surprises." Hence, an understanding

---

3 *See* Markku Rummukainen, et al., *Physical Climate Science since IPCC AR4* 67 (2010).
4 *See* id. at 71 (stating that our robust qualitative understanding of time lags in the climate system tells us that emissions must be reduced well before we feel "their full effects").

of climate disruption's dynamics helps guide policymakers by giving them some sense of the problem's nature, its resistance to precise prediction, and, with the aid of scenario analysis, its very rough magnitude, without disguising uncertainty.

COST-BENEFIT ANALYSIS

CBA has produced wildly varying estimates of the costs and benefits of proposals to address global climate disruption. Furthermore, both the cost and benefit estimates remain dangerously incomplete, because they rely only on factors economists can model, thereby leaving out some of the most important information.

Economists' estimates of the cost of U.S. compliance with the Kyoto Protocol ran the gamut from a loss of 4.2 percent of gross domestic product (GDP) to a gain of 2.5 percent of GDP.[5] The disparities seen in these and other carbon abatement cost estimates stem from a number of sources. Most fundamentally, economists have no way of knowing what the future cost of employing technologies to prevent greenhouse gas emissions will be, since nobody knows what the cost of solar or nuclear power, for example, will be in 2020, 2030, or 2050, let alone what new technology might emerge in the next 50 or 100 years. So they cover up their lack of knowledge with reasonable assumptions, which vary.[6] Some economists use "top-down" approaches that use macroeconomic data, such as data from the 1970s about the influence of rising oil prices on energy consumption, to derive estimates of the cost of reducing carbon dioxide. Others employ "bottom-up" approaches based on current prices of greenhouse gas abatement technologies, which tend to produce lower cost estimates.[7] Both of these approaches are often static and can fail to account for technological advances likely to reduce abatement cost over time.

Economists often use static approaches because they cannot predict the rate of future cost decreases. Some economists, however, recognize that the static approach implicitly uses a number extremely likely to incorrectly estimate the rate of technological progress – zero – and hazard guesses about the rate of future price decreases stemming from technological innovation. In order to have some mathematical basis for doing this, adventuresome bottom-up

[5] *See* Thomas O. McGarity, "The Cost of Greenhouse Gas Reductions," in *Economic Thought, supra* note 1, at 215.

[6] *See* id. at 216 (describing cost estimation as based on "huge simplifying assumptions").

[7] *See* Richard Richels, "Comment: The Costs of Greenhouse-Gas Abatement and Carbon Emissions Reductions," in *Economics and Policy Issues in Climate Change* 216 (William D. Nordhaus, ed., 1998) [hereinafter *Economics & Policy*].

modelers use "rate-of-progress" ratios, data about how prices of abatement technologies have fallen in the past, to predict how rapidly they will decline in the future. For example, policies supporting renewable energy have caused prices to decline over time. Economists can feed data about prior cost declines per unit of time into a model, but, of course, they have no way of knowing whether the implicit assumption that the future will imitate the recent past over or under predicts future price changes. The assumption that some technological innovation will occur, however, tends to produce much lower cost estimates than models based on static assumptions.[8]

Frank Ackerman has shown how the modelers' assumptions drive policy conclusions.[9] For example, William Nordhaus's Dynamic Integrated Climate Economy (DICE) model assumes that the cost of climate abatement comes down over time, whether or not any policy intervention occurs. His model does not allow for the possibility that policy intervention might accelerate a decline in abatement cost, as it almost always does with respect to environmental technology. As a result of this static assumption about policy's lack of influence, Nordhaus's model "shows" that it pays to wait to adopt climate policies. By contrast, some models that assume that policies produce significant cost-saving technological change conclude that limiting greenhouse gas emissions produces economic gains.[10]

Great variation arises on the benefits side as well. Economists' estimates of the dollar value of a ton of greenhouse gas emission reduction vary from as little as $5 a ton to almost $900 a ton by 2010 (although most estimates lie in the $5 to $125 range).[11] Choice of a "discount rate," which devalues future benefits of greenhouse gas abatement, heavily influences these results.[12] Because of greenhouse gases' long residence times, many of the benefits of

---

[8] *See* Terry Barker et al., "Avoiding Dangerous Climate Change by Inducing Technological Progress; Scenarios Using a Large-Scale Econometric Model," in *Avoiding Dangerous Climate Change* 362–64 (Hans Joachim Schellnhuber et al., eds., (2006)).

[9] *See* Frank Ackerman, "Cost-Benefit Analysis of Climate Change: Where it Goes Wrong," in *Economic Thought, supra* note 1, at 61–81.

[10] *See* Richels, *supra* note 7, at 216.

[11] *See* Frank Ackerman & Elizabeth A. Stanton, *Climate Risks and Carbon Prices: Revising the Social Cost of Carbon* 2 (2011); Frank Ackerman & Elizabeth A. Stanton, *The Social Cost of Carbon: A Report for the Economics for Equity and the Environment Network* 9 (2010) [hereinafter 2010 *Social Costs*]; Douglas Kysar, "Some Realism about Environmental Skepticism: The Implications of Bjorn Lomborg's The Skeptical Environmentalist for Environmental Law and Policy," 30 *Ecology L. Q.* 223, 263 (2003) (discussing these numbers, given in 1990 U.S. dollars).

[12] *See* Charles Kolstad, in *Economics & Policy, supra* note 7, at 276 (noting that the choice of discount rate can account for the difference between a recommendation to do very little about climate disruption and a recommendation for 50% emission reductions).

today's greenhouse gas abatement will occur in the future, with the largest benefits occurring several generations hence. Economists typically discount these future benefits by creating a discount rate reflecting the sum of a "rate of pure time preference" and a "wealth-based" component.[13]

The "pure time preference" values human lives from the perspective of the market behavior of those currently living, even though climate disruption will affect people not yet born. Since market behavior suggests that people value current benefits more than future benefits, economists usually discount future benefits using a rate of pure time preference reflecting such things as interest rates, which they believe measures people's discounting of future benefits. Using this approach in the context of the very long time frames involved in climate disruption, however, has the effect of devaluing the lives of future generations relative to those currently living.[14] But economists have varying views about what the pure time preference component of a discount rate should be, and because discount rates over a long period of time have a huge effect on value, the variations of their views produce large disparities in valuation. Nicholas Stern, the author of a famous 2006 CBA, which produced relatively high values for the benefits of reductions compared with other studies, accepted arguments by critics of discount rates that all generations have equal value and therefore discounting across generations to reflect only this generation's preferences is not appropriate.[15] Others using high discount rates get much lower valuations of greenhouse gas reductions' benefits.

The "wealth-based" component of a discount rate reflects the view that future generations will likely be richer than current generations[16] and therefore more able to adapt to or compensate for climate disruption than our relatively poor generation. This implies that climate benefits are less valuable to future generations than they are to us and therefore justifies (supposedly) further discounting future benefits based on our estimates of future generations' wealth. The amount of the wealth-based component of the discount rate depends on uncertain estimates of economic growth and the amount of decline in the utility of consumption per increase in unit of economic growth,

---

[13] See 2010 *Social Costs, supra* note 11, at 7.

[14] See William D. Norhaus & Joseph Boyer, *Warming the World: Economic Models of Global Warming* 11 (2000) (admitting that a positive discount rate favors the current generation over future generations); Amy Sinden, "The Abandonment of Justice," in *Economic Thought, supra* note 1, at 119.

[15] Richard L. Revesz, "Environmental Regulation, Cost-Benefit Analysis, and the Discounting of Human Lives," 99 *Colum. L. Rev.* 941, 988–1006 (1999) (rejecting intergenerational discounting); Lisa Heinzerling, "Discounting Our Future," 34 *Land & Water L. Rev.* 39, 40–41 (1999).

[16] See Ackerman, *supra* note 9, at 69.

so this factor varies in competing analyses as well.[17] Economists' confidence that future generations will be wealthier than the current one reflects the habit of mathematical modelers of assuming that past trends will continue, but seems inconsistent with taking climate disruption seriously, as a host of floods, violent hurricanes, and pestilence might decrease wealth.[18] Many scientists have argued that our current wealth is based on abundant cheap fossil fuel, which might imply that our wealth will diminish rapidly in the years ahead as cheap oil becomes scarcer, even without substantial climate disruption.[19] Furthermore, economists, in coming up with dollar values for the deaths climate disruption will cause, typically use per capita income as a proxy for the value of human life. This has the troubling result of devaluing life in poor countries with low per capita income, where most climate-related deaths will likely occur. If economists applied this same methodology to future generations, they might end up with a negative discount rate component augmenting the value of future lives saved to reflect the increased economic value of people with higher per capita incomes.[20]

Hence, CBA's results depend on the policy views of the economist conducting the analysis. Some of these policy views, such as the view that observed market behavior should govern discount rates, instead of philosophy about the worth of future generations or observations about how much we care for our children or grandchildren, enjoy widespread, although not universal, support among economists. Other policy-relevant analytical choices, such as decisions about which discount rate to choose, vary widely even among economists who share optimism about future wealth and a belief that time preferences revealed by interest rates should lead to discounting.

CBA of environmental impacts usually leaves out very important aspects of the problem under analysis, because only a few aspects of environmental problems lend themselves to mathematical modeling, and climate disruption provides no exception to this rule. William Nordhaus's estimate of climate disruption's health impacts relies upon a study of climate-related disease

---

[17] *See* Helen Scarborough, *Decomposing the Social Discount Rate* 7 (2010), http://ageconsearch .umn.edu/bitstream/59156/2/Scarborough,%20Helen.pdf.

[18] *Cf.* Julie Nelson, "Ethics and the Economist: What Climate Change Demands of Us" 28 (Global Development and Environment Inst., Working Paper No. 11–02, 2011).

[19] *See* Charles A. S. Hall et. al., "The Need to Reintegrate Natural Sciences and Economics," 51 *Bioscience* 663 (2001).

[20] *See* Sinden, *supra* note 14, at 120 (pointing out that employing the logic of per capita income as a measure of the value of life to future generations would cause us to treat future lives as more valuable than our own); Kysar, supra note 11, at 266 (noting that pegging the value of life to per capita income implies that "a future person should be weighted more, not less, than a presently living person").

vectors only.[21] He ignores IPCC predictions, with high confidence, that climate disruption will produce deaths and other health impacts from heat waves, flooding, and malnutrition in areas suffering climate-related declines in crops. CBA almost always ignores significant environmental impacts, not because economists deliberately ignore science, but because economists cannot find data or even semi-credible estimates of the magnitude of many known impacts. Scientists present a clear picture of the dynamics causing sea level rise and therefore flooding, as shown above. But the number of people who die in the floods depends on such imponderables as where and when floods strike, how well public authorities prepare for them, and how large the floods are. Thus, CBA loses more information than most other forms of analysis, because it has no use for information that does not lead to dollar-value approximations.

  Climate disruption, however, has attracted an unusually large amount of attention from economists, thereby generating much more sophistication about science than one typically sees in economic analysis. This growing sophistication has recently manifested itself in some skepticism about CBA's value in this context, even among economists and economic-minded legal scholars, who generally love CBA. Harvard's Martin Weitzman has written that the problem of "fat-tailed distribution" – the potential for feedback loops to generate a large-scale disaster not amenable to quantification – makes CBA of little value for climate disruption.[22] On the law and economics side, Eric Posner and Jonathan Masur consider CBA of climate disruption an unsuitable basis for agency action because of uncertainties regarding the extent of climate disruption's harms and because of the problem's global nature.[23] Even William Nordhaus and Joseph Boyer, although stoutly defending Nordhaus's pioneering but controversial CBA and the neoclassical approach to the problem in general, concede that their damage function is "extremely conjectural, given the thin base of empirical studies on which it rests."[24] Yet the problem of some of the most serious consequences of an environmental problem either completely resisting quantification or permitting it only under very dubious assumptions[25]

[21] Kysar, *supra* note 11, at 264.
[22] *See* Martin L. Weitzman, "On Modeling and Interpreting the Economics of Catastrophic Climate Change," 91 *Rev. Econ. & Statistics* 1 (2009); Martin L. Weitzman, "A Review of the Stern Review on the Economics of Climate Change," 45 *J. Econ. Lit.* 703 (2007).
[23] Jonathan S. Masur & Eric A. Posner, "Climate Regulation and the Limits of Cost-Benefit Analysis," 99 *Cal. L Rev.* 1557, **1563, 1599** (2011).
[24] Nordhaus & Boyer, *supra* note 14, at 41–42.
[25] Masur & Posner, *supra* note 23, at 19–20 (discussing economic models' "weakly defended assumptions" and the FUND model's failure to account for catastrophic outcomes); *See, e.g.* Ackerman, *supra* note 9, at 72–73 (explaining that the PAGE and DICE models arbitrarily characterize a catastrophe as representing 5% to 20% of GDP and increase the probability

is not unique to climate disruption.[26] The "thin base" of empirical studies that Nordhaus and Boyer lament reflects one of the most intensive programs of environmental science research the world has ever seen, generating countless empirical studies, but few quantitative estimates, with those produced likely to prove erroneous, because of climate disruption's nonlinear complex nature.

Any individual CBA usually produces a single point estimate of the benefits of addressing climate disruption, thereby creating the very misleading impression that the underlying analysis is reasonably complete. Even when CBA presents a range of outcomes, it greatly understates the uncertainties involved. Although scientists have produced more than 20 recognized models of climate disruption, economists' work generally relies on only one or two of these models.[27] Because no scientific basis exists for favoring the models economists happen to choose, climate scientists disregard CBA as hopelessly unscientific and likely downward biased.[28] A good scenario analysis, by contrast, would consider the full range of models in constructing an adequate range of scenarios, as scientists do routinely when describing uncertainties in prediction of climate disruption's effects.[29]

NEOCLASSICAL LAW AND ECONOMICS' POLICY INFLUENCE

Neoclassical law and economics has contributed enormously to the United States' failure to adequately address the most significant environmental problem of our age.[30] Most obviously, the deregulatory climate that neoclassical law and economics helped create led to two decades of federal inaction on the problem.[31] The United States, which had been a leader of efforts to address international environmental problems in the past, played a mostly obstructionist role in international negotiations of the climate regime and the federal government did nothing significant to address climate disruption domestically,

---

of such an event occurring by 10% for each additional degree of warming). *Cf.* Richard A. Posner, *Catastrophe: Risk and Response* 52–53 (2004) (noting, accurately, that "climatologists cannot . . . assess the probability" of a catastrophe).

[26] *See* Paul R. Portney, "Applicability of Cost-Benefit Analysis to Climate Change," in *Economics & Policy, supra* note 7, at 117–20.

[27] Marshall Burke et al., "Incorporating Climate Uncertainty into Estimates of Climate Change Impacts, With Applications to U.S. and African Agriculture," 2 (NBER Working Paper 17092, 2011).

[28] Id. at 3.

[29] *See* id. at 6.

[30] *See Economic Thought, supra* note 1 (detailing the nature of the influence).

[31] *See* Christopher Schroeder & Robert L. Glicksman, "The United States' Failure to Act," in *Economic Thought, supra* note 1, at 21–38.

until 2010, when the EPA issued a regulation applying strict California vehicle standards for carbon dioxide emissions from vehicles to the entire nation
(with minor variations). In particular, the United States successfully opposed
mandatory targets for greenhouse gas reductions in negotiations leading up
to the adoption of the Framework Convention of Climate Change in 1992.
The United States also resisted strict mandatory targets in the Kyoto Protocol, but then-Vice President Al Gore brokered a compromise in which the
United States appeared to accept a 7 percent reduction below 1990 levels to
save those negotiations from collapse. President Bush, however, with strong
support in Congress, repudiated the Kyoto Protocol outright, stating, "Kyoto
would have wrecked the economy." This statement invoked the deregulatory
spirit he helped champion and neoclassical law and economics supported, suggesting that markets do not dynamically adapt to a policy addressing climate
disruption, but instead simply wither because of interference.

Moreover, then-contemporary CBA supported Bush's policy decision.
William Nordhaus had modeled compliance with the Kyoto Protocol and concluded that its costs outweighed its benefits.[32] Subsequent analysis, employing
different assumptions, however, reaches the conclusion that much more drastic actions than Kyoto contemplated produce benefits exceeding costs on a
global basis.[33]

Even after Barak Obama became president of the United States, the anti-
regulation gestalt that neoclassical law and economics supported lived on.
Congress failed to pass comprehensive climate disruption legislation, largely
because of fears about its economic impact.

AN ECONOMIC DYNAMIC APPROACH TO CLIMATE POLICY

Although a neoclassical economic approach leads to a maze of unsolvable
puzzles and helps support a political climate hostile to regulation, an economic
dynamic approach yields a simple straightforward conclusion. The world's
current path of continuing reliance on increasing fossil fuel consumption
leads to a set of serious problems and may bring us outright catastrophe. We
need to take actions to reverse the trajectory and ameliorate systemic risks by
moving away from use of fossil fuels as best we can.[34]

The economic dynamic focus on long-term trajectories makes the case for
addressing climate disruption vigorously quite strong. Fossil fuels are finite

---

[32] *See* William Nordhaus & Joseph Boyer, "Requiem for Kyoto: An Economic Analysis of the
Kyoto Protocol" (Cowles Foundation Discussion Paper No. 1201, 1998).
[33] Nicholas Stern, *The Economics of Climate Change: The Stern Review* (2007).
[34] *See* Nelson, *supra* note 18, at 27–29.

nonrenewable resources that will run out. As they become scarce, their prices will rise, perhaps abruptly.

Accordingly, we will phase out fossil fuels eventually, either through policy decisions or disappearance of the resource. Hence, the question we face is not whether to phase out fossil fuels – we will phase them out whether we like it or not – but whether we will do so deliberately early enough to avoid sudden unexpected price increases and many of climate disruption's most dangerous effects, or whether we will be forced to do so after suffering from serious, and perhaps catastrophic, climate disruption and abrupt price shocks that we are ill-prepared for. Admittedly, coal will not run out nearly as soon as oil, but still, this remains the fundamental long-term question we face.

Understanding the direction of change over time, a world of rising fossil fuel prices and growing environmental calamities provides us with solid information on which to base a policy. Economists' feeble, albeit well-intentioned, efforts to quantify future costs and benefits tell us precious little, and that little is probably misleading. We cannot know the costs of switching from finite nonrenewable resources to renewable ones, because the costs of both will change at unpredictable rates, but we do know that over the long term, a switch to renewable resources makes a lot of sense.

The economic dynamic approach has indeed animated much of the international community outside the United States and has influenced some actors within the United States, especially recently. The international community, including the United States, adopted a goal of preventing dangerous climate change in the Framework Convention on Climate Change. This admonition to avoid systemic risk appeared very hard to operationalize, so the IPCC undertook an effort to define dangerous climate change in terms of an amount of temperature increase and to quantify the emission reductions needed to avoid dangerous atmospheric concentrations of greenhouse gases. Although this effort too, involves substantial uncertainties, it does not demand quantification and monetization of all of climate disruption's many consequences. And a scientific consensus indicates that the world must realize something along the order of magnitude of a 50 percent cut in global greenhouse gas emissions by 2050 to prevent dangerous climate disruption.[35]

This implies that a goal of avoiding systemic risk can generate rough agreement about the magnitude of reductions required to meet economic dynamic theory's primary goal. By contrast, in the climate arena, as we have seen, the disparity of analysts' CBA results precludes a reasonable consensus about "optimal" levels of greenhouse gas emissions. Furthermore, since scientists

---

[35] *See* David M. Driesen, "Capping Carbon," 40 *Envt'l L.* 1, 33–35 (2010).

and economists cannot quantify important benefits of greenhouse gas emission reductions, even a consensus about the value of quantifiable reductions could not generate a logically coherent conclusion about optimal pollution levels. If the quantified benefits of a proposed reduction outweighed the costs, it would be possible to say that the proposed reductions would be worthwhile. But it would not be possible to determine whether the unquantified benefits justified more reductions. Conversely, if the monetized costs of a proposed cut outweighed its benefits, one cannot determine whether the proposal would prove suboptimal, since the unquantified benefits might justify the proposed cut.[36]

In this arena, CBA does not materially aid calibration of response, but a goal of avoiding systemic risk does. The scientists' 50 percent reduction goal heavily influenced the European Union's domestic climate policies and its international stance, thereby demonstrating that the EU supports economic dynamic theory's goal of avoiding systemic risk.[37] A decision to adopt such a goal does not by itself tell one exactly what to do, but it provides some conceptual clarity about direction and some degree of guidance about actions. For the most part, the international community has embraced the notion that the bulk of the reductions, about 80 percent by 2050, should come from developed countries, since they have greater historical responsibility for the problem and greater capacity to address it than developing countries.

The economic dynamic approach has also made policymakers realize the value of establishing long-term targets in law now, even though compliance with them is decades off. These targets send a signal that those who start shifting toward low-carbon technologies will eventually find that their investment pays off. An understanding of the economic dynamics makes this signal's importance clear. The most significant sectors for climate disruption include sectors that make large capital investments and change slowly, if at all. Delaying greenhouse gas emission reductions may mean that electric utilities build new coal-fired power plants, in spite of coal's high carbon intensity. Once utilities build these capital-intensive facilities, their owners will acquire incentives to resist emission reduction requirements that might interfere with their operations. This means that absent some policy intervention, emissions will tend to increase drastically and the world will irretrievably lose opportunities to move in a safer direction.

---

[36] Ronnie Levin, "Lead in Drinking Water," in *Economic Analysis at EPA* 205, 230 (Richard D. Morgenstern, ed., 1997).

[37] *See* David Campbell & Matthias Klaes, "Copenhagen, Cancún and the Limits of Global Welfare Economics," 31 *Econ. Aff.* 10, 11 (2011); Driesen, *supra* note 35, at 33–35 (describing the goal's scientific basis and influence).

Furthermore, the economic dynamics of progress on an issue like this suggest that reaching such an ambitious goal in the long term requires some significant emission decreases in the short term, leading to European proposals for an interim goal of 30 percent developed country reductions by 2020 and a EU legislative decision to make a 20 percent cut even if other developed countries do not follow suit. The idea of a short-term target also reflects a dynamic understanding of how firms and individuals will respond to climate policies. If we wait and then suddenly try to meet an ambitious target, it will appear hopeless. Some experience in making progress and seeing costs decline (as they usually have when ambitious actions have been undertaken) can make realization of ambitious targets in the future feasible. This commitment to short-term reductions also reflects the fundamental economic dynamic that Nordhaus's DICE model denies, that near-term investments in new technology will lower long-term costs.

Indeed, in the environmental area, what economists call "learning-by-doing" – the idea that producers learn how to make technology better and cheaper from experience with its production for a real market – provides a key to understanding cost decreases' dynamics. Policy can change behavior in ways that lower costs and therefore make ambitious policies in the future more feasible. An economic dynamic approach has the advantage of treating cost not as a fixed constraint, but as a dynamic factor subject to policy's influence. This has certainly been the case with renewable energy, for which costs have fallen when policymakers have supported its use.[38]

In keeping with an economic dynamic approach envisioning policy as a demand factor to encourage technological improvement, Europe has adopted aggressive targets for renewable energy, calling for 20 percent renewables by 2020. This target seems to reflect a conviction that if we wish to move away from fossil fuels, we must encourage activities that help us learn about how to produce substitutes. Europe's most successful programs rely heavily on feed-in tariffs, which offer an above-market price for renewable energy. This has set in motion a dynamic increasing the supply and generally lowering the cost of renewable energy. Some European countries have employed "green quotas" (called *renewable portfolio standards* in the United States) toward this same end of stimulating learning by doing. Green quotas require the provision of a specified percentage of renewable energy.

An economic dynamic analysis shows, however, that absent policy support, producers rarely adopt environmentally friendly technologies on their own, at

---

[38] *See* David M. Driesen, "Sustainable Development and Market Liberalism's Shotgun Wedding: Emissions Trading under the Kyoto Protocol," 83 *Indiana L. J.* 21, 42–43 (2008).

least not ones having positive costs, because they must pay more for them than for conventional "dirty" approaches without capturing their environmental benefits. Hence, private research and development will likely become significant only if there is a clear policy commitment – manifested by operational targets, subsidies, or carbon taxes – making it seem economically worthwhile. The essential point that technological progress to address climate disruption will remain tepid absent a policy demanding (through incentives or otherwise) deployment of environmentally superior technologies seems to elude some economists because they view technological evolution as a broad spontaneous market process, as it often is outside the environmental realm. In the environmental area, however, government regulation, not spontaneous consumer purchases, serves as the sources for demand for technologies improving environmental performance.

The European Union has also adopted a 20 percent target for energy efficiency improvement, even though Europe already has become much more energy efficient than the United States. An economic dynamic framework justifies massive investments in energy efficiency. Energy efficiency improvements usually pay for themselves. As a result, they would prove worthwhile economically even if climate disruption did not present a serious problem, and they provide a key to lowering energy demand, thus reducing the scale of the necessary project of substituting clean energy for fossil fuels. They represent the happy case where environmental measures generally increase wealth (by reducing costs), a case of what business people call win-win solutions, rather than an example of the stark tradeoffs that dominate the neoclassical law and economics imagination.

An economic dynamic framework firmly rooted in the concept of bounded rationality helps explain why we need policies to encourage energy efficiency. Consumers and, to a lesser extent, businesses tend to underinvest in energy efficiency, because they do not know of the opportunity, lack the necessary capital to make the needed investments, or do not properly calculate the savings available from energy efficiency investments. Business owners and consumers often tend to focus their attention on their daily activities, and not necessarily on the potential energy savings available from changing the buildings they inhabit or the lighting that illuminates their evenings (and days). No business or person can pay attention to all potentially available opportunities for economic gains through reduced expenditures, because there are not enough hours in the day to consider them all. When they do pay attention, they often lack the expertise necessary to identify the best energy saving opportunities. David Goldstein has pointed out that this expertise problem exists even within U.S. businesses because of a dearth of well-qualified process engineers, and, of course, consumers usually have even less expertise.[39] As a result, government programs that simply provide information, such as the EU's ecolabeling program, have some potential to spur energy efficiency improvements that produce cost savings.

Moreover, some consumers and businesses simply do not have the capital to make investments that would pay for themselves over time. Because of this, many governments finance energy efficiency improvements for low-income and sometimes even middle-class homeowners. Even when aware of opportunities and in possession of sufficient capital to take advantage of them, consumers especially tend to fixate on high current costs, rather than sensibly compare them to a stream of future benefits. Energy efficiency investments tend to produce high immediate costs ($10 light bulbs, for example, or $5,000 for a new energy-efficient furnace) and a stream of cost savings thereafter as electricity and fuel bills drop. Consumers tend to react very negatively to the high upfront cost and to pay little attention to the potential for energy efficiency to pay for itself after a few years and then generate additional savings.

An economic dynamic analysis of incentives also reveals decoupling of costs and benefits in the economy that destroy incentives for some market actors to invest in energy efficiency. So, for example, a homeowner who does not expect to live in a house for more than a few years will find an energy efficiency investment that makes perfect economic sense for society unattractive, because the homeowner will pay for all the upfront cost, but reap only a fraction of the future benefits. Another example of this decoupling involves vehicles. Vehicle manufacturers incur the costs of improving vehicle energy efficiency, but reap no benefits. The purchasers of the vehicles reap the benefits. When the EPA finally enacted carbon dioxide standards for vehicles, it found that the fuel savings more than paid for the costs of improving vehicles' energy efficiency (primarily through hybrid technology).[40]

Neoclassical law and economics tends to deny all of this. The assumption that market actors make wholly rational choices based on perfect information leads to the conclusion that the market will make all economically worthwhile energy efficiency improvements on its own. It follows that any energy efficiency improvement not already made must have economic costs exceeding the benefits. William Nordhaus's Regional Integrated Climate Economy (RICE)-99 model, consistent with this tendency to assume that if dollar bills lay on the street somebody would have shined a lamp on them and picked them all

---

[39] David B. Goldstein, *Saving Energy Saving Jobs* 64, 79–83 (2007).
[40] *See* David M. Driesen, Robert W. Adler, & Kirsten H. Engel, *Environmental Law: A Conceptual and Pragmatic Approach* 260 (2011).

up, makes the potential for win-win solutions to at least some of the climate disruption problem disappear, by assuming that they do not exist. He models "carbon-saving technical change... [i.e., energy efficiency]" so that it has no output-enhancing effect.[41] An economic dynamic approach shows these opportunities exist and that climate policy should employ a variety of tools to take advantage of them.[42]

Sophisticated neoclassical economists know some of the abundant evidence that consumers (and, to some extent, businesses) tend to fixate on the upfront costs of energy efficiency improvements. But instead of regarding this fixation as a kind of myopia that policymaking should counteract, they tend to regard it as evidence of an implicit high discount rate that lawmakers should incorporate into cost–benefit models to guide policy choices. An economic dynamic approach, however, regards market actors' myopia as a problem governments should address, not as something for policy to emulate. This follows from economic dynamic theory's rejection of preferences as the basis for policy in favor of choosing sensible long-term trajectories.

Some government officials have adopted or proposed policy measures consistent with an economic dynamic approach. For example, the House of Representatives passed a climate disruption bill in 2010 that resembled the European model, in that it contained targets that seemed aimed at avoiding systemic risks. Similarly, the federal government has run a "green lights" program that has helped businesses save money with energy efficiency improvements that the EPA has helped them identify. Most states in the United States have adopted "renewable portfolio standards," another term for green certificates. And some states, such as California, have made massive investments in energy efficiency.

INSTRUMENT CHOICE

Those steeped in the law and economics of climate disruption have tended to favor carbon taxes or environmental benefit trading as the means of addressing climate disruption, viewing these measures as "market-based solutions." These scholars have enjoyed enormous influence, making environmental benefit trading a centerpiece of international and many domestic efforts to address climate disruption.

Law and economics thinking about "instrument choice," the choice of means to address environmental problems, constitutes one of its most constructive contributions to policymaking. Environmental benefit trading and

---

[41] Nordhaus & Boyer, *supra* note 14, at 19.

[42] *Cf.* Goldstein, *supra* note 39, at 54 (explaining that because energy efficiency reduces consumer costs, it increases economic output).

pollution taxes provide methods for making environmental policy more "cost-effective" than more traditional regulatory approaches. Environmental benefit trading programs require regulators to establish emission limits, but then authorize any owner of a pollution source wishing to avoid its limit to pay another polluter to make extra reductions instead. This ability to trade around pollution reduction obligations leads to lower costs, as those that have cheap abatement opportunities make extra reductions and those with expensive abatement problems buy their way out of expensive local abatement. The U.S. acid rain program, moreover, shows that this approach can, under the right conditions, prove environmentally effective.

Pollution taxes also provide cost-effective abatement. Polluters with abatement options costing more than the tax will probably pay the tax and forgo abatement, whereas those with abatement options costing less than the tax will frequently employ abatement measures to avoid the tax. Thus, in this area, environmental economists and their allies in law schools have made a solid contribution to environmental policy.

Unfortunately, however, the market glorification that frequently goes with the adoption of "market-based measures" has had a pernicious effect on global climate disruption policy, leading to poor design of programs, a failure to learn lessons from past experience about when these sorts of measures do not work, and a lack of imagination about how to stimulate innovation desperately needed to make minimization of climate disruption's huge systemic risks feasible. An economic dynamic approach facilitates better design of these measures and helps us envision superior tools for encouraging innovation.

Economic dynamic analysis' requirement to pay attention to legal detail and how it influences incentives helps reveal why environmental benefit trading works poorly when applied to activities not reliably monitored and program rules allow trades with sources not subject to caps. The acid rain program succeeded partially because of a requirement to employ continuous emissions monitors. Previous trading programs involving hard-to-monitor volatile organic compounds have failed environmentally.[43] An economic dynamic analysis shows that trading programs applied to poorly monitored pollutants will tend to prove fraudulent.[44] Trading creates an incentive for polluters generating "extra" emission reductions to strategically use choices about estimation

---

[43] *See* David M. Driesen, "Is Emissions Trading an Economic Incentive Program?: Replacing the Command and Control/Economic Incentive Dichotomy," 55 *Wash. & Lee L. Rev.* 289 (1998).

[44] I use the term *fraudulent* in a broad sense, not confined to deliberate deception, the focus of fraud's legal definition. For example, emissions trading programs can lose reductions because regulators allow polluters to choose among emission estimation methods and polluters use this

methodologies to exaggerate the amount of reductions they have made.[45] It also creates an incentive for polluters forgoing local reductions (substituting purchased allowances reflecting efforts elsewhere) to understate the amount of reduction foregone, the debit. Hence, trading, as applied to poorly monitored pollutants, will likely fall short of program goals.

Most law and economics scholars recognize that trading needs good monitoring to succeed, but they have been reluctant to embrace that concession's implications. Carbon dioxide, the chief greenhouse gas, lends itself to very reliable estimation and therefore is probably a suitable gas for a trading program. Largely at the market-loving U.S. government's insistence, however, the climate environmental benefit trading programs have expanded to embrace gases that we cannot reliably measure and even to accept, at least in principle, the idea of granting credits for very hard-to-measure efforts to "sequester carbon," for example, by growing trees. This "markets über alles" (everywhere) approach sets up programs for failure.[46] Taxation of pollutants resisting reliable measurement likewise will work poorly, as polluters will tend to underestimate emissions to escape tax liability. Hence, a neoclassical law and economic approach tends to lead to the simple conclusion that markets are great, whereas an economic dynamic analysis produces fine-grained conclusions about where they can prove productive and where they may fail.

The market glorification project has also tended to exaggerate trading's utility at encouraging innovation. A tension exists between short-term cost effectiveness and long-term cost effectiveness and efficacy, as some economists have begun to recognize in recent years.[47] A trading program encourages the use of least-cost measures, at the expense of more costly measures. But the economic dynamics of innovation show that, often, initially costly measures produce the technical progress that lowers long-term costs and increases productivity. Hence, ludicrously expensive supercomputers preceded PCs and expensive handcrafted private automobiles preceded the mass-produced item that became a middle-class staple. The climate disruption equivalents might be nuclear and solar power, which have great long-term potential as substitutes for fossil fuels, but high current costs. Significant investments in either

---

flexibility strategically to overstate the reductions made. I intend the term *fraudulent* to apply to this sort of practice, even though it may not amount to deliberate deception.

[45] *See* Kenneth Richards & K Anderson, "Implementing an International Carbon Sequestration Program: Can the Leaky Sink be Fixed?," 1 *Climate Pol'y* 41 (2001).

[46] *See* Campbell & Klaes, *supra* note 37, at 12–13.

[47] *See* David M. Driesen, "Design, Trading, and Innovation," in *Moving to Markets in Environmental Regulation: Lessons from Twenty Years of Experience* 436–437 and n. 4 (Jody Freeman & Charles D. Kolstad, eds., 2007); *see also* Kenneth Richards, "Framing Environmental Policy Instrument Choice," 10 *Duke Envt'l L. & Pol'y Forum* 221 (2000).

or both should lower long-term incremental costs, especially in light of the eventual rise in fossil fuel prices. Environmental benefit trading, however, will do nothing to promote nuclear power and relatively little to promote solar power. Accordingly, governments that are serious about encouraging innovation have employed other strategies to encourage key technologies. These innovations include the French government's control of nuclear design to provide sufficient safety to gain public acceptance, at least within France, of a large nuclear power industry, and feed-in tariff programs to subsidize renewable energy, thereby leading to vast price decreases over time. An economic dynamic analysis shows that rational market actors will not respond to trading with expensive innovations having great long-term value to society and provides tools for evaluating alternatives or supplements to trading programs.

Once one abandons efficiency, in the sense of near-term cost effectiveness, as the major goal and uses economic dynamic analysis to figure out how to encourage needed innovation over time, some interesting alternatives emerge. The economic dynamics of environmental innovation differ from those of other kinds of innovation. Makers of consumer goods in competitive markets, for example, see innovation as a means to potentially get rich and a failure to innovate as a potential way to lose market share and, therefore, revenue. For these reasons, firms sometimes invent products that nobody asked for in hopes that demand will materialize. Almost nobody, however, buys environmental innovations with positive costs absent government regulation demanding them. Hence, government regulations (including taxes and trading), not individual consumers, provide the demand that might create an impetus for innovation and speculative innovation in anticipation of new demand materializing occurs rarely, if at all.

Government officials' timidity, however, often impedes establishing robust demand, whether in the form of taxes, trading, or traditional regulation. Governments must decide how high a tax to levy or what cap to set (for a trading or traditional regulatory program). But they face significant opposition to stringent policies from polluters, and they cannot readily predict the cost savings that complying companies might produce to adapt to strict standards, as government has limited knowledge of private industry's technological capabilities.

An environmental competition statute – designed to mimic the dynamics, not the hypothetical efficiency, of competitive markets – can solve this problem. Such a statute creates a simple rule: any emitter of greenhouse gases that anticipates society's needs by reducing emissions can obtain reimbursement for the cost of abatement plus a predetermined profit margin from any competitor with higher emissions. Thus, for example, if a new company establishes a solar plant, it can collect the costs of creating the plant from the owner of a coal-fired power plant with higher emissions plus 10 percent (for example). This mimics the structure of competitive markets, where worthwhile innovation can shift market share to the innovator from less innovative competitors, thereby causing wealth increases for those becoming more productive and losses for less productive companies. This statute emulates the dynamics of market share shifts by shifting wealth to environmentally productive companies from those that produce little or no environmental improvement.

I have discussed elsewhere the design issues this environmental competition statute raises and defended it as a policy tool.[48] For present purposes, however, it suffices to say that this idea demonstrates the capacity of economic dynamic thinking to generate imaginative solutions that favor long-term movement over static efficiency. An environmental competition statute, if properly designed, would stimulate a race to the top, encouraging firms to develop and apply their best ideas for ameliorating climate disruption.

CONCLUSION

Neoclassical law and economics contributed to the United States' failure to take meaningful action addressing global climate disruption. It has also contributed to poor design of environmental benefit trading programs addressing climate disruption. An economic dynamic approach, however, has begun to take hold responsive to climate disruption's dynamics and taking into account significant uncertainties through scenario analysis.

An economic dynamic approach can produce an innovative and effective response to climate disruption and provides much clearer and more scientifically sound guidance than an approach too beholden to neoclassical law and economics.

---

[48] *See* David M. Driesen, "An Environmental Competition Statute," in *Beyond Environmental Law: Policy Proposals for a Better Environmental Future* 173–98 (Alyson C. Flournoy & David M. Driesen, eds., 2010).

12

Conclusion: On Economic Dynamics' Value and Limits

This conclusion sharpens the case for the economic dynamic approach based on lessons from the subject-matter-specific chapters, delineates its scope and limits, and responds to some potential criticisms best addressed with the benefit of Part Two's contextualization. It begins by drawing out a few lessons about the problems with the neoclassical theory of law and economics that came into focus as the book reviewed neoclassical law and economics' influence in particular areas. It then examines the economic dynamic theory's scope, arguing that it applies more widely than one might anticipate and that practitioners and scholars have made more use of this theory's elements than one might initially suspect. This final chapter then develops some caveats acknowledging the theory's limits. Finally, this chapter addresses some possible objections to the theory, especially those implicit in some of Richard Posner's responses to advocates of behavioral economics, an element of which plays a role in economic dynamic analysis. This discussion also helps the reader situate the economic dynamic theory in the context of more familiar theories, namely those of institutional and behavioral economics and sharpens the case for employing it widely.

ADDITIONS TO THE CRITIQUE OF NEOCLASSICAL
LAW AND ECONOMICS

Part Two shows that neoclassical law and economics scholars' most important recommendations do not flow from actually carrying out CBA. Indeed, Robert Bork and Richard Posner specifically reject using CBA to evaluate mergers in the antitrust arena, an area that gave birth to neoclassical law and economics. Stephen Breyer and Richard Posner both approach intellectual property with balancing metaphors and some talk about CBA, but they do not carry any out. Harold Demsetz argues that CBA often shows private property's superiority, but carries out no CBA to support this idea. More radical law and economics-minded scholars seeking to reform intellectual property law simply assume the superiority of markets and do not even rely upon balancing metaphors. Analysts of the choices between property and liability rules do not carry out CBA either.

The invocation of CBA, and its cousin, optimality, gives the neoclassical law and economic enterprise a veneer of neutrality and objectivity. But the actual work of the analysis comes from thinking about economic incentives' influence on rational choices of actors with perfect information. In the case of antitrust law, Chapter 9 showed that the real work in justifying neoclassical law and economic reforms comes from focusing on firms as rational actors with perfect (or nearly perfect) information. The Chicago School's radical intellectual property and security law reformers reach conclusions favoring strengthening intellectual property protection and weakening disclosure requirements by focusing on the positive incentives in the market to do the right thing. This suggests that law and economics scholarship might bear more direct responsibility for the market worship it helped spawn in the policy arena than seemed initially apparent in Chapter 2.

This does not necessarily prove that CBA never figures in the work of law and economics scholars. But it does show that the principal policy proposals stem from analysis of economic incentives under assumptions tending to glorify markets, not from law and economic scholars' CBA of legal rules.[1]

In the policy realm, CBA serves a similar function, justifying a series of reforms whether or not formal CBA supported them. This book already suggested that some policymakers tend to embrace market glorification to an even greater extent than do sensible law and economics scholars, like Richard Posner. We saw in Chapter 10, for example, that in the national security arena market glorification has contributed to some problematic privatization with no use of CBA. We also saw that OMB used its CBA-based authority to campaign against strict regulations on a variety of grounds, sometimes in the teeth of CBA suggesting that regulations needed strengthening.

Neoclassical law and economics obtains much of its prestige from its apparent coherence and unity. Seen close up, in a variety of fields, however, it

---

[1] Law and economics scholars have produced numerous "empirical studies" that purport to demonstrate that regulations produce no benefits at all. *See* Mark Kelman, "On Democracy-Bashing: A Skeptical Look at the Theoretical and 'Empirical' Practice of the Public Choice Movement," 74 *Va. L. Rev.* 199, 238–255 (1988) (faulting Gary Becker for failing to provide evidence to support his theories and for failing to explain discordant data). These studies tend to rely on very unconvincing application of rational actor assumptions in order to overcome skepticism about the thin data purporting to justify the results. *See id. Cf.* id. at 255–60 (criticizing one very incomplete and problematic cost-benefit analysis in the law and economics literature).

appears rather ad hoc. We saw that some neoclassically oriented intellectual property scholars tended to favor existing law as reasonably balanced, while others sought radical reforms extending intellectual property law's reach. Similarly, while economic theory would seem to provide an adequate basis for approving security law's disclosure requirements, faith in free markets led law and economics scholars to oppose mandatory disclosure. Even in highly specialized fields where unity might appear among neoclassical law and economics scholars, as in the antitrust area, this unity seems to reflect agreement to a series of discrete and highly contestable arguments for deregulation (e.g., firms will employ predatory pricing seldom and with little effect) rather than the results of a rigorous CBA.

Law and economics types often imagine that CBA, when actually deployed, at least provides a means of specifying a level of effort appropriate to optimally address a problem. But the material in these chapters casts doubt even on CBA's capacity to calibrate government efforts. We saw in the military and antitrust contexts (Chapters 9 and 10) that it provided no help at all. Perhaps surprisingly, Chapter 11 showed that the seemingly vague requirement to avoid dangerous levels of greenhouse gas emissions, a synonym for the economic goal of avoiding systemic risk in this context, provides more concrete guidance to calibration of emission levels than CBA. CBA's inability to support calibration in this area owes something to the uncertainties that plague efforts to address environmental problems. It is possible that some area exists where CBA offers concrete guidance. But its capacity to guide calibration of efforts to address systemic risks (and many other risks) in addressing an uncertain future usually varies between very weak and none at all.

ON ECONOMIC DYNAMIC THEORY'S SCOPE AND LIMITS

At the outset, this book defined the economic dynamic theory in terms of three parameters:

1) **Focus:** Change over time (the macroeconomic focus)
2) **Goal:** Avoiding systemic risk while keeping a robust set of economic opportunities open
3) **Method:** Economic dynamic analysis to analyze problems and proposed legal reforms

These parameters contrast with neoclassical law and economics' focus on transactions, goal of maximizing short-term efficiency, and ostensible reliance on CBA as its principal method.

As I wrote this book, I was surprised to find that the economic dynamic theory applied as broadly as it did. It turns out that economic dynamics play an important role even in the common law areas of property and contract, which one tends to think of as static. Contract law has little to do with ensuring efficiency; indeed, litigants usually invoke it to enforce inefficient bargains. But it has everything to do with creating an economic dynamic conducive to seizing economic opportunities. Hence, the macroeconomic focus provides a fruitful lens through which one can view contract law. Furthermore, leading contracts scholars have employed economic dynamic analysis in their work, albeit without giving it a label. In the property field we saw that many of the field's most important subjects and insights stem from an analysis of the dynamics of change over time to address macroeconomic issues. We also saw that property law aims to provide economic opportunities and at times plays a role in addressing systemic risks. Chapter 7 argues for more conscious use of economic dynamic analysis and for a shift in scholarly attention from an old debate on remedial efficiencies to problems more crucial to achieving important macroeconomic goals.

As Part Two moved beyond traditional common law areas, we saw even clearer examples of economic dynamic theory's centrality. Attention to change over time to provide macroeconomic opportunities constitutes something of a consensus approach among leading intellectual property scholars. And many of them analyze the economic dynamics of legal and sociological questions by considering explicitly the bounds of relevant actors' rationality. The antitrust chapter (Chapter 9) provided an account of empowerment analysis, a component of economic dynamic analysis, drawn from scholarship on antitrust law's social and political values. It also found an important school of scholarship, with roots going back at least to Louis Brandeis, emphasizing change over time and the creation of economic opportunity. Some experts in the field have also suggested that antitrust has a role to play as a tool to limit systemic risk in the financial sector. Good national security analysts employ scenario analysis and other components of economic dynamic analysis to address change over time as we seek to avoid serious systemic risks endemic in this area. Countries around the world have employed an economic dynamic approach explicitly aimed at avoiding systemic risk to design appropriate climate policy.

If scholars regularly and consciously focused on change over time, recommended policies aimed at avoiding systemic risk while keeping open significant economic opportunities, and employed a full-blown economic dynamic analysis to justify their recommendations, this book would add very little to law and economics. Instead, Part Two showed that leading scholars employ elements of the theory unconsciously, but rarely apply all of its elements together. Thus, Ian Ayres and Robert Gertner employ economic dynamic analysis to analyze default rules, but aim it at an efficiency goal. Garrett Hardin focuses on change over time and avoiding systemic risk in developing the idea of the tragedy of the commons, but implicitly employs a rational actor model.

The fact that even unconscious piecemeal application of this theory has yielded so many important results suggests that it has great value. Putting it all together into a conscious approach would have even more value.

Yet the entire theory does not apply perfectly to every problem. While systemic risk turns out to matter in a wider variety of contexts than one might think, such as some property law contexts and potentially in antitrust, it does not figure in every legal problem. The focus on change over time will frequently prove valuable in contexts where systemic risks do not loom as a primary concern, such as in many areas of contract law. (Note, however, that systemic risks do matter to contracts at times; for example, contracts created the subprime crisis by creating and selling derivatives). And economic dynamic analysis can help, as pointed out in the property chapter, even when we wish to analyze law's effect on noneconomic values (such as the social value of property). Even a simple shift to more attention to change over time by itself can profoundly help legal scholarship, as the value of the tragedy of the commons metaphor, the macroeconomic research program advocated in the property law chapter, and the macroeconomic view of contract law articulated in Chapter 6 suggest (to take but a few of many examples in Part Two). Thus, this book's macroeconomic perspective proves valuable even in areas of the law where systemic risk does not loom large as a primary concern, but economic opportunity matters (e.g., contract law and intellectual property).

A fairly complete application of economic dynamic analysis would greatly improve legal scholarship. Ian Ayres and Robert Gertner's work on contract default rules provides an example of rather complete economic dynamic analysis. But in many cases – for example, Robert Ellickson's use of the bounded rationality assumption to flesh out the case for cooperative norms among neighbors – we see only some elements of economic dynamic analysis being employed. Without calling into doubt the capacity of some elements in the right context to provide good insights (for example, by simply fleshing out the bounds of a particular group's rationality, as Ellickson does), policy and legal analysts should self-consciously try to employ a full economic dynamic analysis when analyzing major problems with an eye toward making specific recommendations for major legal and policy changes. This would include:

1) Attention to legal detail
2) Analysis of the bounds of relevant actors' rationality
3) Analysis of how actors will respond to the law's incentives given these bounds

4) Analysis of how countervailing incentives might defeat the law's objectives
5) Empowerment analysis
6) Scenario analysis

As the book suggests, analysts may dispense with this last element when addressing proposals of lesser importance or where uncertainty does not loom large.

By decoupling analysis of economic incentives from the efficiency goal so often invoked when traditional law and economics scholars address economic incentives, this book increases the potential utility of analysis of economic incentives. At the same time, by choosing macroeconomic goals that matter a lot, it focuses legal analysis on more important questions than that of efficiency. Part One already showed that macroeconomics matter much more to wealth maximization than efficiency. Chapter 9 showed that for 90 percent of Americans, efficiency increases may have no wealth-increasing effect at all. The more modest justification sometimes offered for focusing tightly on efficiency – that economists are not well equipped to analyze anything else – rings hollow in light of the critique of neoclassical law and economic developed earlier and some of the information conveyed in Part One. First of all, law and economics scholars more often base their reform proposals on an impoverished analysis of economic incentives (impoverished because insufficiently attentive to bounded rationality, countervailing incentives, empowerment, and unquantifiable uncertainty) rather than on a convincing demonstration that CBA demonstrates the superior efficiency of a particular legal rule. Second, economists have developed tools, such as game theory, that work perfectly well when not aimed at efficient outcomes. Third, if existing economic tools do not sufficiently inform legal analysis, lawyers should develop tools that work to aid in the construction of law. Although it may be too much to claim that I have developed economic dynamic analysis out of whole cloth, in light of its deployment (albeit sometimes in a partial way) by lawyers, economists, scientists, and others, this theory puts together certain approaches that play a big role in some of the most perceptive legal scholarship. This tool provides a means of systematically examining economic incentives' effects while taking into account law's generality and future-oriented nature.

At the same time, no analytical method works well in all legal contexts. While Congress and academics remain free to use any methods they wish in crafting legislation or recommending policy reforms respectively, administrative agencies must use analytical methods that fit the statutory criteria under which they operate. Thus, the Supreme Court held in *Whitman v. American Trucking Ass'ns* that the EPA may not consider cost in crafting rules protecting public health with an "adequate margin of safety."[2] It follows that the EPA may not consider CBA in the context of health-based standard setting, but instead must analyze health impacts. This illustrates the more general principle that statutory criteria appropriately limit analytical methods, commanding conscientious agencies to focus their analysis on questions the statute makes relevant. The same principle would limit the application of economic dynamic analysis. That said, some limited forms of economic dynamic analysis might prove more widely useful than CBA in an administrative setting. For example, it might be useful to analyze dynamic factors that might change what people do in ways that change the amount of pollution or cause people to engage in more activities influencing their exposure to pollutants in analyzing a proposed standard to protect public health. Still, recognition that statutory criteria sometimes limit the scope and form of appropriate analysis remains an important caveat to this book's endorsement of economic dynamic analysis.

DEFENSES TO POSSIBLE CRITICISMS

Because economic dynamic analysis places some emphasis on the bounded rationality assumption, it must confront Richard Posner's criticism of behavioral law and economics, which also relies upon and elaborates this concept. At the core of Posner's criticism lies an argument that played a big role in his analysis of the 2008 economic crisis – that a rational actor model can operate fairly well even in the face of a lot of irrational behavior.[3] Specifically, Posner contends that rational choice analysts can take preferences as a given and proceed from there, even if some of these preferences reflect an irrational cognitive process.[4] Posner's contention envisions construction of a utility function based on data about present (or, more precisely, past) preferences. Posner engages in something like this approach when he argues, in A *Failure of Capitalism*, that rational actor assumptions adequately explain the observed behavior of economic actors that led to the economic crisis of 2008.[5] By subsuming the panicked reaction of investors and the herd behavior of bankers who should have known better (and sometimes did) within the rubric of rational behavior,

---

[2] *Whitman v. American Trucking Ass'ns*, 531 U.S. 457, 464–65 (2001).

[3] *See* Richard Posner, "Rational Choice, Behavioral Economics, and the Law," 50 *Stan. L. Rev.* 1551, 1554 (1998).

[4] *Id. Cf.* Russell B. Korobkin & Thomas S. Ulen, "Law and Behavioral Science: Removing the Rationality Assumption from Law and Economics," 88 *Cal. L. Rev.* 1051, 1068 (2000) (arguing that one cannot predict legal rules' influence without predicting the content of preferences).

[5] *See* Richard Posner, *A Failure of Capitalism: The Crisis of '08 and the Descent into Depression* 77–100 (2009).

he manifests a very capacious view of rationality.[6] Posner's capacious view of rationality, while perhaps justifiable in some sense, does not capture well what economists usually do when they construct financial models to predict potential futures.

Chapter 5, however, shows that analysts constructing models based on an assumption of rational behavior failed to predict the crisis, but others who looked for potential irrationality in the market predicted it. This fact embarrasses the point Posner's defense of a broad rational actor model leads to, namely an attack on behavioral economics as sacrificing "predictive power" for "descriptive accuracy."[7] Neoclassical economics has little "predictive" power to lose.[8] We have seen, for example, that faith in financial models' "predictive power" blinded bankers and regulators to obvious increased risks. Implicit rational actor models led lawyers like Richard Posner and Robert Bork to "predict" that mergers would generally enhance efficiency, but economists found that mergers often destroyed value, partly because of management egoism. And Eric Posner has pointed out that even in the relatively confined domain of contract law, analysts have been unable to "predict" which rules would prove efficient.[9]

In spite of Richard Posner's prophet-like invocation of "predictive power," he may not mean to claim that rational choice economics actually predicts anything accurately, for he argues that rational choice models yield clear predictions, which we can then test against empirical evidence.[10] This neither suffices as an argument supporting its superiority to economic dynamic analysis nor captures the practice of neoclassical economics (let alone neoclassical law and economics). If rational choice models regularly produce wrong, but testable, predictions, analysts and policymakers should abandon these models in favor of models that provide more predictive accuracy. The preference for simplicity in a model reflects an understandable aesthetic choice, but not

[6] *See id.* at 80–86; Korobkin & Ulen, *supra* note 4, at 1061–62 (characterizing Richard Posner's conception of rationality as the "thinnest" of several competing conceptions).

[7] *See* Posner, *supra* note 3, at 1559.

[8] *See* Korobkin & Ulen, *supra* note 4, at 1066–67 (describing the rational choice model's predictive power as "inadequate").

[9] Eric Posner, "Economic Analysis of Contract Law After Three Decades: Success or Failure?," 112 *Yale L. J.* 829, 830 (2002). *Cf.* Ian Ayres, "Valuing Modern Contract Law Scholarship," 112 *Yale L. J.* 881, 881–82 (2003) (not contesting Posner's descriptive claim about law and economics' failure to "predict" common law rules, but finding more normative value in recent law and economics contract scholarship than Posner does); Richard Craswell, "In That Case, What Is the Question? Economics and the Demands of Contract Theory," 112 *Yale L. J.* 903, 923–24 (2003) (same).

[10] *See* Posner, *supra* note 3, at 1559.

one that society can safely employ in addressing systemic risks. Moreover, many scholars have criticized rational choice economics precisely because economists often fail to examine empirical data with an eye to falsifying and modifying their assumptions.[11] Chapter 9, however, shows that economists have tested the Chicago School claims that predatory pricing should prove rare and unsuccessful and that mergers should generally prove efficient, and often found them wanting. Leaders of the law and economics school, however, have not adjusted their views to fit these findings.[12]

Posner correctly points out that reliance on bounded rationality by itself does not provide an adequately specific basis for analysis, but his own capacious view of rationality may suffer from the same problem.[13] In any case, economic dynamic theory addresses this problem by demanding a description of the relevant bounds of rationality. Any adequately specific assumption will yield reasonably clear predictions, not just a rational actor assumption. Hence, economic dynamic models should be, insofar as possible, based on clear descriptions of a particular group's bounded rationality drawn from empirical evidence. We have seen examples in previous chapters of such successes. For example, Ian Ayres and Robert Gertner assume that buyers of real estate will not know the rules for handling escrow money and that retail purchasers will not know the rules regarding breach of promises to buy retail goods in predicting the effects of various potential default rules in contract. As Russell Korobkin and Thomas Ulen have pointed out, legal analysis generally focuses on rules addressing particular groups of actors, so that a description of bounded rationality adequate to inform a particular policy decision need only adequately characterize particular groups, rather than apply perfectly to the entire population.[14] Nor does legal analysis require a complete psychological profile to create a sufficiently accurate model to inform a particular analysis, as shown by the mileage Ayres and Gertner get out of an exceedingly simple observation (Chapter 6) and the somewhat more elaborate suggestions that

---

[11] *See, e.g.*, Charles Hall & Kent Klitgaard, *Energy and the Wealth of Nations: Understanding the Biophysical Economy* (2012) (criticizing economic modeling for not testing economics' key assumptions); James Hackney, *Under Cover of Science: American Legal-Economic Theory and the Test for Objectivity* 106–10 (2007) (discussing the lack of empiricism in foundational law and economics work, and its reliance upon deduction from fixed axioms); Kelman, *supra* note 1, at 206 (faulting Gary Becker for failing to provide evidence to support his theories and for failing to explain discordant data).

[12] *See generally* Donald MacKenzie, *An Engine, Not a Camera* 9–12 (2006) (discussing the tradition within economics of not treating falsification of a model's assumptions as a test of its theoretical value).

[13] *See* Korobkin & Ulen, *supra* note 4, at 1067 (characterizing Posner's thin version of rational choice as offering "no behavioral predictions at all").

[14] Id. at 1072.

Fritz Sharpf developed for the application of game theory to policy (Chapter 4). This may explain why legal analysts implicitly employing a bounded rationality framework have succeeded in making sufficient characterizations of the bounds of rationality to aid prediction. At the same time, we should welcome more work identifying more precisely how one develops sufficiently thick descriptions of bounded rationality to avoid major errors without making the descriptions so complex and multifaceted that bounded rationality becomes unworkable as a predictive tool.

In spite of the overlap between behavioral economics and economic dynamic theory, Posner's criticism of bounded rationality in that context proves less than completely apposite in the economic dynamic context. He characterizes bounded rationality as quirkiness.[15] Posner's reference to "quirks" imaginatively, albeit pejoratively, captures a key element of what behavioral economists study under the bounded rationality rubric. But this book has defined bounded rationality in a manner more in keeping with the thinking of institutional economists, as a recognition that people, including key actors in relevant institutions, pay attention to only some of the information available to them.[16] To some extent, this failure to pay attention to all information simply constitutes an inevitable consequence of information overload in our society. Call this the informational component of bounded rationality. But the economic dynamic theory also recognizes that people's and institution's habits and routines influence which information they pay attention to. This habitual component does overlap with the domain of behavioral economics,[17] although the term "institutional habit" better captures economic dynamic theory's central concerns than the term "quirks." So Posner's critique of basing economic analysis on a set of observations about quirks misses most of what is important in the concept of bounded rationality used in this book primarily by deemphasizing its information component.

Posner, however, makes an argument calling into question the value of the informational component when he argues that rational choice theory has no difficulty assimilating the phenomenon of positive information costs and insists that rationality does not require "omniscience" or that one spend all one's time assimilating information.[18] That may be so, but the standard definition of the perfect information assumption in economics views it as requiring

---

[15] *See* Posner, *supra* note 3, at 1553.
[16] *Cf.* Daniel A. Farber, "Toward a New Legal Realism," 68 *U. Chi. L. Rev.* 279, 299 (2001) (reviewing *Behavioral Law and Economics* (Cass Sunstein, ed., 2000)) (criticizing behavioral economics for too little attention to institutional context).
[17] *See* Korobkin & Ulen, *supra* note 4, at 1113–19.
[18] Posner, *supra* note 3, at 1553.

"complete knowledge of a person's economic environment."[19] And standard neoclassical economics assumes both rationality and perfect information, not just rationality. So standard neoclassical law and economics comes pretty close to assuming omniscience.[20] Still, as Chapter 2 pointed out, economists sometimes relax perfect information assumptions.

If, for purposes of legal analysis, one relaxes perfect information assumptions in order to explicitly take into account what Posner categorizes as "information costs" instead of just ignoring them, one must decide what informational assumptions to use. The economic dynamic theory addresses this problem by demanding an assessment of what sorts of information people will likely pay attention to. Unless economic analysis of legal rules makes explicit assumptions about the precise nature of information imperfections based on empirical study, it will, by default, proceed as if relevant actors possess all the information they could obtain if "information costs" were zero. And this is precisely what analysis employing a perfect information assumption does.

Economic dynamic theory builds on the Chicago School insight that economic incentives matter a lot. The Chicago School of law and economics, however, has no theory about how to apply this insight to the analysis of legal rules. Instead, its theory locates the methodological justification for its conclusions in CBA, which does little actual work. Economics, of course, offers a broad toolkit analyzing economic incentives, including game theory and other techniques. But the lawyers leading the law and economics movement have not specified how one goes about systematically analyzing economic incentives from legal rules, except that in doing so one should assume that actors are rational and possess perfect information.

Those assumptions work wonderfully to glorify markets and therefore helped spur an economic collapse made possible by deregulation. But employment of those assumptions hinders development of capacity to cope with systemic risks and provide economic opportunity in a world of information overload that demands bounded rationality. Nor does the neoclassical approach provide an analytical method for understanding economic incentives' impacts, even if its assumptions were adequate. Economic dynamic theory's requirements that analysts pay attention to legal detail, consider which information relevant actors will pay attention to given their bounded rationality, evaluate countervailing incentives, conduct an empowerment analysis and feed that into the

---

[19] Leonard J. Mirman, "Perfect Information," in *The New Palgrave Dictionary of Economics* (Steven N. Durlauf & Lawrence E. Blume, eds., 2008).

[20] *See* Korobkin & Ulen, *supra* note 4, at 1078 (pointing out that scholars employing rational choice theory rarely consider the possibility that an actor may not optimize utility, because he or she takes mental shortcuts instead of obtaining complete information about choices).

analysis, and, for major proposals with significant future uncertainties, employ scenario analysis to explore the future add up to a rather robust and specific analytical method for analyzing legal rules.

SOME FINAL THOUGHTS

An economic dynamic approach has a number of virtues. By requiring a focus on the long term, it recognizes the fundamental nature of legal rules as long-term commitments and helps law counteract, rather than simply reflect, the myopia that a transactional approach can reinforce. By calling for a focus on avoiding systemic risk while preserving a reasonably robust set of economic opportunities, economic dynamic theory chooses an important and plausible role for government.

Finally, economic dynamic analysis provides a good method for making important choices in pursuing these valuable long-term objectives. No wonder that we see this method, or some of its elements, surface in the most perceptive work of academics and policymakers. It helps us confront the future's uncertainty without wishing it away or pretending that we know nothing about the future when we cannot quantify law's costs and benefits over time. It forces us to use the knowledge we have about actors' bounded rationality and encourages us to develop more of this knowledge, instead of just employing the convenient, but dangerous, assumption that market actors know what they are doing.

The founders of neoclassical law and economics deserve credit for changing the way we think about law and introducing some important insights. But this approach has begun to fragment as legal scholars find that simple models based on rational actors and perfect information do not adequately address even fairly basic legal problems. And the market glorification project it gave rise to has contributed to decades of economic failure for most Americans and neglect of the greatest environmental challenge we have ever faced. This book's theory provides a way forward. It seeks to take these founders' key insight – that economic incentives matter – and provide a framework for using it systematically to address key long-term problems that we neglect at our peril.

Index

Printed in the United States
by Baker & Taylor Publisher Services